the art of inn

photo : Getty Images / Tim Flach

www.petzl.com

EL PISÓN, MALLOS DE RIGLOS, ESPAÑA.

GUIDEBOOK TRADE DISTRIBUTORS

BRITISH ISLES & GENERAL WORLD
CORDEE
3a De Montfort Street,
Leicester. LE1 3HD, Great Britain.
Tel: 0116 254 3579   Fax: 0116 247 1176
sales@cordee.co.uk
www.cordee.co.uk

BERGVERLAG ROTHER
Haidgraben 3,
D-85521 Ottobrunn (München),
DEUTSCHLAND
distributor-publisher as
Licensed by Jingo Wobbly-Euro Guides for
Deutschland, Österreich, Schweiz, Italia(South Tyrol).

FREYTAG & BERNDT - PRAHA
Varhulíkové 120
170 00 Praha 7 – Holešovice,
CESKA REPUBLIKA
distributor-publisher as
Licensed by Jingo Wobbly-Euro Guides for
Ceska Republika, Slovenska Republika, Hungary.

FRANCE – Main Distributor:
RANDO diffusion IBOS
4, rue Maye Lane, F 65420 IBOS-TARBES,
tél; 00 33 5 62 90 09 96
RANDO diffusion PARIS
2bis, place du puits de l'ermite, F75005 Paris.
tél; 00 33 1 44 08 78 10

NETHERLANDS – Main Distributor:
NILSSON & LAMM
Pampuslaan 212, Postbus 195
1380 AD Weesp (NL)
www.nilsson-lamm.nl
00 31 294-494 949

JAPANESE AGENCY:
Sport Climbing Center PUMP
Frontier Spirit, Inc.
2-20-10 Higashimotomachi Kokubunzi-shi,
Tokyo, Japan.
www.pump-climbing.com
Tel/fax 0081-42-324-6762

David Atchison-Jones
Chief Editor

Europe – Sport Vertical

ESV-1-2 printed January 2003

Jingo Wobbly – Euro Guides
First Published in March 2002 by Jingo Wobbly Euro Guides
(An imprint of Vision PC).
Holmwood House, 52 Roxborough Park,
Harrow-on-the-Hill, London. HA1 3AY

Copyright © David Atchison-Jones
Computers built by Vision PC.
Image Scanning – Professional Film Company, London.
Graphics with a touch of Botticelli, Digital Colourmill at Vision PC.
Printing – Fratelli Spada SPA, Roma.

A CIP catalogue record is available from the British Library

ISBN   1-873 665 21-0

Cover Photos: <p221; >p249;
Bottom - Rifugio Cinque Torri, Cortina d'Ampezzo;

EUROPE
SPORT VERTICAL

CARTE BLANCHE 8a, Céüse. Stevie Haston

JINGO WOBBLY EURO-GUIDES
LONDON - FONTAINEBLEAU - FRANKENJURA - CÉÜSE
ABLON - VERDON - RIGLOS - BUOUX

CONTENTS - PORTUGAL-ESPAÑA

ACKNOWLEDGEMENTS

I would first like of course to dedicate this book to my wife Carrie Atchison-Jones, who had helped me enormously over many years, in collecting the majority of information in this book. Carrie has been my happy and chirpy travelling companion, on our whacky wingo Wobbly Tours; down all those whong widdley windey woads, to the wong location!

There have nearly always been, 2-3 climbers that have helped me at every cliff I have visited, which makes a list of acknowledgements, around 7500 names! I just have to say a huge thank you to everyone collectively, for all the help that they have given to me.

The writing of this book has taken many years, and I have really enjoyed doing it. The climbing has always been excellent, but it is mostly the people that I remember of course, and my thanks to all those that I share such fond memories, you all know who you are. If I can remember 2700 cliffs, I can also remember the friends – it is often the easiest way to remember the places I have been to.

My other acknowledgements must be to mention those people who have effectively – been there before me and lead the way. We are all on a discovery trip, and rely on previous information in whatever form; guidebooks, magazines, first hand knowledge, pub talk. This is how we first come to know of a new place to climb, and where our inspiration is first ignited. So it is with particular importance, that I both acknowledge and thank, the brilliant efforts of past climbers in giving so much information.

Portugal; Nuno Soares, Francisco Ataide, José Teixeira, Paulo Alves, Alda Vieiera, Sandra Mendes, Nuno Seabra, Emílio Andrade, Rui Carvalheira, Carlos Simes and Andy Reid.

España: A giant thank you to Darío Rodríguez and Ernesto López; David Munilla, Chris Craggs, Alan James, Alan Cameron-Duff, Rab Anderson, Miguel Seaone, Javier Carreras, Mark & Isabel Quiros, Racquel Perez, Mark Glaister, Emma Williams, Juan Carlos Sarasa & Marisa, Eva & Juan Carlos, Daniel Ascaso, Carlos Longroño, Jon Biddle, Felipe Guinda Polo.

France: A great memory of Bruno Cormier; big thank to Jean-Pierre Bouvier, Jacques Glénat, Jean-Michel Asselin, Patrick Edlinger, Jean-Baptiste Tribout, Daniel Taupin; not to forget – Nico Mailänder, Candice Piechaud, Jean-Michel Larricq, Jean-Luc Archelli, Serge Casternan, Christine Coquio, Maurice Martin, Roland Truffaut, Jacky Godoffe, Jo Montchaussé, Jean-Yves Gerbet, Jacques Dreyer, Michel Piola, Stevie Haston, Philippe Mussatto, Robert Durieux, Christian Emprin, Philippe Deslandes, James Merel, Patrick Col, Jérôme Meyer, Jean-Jaques Rolland, Ian & Claudie Dunn, Denis Garnier, Jean-Marc Troussier, Alex Duboc, Nanette Raybaud, Nathalie Richer, David Belden, Christine

de Colombel, Marc Baudemont, Thomas Verpillot, Raphaël Deschamps, Mathieu Midonet.

Italy: Matteo Gamberro, Marco Marzialle, Maurizio Oviglia, Piero Ledda, Andrea Gennari Daneri, Andrea Gallo, Alessandro Quagliolo, Flavio Fosson, Pietro Bagnara, Pietro Corti, Edgardo Quadri, Roberto Capucciati, Bruno Quaresima, Euginio Pesci, Bruno Tassi, Guido Lisignoli, Graziano Alberti, Flavio at Arco, Antonio Prestini, Hubert Moroder & Tania, Roberto Casanova, Mario Lacedelli, Flavio Faoro, Arianna Sitta, Gigi da Pozzo, Marcella Santuz.

Alps: A giant thank to Timo Marschner; Jean-Claude & Yves Remy, Jürg Von Känel, Philippe Steulet, Patrick Andrey, Andreas Luisier, Mike Tscharner, Kurt Schall, Ingo Neumann, Wolfgang Haupolter, Andrea Kinauer, Heinz Zak, Michael Nedetzky, Andrea Leitgeb.

Germany-Czech: A giant thank to Richard Goedeke; Achim Panico, Bernard Thum, Sebastien Schwertner, Hans-Dieter Brunner, Martin Lochner, Jürgen Wesley, Markus Stadler, Pádlo Werdermann, Berndt Arnold, Mikail Skyora, Bohmiel Skyora, Dan Stransky, Alice Flesarova, Michal Burda.

Britain: Terry Tullis, Frank Shannon, Barry Knight, Guy McLelland, Malcolm McPherson, Robin Makinze, Rowland & Mark Edwards, Pete Oxley, Sandy Ogilvie, Dave Viggars, Steve Findlay, Richard Harrison, John Harwood, Fliss Butler, Jon Kenton, Paul Williams, Andy Pollitt, John Redhead, Gerry Lynch, Paul Pritchard, Ron James, Jerry Moffatt, Ben Moon, Simon Nadin, Chris Plant, Geoff Birtles, Mark Pretty, John Hart, Seb Greive, Sean Myles, Niall Grimes, Joe Healey, Matt Saunders, Alan James, Chris Craggs, Fred Simpson, Mark Leach, Gerry Peel, Mick Lovatt, Al Phizaklea, Gordon Stainforth, Bernard Newman, Gary Latter, Dave Cuthbertson, Tom Prentice – and of course Ken Wilson.

My thanks also have to go to the translators, who have had incredible patience in coping with the constant updating, with the design of the guide; Alda Vieira, Eva Bosque, Virginie Bernier, Jérôme Meyer, Matteo Gandini, Rudiger Jooss, Birgit Koenig, Nico Mailänder, Wolfgang Haupolter, Lenka Prenosilova, Naoya Naito.

All the photos in the guide have been taken by myself or Carrie. There are a few exceptions, and I would like to thank Robin Mazinke for the photos in the Alicante section, and Mark Glaister for the Sardegna section.

Last of all, I would like to say thank you, to all our sponsors – both small and large companies, who have given us such great support in this new style of guidebook.

David Atchison-Jones
February 2003

Portugal
Montanha [2] – www.montanhalau.pt
España
Escalar [6]
Desnivel [12] – www.desnivel.es
France
Grimper [12]
Roc'n Wall [12] – www.glenat.com
Montagnes [12]

Italia
Pareti [12] – www.pareti.it
Montagna [12] – www.cda.it
Deutschland
Klettern [12] – www.klettern.de
Great Britain
Climber [12] – www.climber.co.uk
OTE [12] – www.ontheedgemag.co.uk
High [12] – www.highmountainmag.com

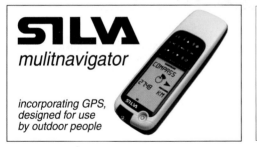
LONDON

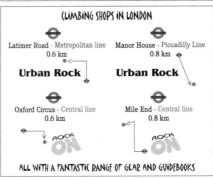

Rock On
@ YHA Adventure Shop
152-160 Wardour Street
London W1F 8YA
Tel: 020-7025 1919

CLIMBING SHOPS IN LONDON

Latimer Road - Metropolitan line
0.6 km
Urban Rock

Oxford Circus - Central line
0.6 km

Manor House - Piccadilly Line
0.8 km
Urban Rock

Mile End - Central line
0.8 km

ALL WITH A FANTASTIC RANGE OF GEAR AND GUIDEBOOKS

Mile End Climbing Wall
Haverfield Road, Bow
London E3 5BE
Tel: 020-8981 5066
Fax: 020-8983 0204

This book is a comprehensive overview, to the climbing in Western Europe. It is written for climbers of all standards, from beginners and weekend enthusiasts, to experts and professional mountain guides. We include all types of climbing, but mainly concentrate on equipped sport routes and bouldering. It is a guidebook that offers an Encyclopaedic level of knowledge on European climbing. However, it is still a book, small enough to be carried in the top of a rucksack. Wherever you may be in Europe, you can find all the really good climbing locations in an instant. On the web, there is simply too much information, and much of it being – unreliable! So, Europe - Sport Vertical, gives the climber quick to use, quality edited and concise information; and is supported by over 350 high quality photographs. It is set to become the trustworthy, happy and colourful, travelling companion for all climbers.

TOM'S CAVE, Stoney Middleton, Peak District, England; A very young Jerry Moffatt in the early 1980's

We have designed the guide to be used by climbers of any nationality and language, open to all from around the world. Therefore, we have to use as little text as possible. All our specialist climbing icons are unique to Jingo Wobbly guides, and have been specially developed from over 30 years of climbing experience. The main icons are described in several languages on the inside covers. (See appendix-4 also)

Sectors

We have chosen to divide Western Europe into 96 European climbing sectors, and they are grouped into 6 main regions (page-indexed on inside cover). Each sector is a different size and shape, but generally they will contain at least 800-1000 routes, and offer plenty of climbing for a 2-week holiday. On a practical level, most climbers need to know all the possible climbing within a 2 hour car journey from their campsite or Gîte. We have used this principle to design most of our sectors. We hope to eventually produce 4 illustrated pages for each sector, but to accurately report on 2600 crags does take a few years!

Layout

We use 3 styles of page; Main data maps, Mini location maps, and Information pages. The main Data map page is specially designed - to give climbers a clear, fast impression to the location of the best climbing in a sector. The most important cliffs are highlighted in yellow boxes, and all good popular cliffs are shown with red dots (40 max. in each area). The total number of cliffs and routes in each sector are listed at the top of the page, and the thin turquoise boxes, show topo guidebook coverage. The maps are not intended to replace high quality cartographic footpath maps; and we always suggest that you purchase an up to date road map, to get the most out of your climbing trip. (1:2-300 000 useful scale)

The icon layout for the data section is explained on the inside cover. It can look complicated at first, but every line uses exactly the same layout principle,

so it should be quick to master. For each crag we include: Number of routes – (colour coded from min to max, or with colour percentage in each grade); cliff orientation and possible summer shade; height of routes and crag altitude; type of rock and different climbing style; walk in time and angle, and the level of difficulty to locate the crag.

Stars

We award colour coded quality stars (1-3), on a European scale that has a very high standard. Green stars illustrate good climbing, but a bad location – such as a dirty quarry or near a busy road. Blue stars show good climbing in a very pleasant location. Red stars are only awarded for superb climbing in an exceptional location. (See appendix-1 for minimum standard examples). We award stars on our personal experience when visiting crags, and visit over 200 different new crags each year.

Mini Maps

When you first visit an area, it may be impossible to find or purchase a guidebook – it may be out of stock, or the shop may be closed. We therefore try to give at least 4 mini maps to good crags. This is so you can at least get to the crag, go climbing, and have a good chance of meeting other climbers. They are small and concise maps, but should prove adequate. They try to show considerate parking locations, correct approach footpaths, cliff direction, forests and local landmarks. They do not show any right of way, and give no indication to any rights of climbing etc. All have North at the top, and try to show a scale. We also have special white limestone rock icons, these show the (climbing) type of limestone at the crag – see back flap for 26 different categories (Appendix 3 – photos).

Information page

We support our data map pages with information pages; Jingo and Wobbly give comments both in English and the local language where possible. Jingo represents a strong muscular climber's point of view, and Wobbly makes suggestions for the more technical and artistic climber. There are over 500 guide-books to Europe! We like to support all the local guidebooks, so we illustrate the topo front covers, along with useful details; Author, date published, pages, size, and a local stockist where you can buy the guide (with days open, Monday-1). We award our quality stars for 5 different categories: General information: Maps to find the cliff for the 1st time; Topo route information; ease of use for those who do not speak the local language; Photographs. Every guidebook takes a huge amount of work and effort to write, so we use our stars and dustbins very, very carefully! Jingo and Wobbly do not do 'camping guides,' but we try to show at least a good campsite that is centrally located, and at least gives you a starting point – like the grades, yellow is basic and purple is exotic.

Europe tips and information:

Sport climbing is the most popular style of climbing in Europe; Climbers mostly use a single 10.5mm 70-metre rope with 12 quickdraws. A helmet can be useful protection, but generally you are better advised to dodge any falling parts of the cliff. The weather will severely affect, when and where you climb; so use the altitude and position of a cliff to shelter from a sun scorching 30 degrees in summer, and pick a low level, South facing cliff in winter. Theft; certainly in the south of France! Car break-ins are popular, so leave your car empty, open and immobilized!!!! Climbing is getting more and more popular; do not rough camp, please. Campsites are not expensive, and they help to keep the environment clean and healthy. No climbing guidebook gives anybody the right to climb or go anywhere; you are always a guest of the local community.

Climbing is highly dangerous, and there are no safety notices or warnings in the countryside and mountains! We do not advise on safety at all. In France for example, there is a general code:

Climbers are responsible for their own security.
Climbers must personally check any safety measures
Climbers must be able to recognise unreliable cliffs and equipment
Climbers must evaluate all the risks, all the time, and never stop evaluating.

Sometimes cliffs can even fall down!!!! If you do have any comments, especially on our star gradings, or feel that any of our information is out of date, please write to us at our publishing address, see details page at the front of the book, or email us on - info@jingowobbly.com

SOSSBLITZ 6a+, Harrison's Rocks (90.9), GB. Frank 'Cool River' Shannon

In this section, I presume that you are travelling to Europe for the first time. My first recommendation is that you should also buy two other guidebooks to Europe. First, get a 'lonely planet' style of book, which will include all the essential basic travel information. Secondly, look at the eyewitness travel series, they are fabulous and really worthwhile tourist guidebooks, and will surely make your trip a special one. Now, I only have to concentrate on good climbing tips.

We have no strict rule for including the particular cliffs in this guide; it could be called 'My favourite 2500 climbing sites in Europe.' I have tried to include a good overall selection from some 50,000 sites, carefully trying not to miss any gems, but leaving out some cliffs with delicate access problems. I have included lots of different styles of climbing; popular bouldering areas, tough gritty sports routes, longer traditional areas, and a few stunning mountain cliffs. You will need different safety equipment for each of these various styles of climbing, and it would be a pity to miss out on any good cliffs, just because you didn't bring some extra gear along. Also be psychologically prepared to climb on lots of different types of rock.

There are not really any specific, good or bad airports to fly into, but crossing between England and France is expensive with a car. Also there are many toll motorways in Europe; Britain, Germany and Holland, are free at the moment. There are different systems for charging, but it roughly the costs per hour are; Spain and Portugal $US 8, France $10, Italy $20. Work it out first, driving from London to Roma could cost you another $750, on top of fuel! You can crank up quite a few extra travel costs if you are not careful.

You do need a car to get the best from climbing in Europe – no doubt at all. You also want to come with quite a bit of luggage, and trolley it straight into the back of the car at the airport. I have found many good freelance companies on the web, who actually rent you the car, via one of the major companies at the airports – and therefore give you the very simple check in procedure for your car, and you get a pretty descent car too. We have also found that the smallest cars on offer, are only good for 2 people, if there are 4 climbers – next size up is essential.

Where do you go for the first visit to Europe? It's your choice of course. You have 3 obvious options. 1. You do a rock and roll style, non-stop tour. Visit a new crag each day, tick the hardest routes and move on. Not the best way to travel and quite exhausting, and you are bound to get your car done over at some point and have everything stolen! 2. Drive to one place and work on a route for 3 weeks, get rained on for the last 2 days, and go home defeated. 3. Pick 3 different sectors, one for each week. You find a nice place to stay, have a chance to climb at a few different cliffs around the area, enjoy the local bars and ambience, and stay long enough to meet people and make friends. We do the 3rd option every time. Do not underestimate the actuality of car break in's! Anything - in our past experience, left in the car, is likely to get stolen. By the time you have gone to the police, found another climbing shop, etc, etc. you have just lost about 10-20% of the time on your trip. Glove box open, parcel shelf out, nothing in car – be sensible and cautious.

If you want to camp – fine. We always travel now with a tent and stove because there are times when you find a great campsite, in a great spot. Stove canister compatability across Europe, is almost impossible- so maybe buy a stove on arrival. But for a good trip in style, most climbers now are going for renting a caravan or mini chalet (called mobilehomes! – but there ain't nothing mobile about them). You can get these for a week at a lot of campsites, and they are certainly not expensive, they have a small lounge, good cooker and fridge (cool beer!), and a hell of a comfy bed. (August is generally considered as "booked solid month.")

Don't over-estimate your climbing ability! Cranking 5.11a down the gym on a route that you know like the back of your hand is comfortable enough. Sport 6c is the equivalent in Europe. But out of the gym, on the crux of a route (always slightly polished holds), 4 metres above the last bolt! will make it feel like 5.13d. For on-sight climbing, red, white and purple grades are purely academic nonsense for 99% of climbers. We use blue to represent 6a-b, and this is still pretty tough for most climbers, so plan the areas for your trip, within your actual on-sight standard. Have a crusin, and not a doggin holiday.

This guide should give you enough basic information to plan your trip. You need some maps of course. We get a motorway-major road map of Europe to do the major navigation. After that you really do want the minimum detail level of a 1:300,000 area map. Less detail than this scale, really does give you a hard time. If you can get a good map before you travel, it really is worth it. Certainly Freytag and Berndt offer very good maps to central Europe – CH,A,CZ; IGN green series to France 1:100,000; Geográfico Nacional 1:200,000 for Spain; Ordnance Survey (explorer series) GB. A compass is pretty useful, but we are finding a lot of new uses for the global positioning system. GPS, is going to be a thing of the future, but for now they are brilliant in bouldering at Fontainebleau. It will remember where your car is! So after 4 hours of bouldering in the forest and getting completely disorientated, you can be home in minuites.

Do you want to climb, with or without route information? I have had a great deal of fun by not using any topo guidebooks, but it does demand a very adventurous spirit. You usually get intimidated by the sheer!!! look of a cliff, so therefore end up climbing the easier lines. But you remain uncluttered by information and weighty guidebooks, and get a far more comfortable sense of freedom. I admit, that it is not the best thing for beginners, but as soon as you climb completely by your own personal instinct, you will be far safer in the mountains; where bad weather and being reliant on following guidebook instructions, is a bad mix!

If you do want a guidebook, there are hundreds, if not thousands. Some are fact, and some are fiction! It is sod's law, that the day before you get to your area, they sell out of guidebooks! Certainly, if you ever get the chance to buy a guidebook, to an area you might go to, get it! Good guidebooks

cost around $30, and therefore a weeks climbing is going to cost you - say $6 a day. It is way cheap, considering the information and the pleasure you will get from the guidebook (not even the price of the gym). We try to list the local guidebooks for each area, but they may not always be in print! Certainly the web is an ideal place to buy a guidebook, and we try to give a fair indication to the quality of the material in the guidebooks that we show. When you get to an area – each country differs from the sales point for guidebooks. Spain has relatively few guidebooks locally, and often you get a topo held behind the bar at the local café – which people copy out (blank pages at the back of this guide); F-local bookshops, local bar or café (bakery etc...) I,CH,A,D – bookshops; GB-generally climbing shops.

A lot of land in Europe is privately owned, and for most of the time there is not a problem with access. Generally climbers want to enjoy the natural areas the countryside, and landowners recognise this. Most farmers we meet, seem to enjoy others appreciating the countryside, but like anyone else – get well upset, when you take their favourite parking spot. So, it is well worth taking the trouble to ask locally, if you car is parked OK. If there is an access problem, you will hear about it straight away, instead of coming back to a duffed up car. As for bird restrictions, you are a bit more than thoughtless, dim, stupit, arrogant, and many worse terms – it you ignore them.

Any accidents in the alpine areas of Europe will be usually dealt with a highly professional service; I can promise you that this is very expensive, ouch! So you must get proper travel and accident insurance, which specifically states that rock climbing is part of the cover. Also make sure there is a good arrangement for payment of anything, should you get injured. At the back of this guide, we have added a page to put in your details of insurance etc, because in the event of an accident, you would be chopper'd straight to the hospital, and in is always handy to have these details with you. Have a great trip, and really safe, enjoyable, climbing.

RIGHT WALL E5 6a, Dinas Cromlech, Llanberis Pass, Wales; Phil Davidson - Solo!

Ce livre donne un panorama détaillé de l'escalade en Europe Occidentale. Il a été écrit pour les grimpeurs de tout niveau, des débutants aux professionels. Tous les types de grimpe sont mentionnés cependant nous avons privilégié les voies équipées et l'escalade à bloc. Ce guide, qui ressemble presque à une encyclopédie de l'escalade en Europe, reste malgré tout assez petit et peut donc être emmené partout. Où que vous soyez en Europe, vous trouverez en un instant et grâce à ce guide, tous les meilleurs sites d'escalade. Internet donne en général trop d'information qui n'est pas toujours mise à jour. Europe – Sport Vertical donne au grimpeur une information concise, de qualité et facile à utiliser, avec en prime plus de 350 photos de qualité. Ce guide a été créé dans le but de devenir le compagnon de voyage de tous les grimpeurs.

Icônes

Notre intention est que ce guide soit utilisé par les grimpeurs du monde entier quelque soit leur nationalité ou leur langue. C'est pourquoi nous

avons utilisé très peu de texte. Nous avons créé des icônes très spécifiques, uniques aux guides Jingo Wobbly, grâce à notre expérience en escalade de plus de 30 ans. Vous trouverez au début de ce livre les principaux icônes traduits en différentes langues (voir également annexe 4).

Secteurs

Nous avons choisi de diviser l'Europe Occidentale en 99 secteurs d'escalade, eux-mêmes regroupés en 6 principales régions (voir index sur la couverture intérieure). Chaque secteur est de taille et de format différent, mais contient en général un minimum de 800 à 1000 voies, ce qui est idéal pour 2 semaines de vacances par exemple. D'un niveau plus pratique, la majorité des grimpeurs souhaitent en général connaître toutes les voies existantes dans un périmètre d'environ 2 heures depuis leur camping ou leur gîte. C'est sur cette idée que la plupart des secteurs ont été créés. Nous espérons, à l'avenir, réaliser 4 pages illustrées pour chaque secteur, mais faire un rapport précis sur 2600 falaises prend quelques années!

St. Antonin-Noble-Val, Tarn-et-Garonne, France - Cahors (25).

Mise en page

Nous avons utilisé 3 types de page dans ce guide: pages avec cartes générales, pages avec petites cartes de location et pages d'information. Les pages avec cartes générales donnent aux grimpeurs, pour chaque secteur, une idée claire et rapide de la location des meilleurs sites. Les falaises les plus importantes sont mises en valeur par des rectangles jaunes et les falaises les plus populaires sont indiquées avec des points rouges (40 max. pour chaque secteur).

Cluses, Savoie, France - Cluses (36).

Le nombre total de falaises et de voies dans chaque secteur est répertorié en haut de la page et les rectangles turquoises indiquent ce que couvre le guide local.

Nos cartes n'ont pas pour intention de remplacer les cartes de type IGN et nous vous conseillons de toujours acheter au moins une carte routière pour vous aider dans vos déplacements (1:2-300 000 est l'échelle la plus pratique). La disposition des icônes pour la section informative est expliquée au dos de la couverture avant. Elle peut paraître un peu compliquée au premier abord mais devrait être maîtrisée rapidement puisqu'elle est identique à chaque section. Vous trouverez pour chaque secteur: le nombre de voies (codé par couleur avec un pourcentage de voies dans chaque cotation); l'orientation de la falaise et l'ombrage offert; la hauteur des voies et l'altitude de la falaise; le type de roche et les différents types d'escalade; la distance depuis le parking; enfin le niveau de difficulté pour trouver les falaises.

Etoiles

Nous avons décerné, pour la qualité, des étoiles de couleur (de 1 à 3). Les étoiles vertes illustrent les voies qui sont bonnes mais mal situées – près d'une carrière sale ou d'une route passagère. Les étoiles bleues indiquent les voies de qualité et bien situées. Les étoiles rouges sont décernées seulement aux superbes voies situées dans des endroits exceptionnels (voir annexe-1 pour les exemples). Ces étoiles ont été données suite à nos visites sur les sites d'escalade et selon notre expérience personnelle.

Page d'information

Les pages avec les cartes générales s'appuient sur des pages d'information. Jingo et Wobbly donnent, autant que possible, des commentaires aussi bien en anglais que dans la langue locale. Jingo donne son opinion pour les grimpeurs forts et musclés, tandis que Wobbly donne des suggestions pour les grimpeurs plus techniques. Il y a sur l'Europe plus de 500 guides d'escalade! Nous souhaitons promouvoir pour chaque pays ces guides locaux, et à cet effet vous trouverez les photos des principaux guides avec quelques informations utiles (auteur, date de publication, nombre de pages, dimensions et endroits où vous pouvez les acheter). Nous avons décerné nos étoiles de qualité pour 5 catégories différentes: informations générales (cartes afin de trouver le site pour la première fois); topo des voies; facilité d'utilisation pour ceux qui ne parlent pas la langue locale; photos. Chaque guide demande à son auteur beaucoup de travail et d'effort, c'est pourquoi nous avons utilisé les étoiles et les poubelles très, très prudemment! Jingo et Wobbly ne font pas de 'guides sur les campings' mais ont néanmoins essayé d'indiquer pour chaque secteur un bon terrain

de camping, bien situé par rapport aux
principaux sites d'escalade – comme pour les
cotations, le jaune est pour le bas de gamme
et le violet pour le haut de gamme.

Petites cartes

Lors d'une première visite dans un secteur,
il est possible que vous ne trouviez pas
ou que vous ne puissiez pas acheter le
guide d'escalade local (rupture de stock
ou magasins fermés par exemple). C'est
pourquoi, et pour les meilleurs sites, nous
avons essayé de présenter un minimum de 4 petites
cartes afin de vous permettre de trouver les sites,
d'aller grimper et de rencontrer d'autres grimpeurs.
Les cartes sont petites et concises et devrait donner
suffisamment d'information. Elles indiquent
également les parkings, les chemins et sentiers
d'approche, l'orientation des falaises, les forêts
et tout autre point de repère indispensable. Elles
n'indiquent pas les droits de passage, et ne donnent
aucune indication sur les restrictions au niveau de
l'escalade. Toutes les cartes indiquent en haut le
nord et ont pour la plupart une échelle. Nous avons
également des icônes spéciaux avec des blocs de
calcaire, ceux-ci indiquent le type de calcaire pour
chaque site - voir volet au dos pour les 26 catégories
différentes. (annexe-3 photos).

Conseil et information:

L'escalade sur voies équipées est le type d'escalade le
plus populaire en Europe. Les grimpeurs utilisent
le plus souvent une seule corde de 10.5mm de
diamètre et de 70 mètres de long et 12 dégaines.
Un casque peut-être utile mais en général nous
vous conseillons d'éviter de grimper sur les parties
instables de la falaise. La mauvaise saison pour
grimper est de novembre à février cependant
l'escalade en Espagne, Italie, Grèce etc est possible;
de mars à mai et octobre sont les mois parfaits pour
l'escalade en basse altitude; en juin et septembre
recherchez les sites aux alentours de 1000m
d'altitude, et en juillet et août aux alentours de
2000m d'altitude. Les effractions de voitures sont
très fréquentes, c'est pourquoi nous vous conseillons

Beaumes-de-Venise, Vaucluse, France
Dentelles de Montmirail - Avignon (44)

de ne rien laisser dans votre voiture et d'utiliser
un dispositif antidémarrage!!!! L'escalade est un
sport de plus en plus populaire, cependant veuillez
éviter le camping sauvage. Les terrains de camping
sont souvent peu chers et permettent de garder
l'environnement propre et sain. Souvenez-vous
que vous n'êtes qu'un 'invité' de la communauté
locale et qu'aucun guide d'escalade donne le droit à
quiconque de grimper ou de se promener n'importe
où.

Grimper est très dangereux et il n'y a pas de notice
de sécurité ou d'avertissement en montagne ou en
campagne! Nous-mêmes nous ne donnons aucun
conseil de sécurité. Cependant il existe un code
général européen:

Les grimpeurs sont responsables de leur propre
sécurité.
Les grimpeurs doivent personellement vérifier les
mesures de sécurité.
Les grimpeurs doivent être capables de reconnaître
les falaises instables et les équipements douteux.
Les grimpeurs doivent évaluer tous les risques tout le
temps et évaluer ces risques sans arrêt.

Si vous avez des commentaires, en particulier sur le
décernement de nos étoiles, ou si vous pensez que
certaines informations ne sont pas à jour, n'hésitez
pas à nous écrire à notre adresse de publication (voir
page d'information à l'avant du livre) ou envoyez
nous un e-mail à – info@jingowobbly.com

Dieses Buch bietet einen umfassenden Überblick über die Klettergebiete Westeuropas. Es ist für Kletterer aller Grade, vom Anfänger und Sonntagskletterer bis zum Hardmover und professionellen Bergführer, geschrieben. Wir haben viele Spielarten des Kletterns integriert, den Schwerpunkt jedoch auf eingebohrte Sportkletterrouten und das Bouldern gelegt. Entstanden ist ein Führer über die Klettermöglichkeiten in Europa mit geradezu lexikalischem Charakter. Dennoch ist er klein genug um in der Rucksack-Deckeltasche mitgenommen zu werden. Wo auch immer ihr in Europa unterwegs seid– mit diesem Führer findet ihr schnell zu den lohnenden Klettergebieten. Im Internet wird schlichtweg zu viel und oft unzuverlässige Information angeboten. Europe – Sport Vertical bietet dem Kletterer schnell erfassbare, sorgfältig recherchierte und präzise Angaben sowie über 350 qualitativ hochwertige Fotos. Dieser Führer soll allen Kletterern ein zuverlässiger, unterhaltsamer und farbenfroher Reisebegleiter sein.

Symbole

Wir haben den Führer so gestaltet, dass er von Kletterern sämtlicher Nationalitäten und Sprachen der Welt benützt werden kann. Deshalb verwenden wir so wenig Text wie möglich. In den speziell für Jingo Wobbly Führer entwickelten Kletter-Symbolen steckt über 30 Jahre Klettererfahrung. Die wichtigsten Symbole werden auf den Umschlaginnenseiten in mehreren Sprachen erläutert. (Siehe auch Anhang 4)

Sektoren & Layout

Wir haben Westeuropa in 99 europäische Klettersektoren aufgeteilt, die 6 Hauptregionen zugeordnet sind (siehe Umschlaginnenseite). Die Sektoren haben jeweils unterschiedliche Größen und Formen, enthalten aber in der Regel mindestens 800-1000

Routen und bieten genügend Klettermöglichkeiten für einen zweiwöchigen Urlaub. Da die meisten Kletterer erfahrungsgemäß Informationen über all die Klettergebiete wollen, die innerhalb von 2 Stunden von ihrem Campingplatz oder ihrer Unterkunft aus erreichbar sind, haben wir die meisten Sektoren nach diesem Prinzip abgegrenzt. Wir hoffen im Laufe der Zeit jeden Sektor mit 4 bebilderten Seiten darstellen zu können, aber 2600 Klettergebiete exakt zu recherchieren dauert nun mal ein paar Jahre!

Wir verwenden 3 Seiten-Layouts: Übersichtskarten, Detailkarten und Informationsseiten. Die Übersichtskarten sind so gestaltet, dass sie dem Kletterer auf einen Blick zeigen, wo in einem Sektor die besten Klettergebiete zu finden sind. Die wichtigsten Gebiete sind mit gelben Kästen hinterlegt und gute, beliebte Felsen sind mit roten Punkten gekennzeichnet (max. 40 in jedem Sektor). Die Anzahl der Klettergebiete und Routen in jedem Sektor ist oben auf der Seite aufgeführt. Türkis umrandet sind die Gebiete, die von lokalen Topo-Führern abgedeckt werden. Die Karten sind nicht dazu gedacht qualitativ hochwertige Wanderkarten zu ersetzen. Wir empfehlen den Kauf einer aktuellen Straßenkarte, damit ihr nicht unnötige Zeit bei der Suche der Gebiete verliert (brauchbarer Maßstab 1: 2-300 000).

Essing, Altmühltal, Kelheim; Regensburg (83)

Goslar, Harz; Hannover (80)

Die Bedeutung der Symbole ist auf den Umschlaginnenseiten erklärt. Diese Legende mag zunächst kompliziert erscheinen, sie wird sich aber schnell einprägen, da für alle Klettergebiete das gleiche Layoutprinzip verwendet wird. Für jeden Felsen werden angegeben: Anzahl der Routen (Farbkodierung des Anteils pro Schwierigkeitsgrad), Exposition der Wände und Beschattung, Länge der Routen und Höhenlage des Felsens, Gestein und Art der Kletterei, Zustiegsdauer und -steilheit sowie die Schwierigkeit den Felsen zu finden.

Sterne

Für die Qualität eines Klettergebiets haben wir farbkodierte Sterne (1-3) vergeben. Grüne Sterne stehen für gute Kletterien, die sich jedoch in unschönem Ambiente befinden, wie etwa in einem Steinbruch oder neben einer stark befahrenen Straße. Blaue Sterne bedeuten gutes Klettern in sehr schöner Umgebung. Rote Sterne wurden nur für Top-Gebiete in außergewöhnlich schöner Lage vergeben. (Siehe Anhang 1 für Beispiele des jeweiligen Mindeststandards). Wir vergeben die Sterne nach unserem persönlichen Eindruck im Klettergebiet und besuchen jedes Jahr über 200 neue Gebiete.

Detailkarten

Beim ersten Besuch eines Klettergebiets kann es passieren, dass man keinen Kletterführer bekommt, z.B. weil er ausverkauft ist oder der Laden geschlossen hat. Deshalb haben wir mindestens 4 Detailkarten von guten Klettergebieten eingebaut. Damit findet ihr immerhin die Felsen, könnt klettern und trefft vielleicht andere Kletterer. Die Karten sind zwar klein und wenig detailliert, sollten jedoch für diesen Zweck genügen. Sie zeigen Parkmöglichkeiten, korrekte Zustiege, die Lage der Felsen, Waldgebiete und lokale landschaftliche Besonderheiten. Nicht enthalten sind Fahr-, Betretungs- oder Kletterverbote o.ä. Alle Karten sind eingenordet und grob maßstabsgerecht. Für Kalksteingebiete gibt es zusätzliche Symbole, die genauer über die Art der Kletterei Auskunft geben – die 26 Kategorien sind auf der hinteren Umschlaginnenseite erläutert.

Informationsseite

Wir haben die Übersichtskarten mit Informationsseiten ergänzt. Jingo und Wobbly geben Hinweise sowohl in Englisch wie auch – wo möglich - in der Landessprache. Jingo vertritt die Meinung eines starken, athletischen Kletterers, während Wobbly Tipps für eher technische und akrobatische Kletterer gibt. Für Europa sind derzeit über 500 Kletterführer veröffentlicht! Da wir die lokalen Führer unterstützen wollen, zeigen wir deren Titelseiten und geben nützliche Hinweise zu Autor, Erscheinungsjahr, Seitenzahl, Größe und Kaufmöglichkeit (mit Öffnungszeit, Montag-Sonntag?) Bei der Sternvergabe haben wir 5 Kategorien berücksichtigt: allgemeine Informationen, Karten für die Felssuche, Klettertopos und –informationen, Verwendbarkeit ohne Kenntnisse der Landessprache und Fotos. (Siehe Anhang 3 für die besten Kletterführer Europas). Einen Kletterführer zu schreiben ist eine Wahnsinnsarbeit, deshalb haben wir unsere Sterne und Mülleimer sehr, sehr sorgfältig vergeben! Jingo und Wobbly veröffentlichen keine ‚Camping-Führer‘, aber wir versuchen zumindest einen zentralen Campingplatz als ersten Anlaufpunkt zu nennen – wie bei den Schwierigkeitsgraden steht dabei Gelb für einfach und Violett für außergewöhnlich.

Tipps und Informationen über Europa

Das Sportklettern ist die populärste Spielart des Kletterns in Europa; die meisten Kletterer verwenden ein 70 Meter langes 10,5 mm-Einfachseil und 12 Expressschlingen. Ein Helm kann sinnvoll sein, aber ihr solltet generell versuchen steinschlaggefährdete Routen zu meiden. Höhenlage und Exposition der Felsen solltet ihr so wählen, dass ihr im Sommer keine 30 Grad ertragen müsst und euch im Winter an einer tief gelegenen Südwand vergnügen könnt. Diebstahl: Zumindest in Südfrankreich ist Autoknacken weit verbreitet; das Auto sollte nur leer, offen und mit

Wegfahrsperre allein gelassen werden!!! Klettern wird immer populärer, deshalb bitte nicht wild zelten. Campingplätze sind nicht teuer und tragen dazu bei, dass die Umwelt sauber und intakt bleibt. Kein Kletterführer gibt euch das Recht überall zu klettern oder herumzulaufen; ihr seid immer Gäste der Einheimischen vor Ort. Klettern ist sehr gefährlich und es gibt vor Ort an den Felsen keine Sicherheitshinweise oder Warnungen! Wir geben keinerlei Sicherheitsinformationen. In Frankreich beispielsweise gelten folgende Regeln:

Kletterer sind für ihre Sicherheit selbst verantwortlich.
Kletterer müssen persönlich alle Sicherheitsvorkehrungen überprüfen.
Kletterer müssen in der Lage sein unsichere Felsen und Ausrüstung zu erkennen.
Kletterer müssen ständig und in jeder Situation alle Risiken einschätzen.

Manchmal können sogar ganze Felsblöcke abstürzen !!! Wenn ihr uns Kommentare zukommen lassen wollt, etwa über die Sterne-Bewertung, oder wenn Ihr der Meinung seid, unsere Informationen seien veraltet, schreibt uns bitte an die Adresse im Impressum am Anfang des Buchs oder mailt uns an – info@jingowobbly.com

Hohnstein, Elbsansteingebirge; Dresden (81)

Questo libro è una ricerca completa sull'arrampicata nell'europa occidentale. È stato concepito per alpinisti di tutti i livelli, da chi inizia e si diverte solo nel weekend, fino agli esperti e a chi pratica la professione di guida alpina. Consideriamo tutti i tipi di arrampicata, ma in questo lavoro ci siamo concentrati su vie di arrampicata sportiva e bouldering. È una guida che offre un livello enciclopedico di conoscenze sull'arrampicata in Europa. Tuttavia rimane un libro, piccolo abbastanza da essere portato nella tasca del vostro zaino. Ovunque voi siate in Europa, potete trovare in un istante tutti i migliori posti per arrampicare. Se cercate informazioni in rete ne trovate semplicemente troppe, e molte di queste inattendibili. Così Europe - Sport Vertical dà all'alpinista informazioni veloci da usare, concise e qualitativamente curate; è supportato da oltre 350 fotografie di alta qualità. Si appresta a diventare un fidato simpatico colorato compagno di viaggio per tutti gli arrampicatori.

Icone

Riteniamo che questa guida verrà usata da alpinisti provenienti da tutto il mondo. Abbiamo perciò utilizzato una quantità di testi contenuta. Tutte le nostre speciali icone di arrampicata sono uniche delle guide Jingo Wobbly, e sono state specialmente studiate in oltre 30 anni di arrampicata. Le icone principali sono descritte in alcune lingue sulla copertina interna. (vedi anche l'appendice 4)

Settori

Abbiamo deciso di dividere l'Europa dell'ovest in 99 settori europei di arrampicata, e raggruppati in 6 principali regioni (trovate l'indice sulla copertina interna). Ogni settore ha una forma e un taglio differenti, ma generalmente tutti contengono almeno 800-1000 vie, offrendo molte arrampicate per una vacanza della durata di due settimane. Infatti la quasi totalità degli alpinisti ha bisogno di sapere tutte le possibili arrampicate racchiuse nell'area raggiungibile con due ore di macchina dal campeggio. Abbiamo usato questo principio per descrivere la maggior parte dei nostri settori. Ci auguriamo in futuro di produrre quattro pagine illustrate per ogni settore, ma riuscire

a catalogare accuratamente 2600 guglie sarebbe un lavoro di alcuni anni!

Impaginazione

Usiamo tre stili di pagina: cartine con i dati principali, cartine per individuare la posizione, e pagine informative. Le cartine sono state concepite per fare capire agli arrampicatori in modo chiaro e veloce dove sono situate le migliori arrampicate in una determinata area. Le falesie più importanti sono evidenziate con riquadri gialli, quelle più popolari sono riconoscibili per la presenza di punti rossi (massimo 40 in ogni area). Il numero totale delle falesie e delle vie in ogni settore è elencato all'inizio della pagina, mentre fini riquadri turchesi mostrano la topografia del luogo. Le cartine non hanno la pretesa di rimpiazzare le cartine cartografiche di alta qualità; vi suggeriamo infatti acquistare una recente cartina dei sentieri, per avere il massimo dalla vostro viaggio. (scala consigliata 1:2-300000)

Troverete la spiegazione di come sono organizzate le icone nella copertina interna. Può sembrare complicata all'inizio, ma ogni linea utilizza esattamente lo stesso principio dell'impaginazione, così dovrebbe essere veloce da padroneggiare. Per ogni guglia includiamo: numero delle vie (codificate con colore e con il grado rispettivo); orientamento della falesia e ombra offerta; lunghezza delle vie e altezza della guglia.

Stelle

Assegnamo stelle con differenti colori indicanti la qualità (1-3), su di una scala europea ad alto standard. Le stelle verdi illustrano una buona arrampicata ma in un cattivo posto, come ad esempio in una cava sporca o vicino ad una strada trafficata. Quelle blu mostrano un'arrampicata in un posto molto bello. Le stelle rosse sono solo assegnate ad una arrampicata superba in un posto eccezionale. (vedere appendice 1 per esempi ….) Assegnamo stelle in base alla nostra personale esperienza, e sulla possibilità di visitare più di duecento nuove differenti guglie ogni anno.

Pagina di informazione

Le carte sono supportate da pagine informative; Jingo e Wobbly forniscono commenti sia in inglese che nella lingua locale quando possibile. Jingo rappresenta il punto di vista di un forte arrampicatore muscolato, e Wobbly crea suggestioni per l'alpinista più tecnico e artistico. Offriamo più di 500 guide per l'Europa! È nostra intenzione supportare tutte le guide locali, così da illustrare la copertina con utili dettagli: autore, data di pubblicazione, pagine, formato, e un fornitore locale dove potete acquistare la guida (con i giorni di apertura). Assegnamo le nostre stelle per 5 differenti categorie: informazioni generali come ad esempio cartine per trovare la falesia al primo tentativo; informazioni sul luogo della via facile da usare per quelli che non parlano la lingua locale; fotografie. È sempre un grosso lavoro ed un grande sforzo completare una nuova guida, così stiamo molto attenti nell'usare le nostre stelle ed i nostri "cestini". Jingo e Wobbly non forniscono guide per il campeggio, cerchiamo però almeno di indicare un buon campeggio che sia situato centralmente, e con i colori giallo e viola indichiamola qualità: giallo identifica un servizio minimo, viola condizioni esotiche! Inoltre abbiamo speciali icone raffiguranti roccia calcarea, che vi faranno capire il tipo di calcare presente sulla guglia (guardare la tasca posteriore per le 26 differenti categorie-photo Appendix 3).

Mini cartine

Quando visitate un'area, è possibile che non riusciate a trovare o acquistare un guida perchè esaurita o perchè il negozio potrebbe essere chiuso. Noi perciò proviamo a dare almeno 4 mini cartine per affrontare buone arrampicate. Questo perché così possiate almeno raggiungere la guglia, andare ad arrampicare e avere la possibilità di incontrare altri arrampicatori. Sono concise e piccole mappe, ma si dimostrano adeguate. Mostrano dove sono situati i parcheggi, le corrette vie di accesso, la direzione delle falesie, i principali punti di riferimento. Ricordate però che non riportano nessuna via di salita, e non danno indicazioni riguardanti l'arrampicata. Tutte riportano il nord sul bordo superiore ed una approssimativa scala.

Informazioni e suggerimenti sull'Europa

L'arrampicata sportiva è il più popolare stile di arrampicata in Europa; i climbers usano soprattutto una corda da 70 metri con un diametro di 10.5 mm da 12 intrecci . Un casco è sempre una protezione utile, ma generalmente è più consigliato cercare di scansare qualsiasi cosa che cade! Il periodo peggiore per arrampicare è da novembre a febbraio, tuttavia è possibile arrampicare in Spagna Italia Grecia...; i mesi di Marzo Aprile Maggio e Ottobre sono ottimi a basse altitudini; in Giugno e settembre è opportuno cercare zone attorno ai 1000 metri di altitudine, mentre in luglio e Agosto è meglio recarsi in falesie il più vicino possibile ai 2000 metri s.l.m. Furti: lasciate le vostre automobili vuote, i furti all'interno delle automobili sono molto frequenti. L'arrampicata sta diventando sempre più popolare, i campeggi sempre più affollati, abbiatene rispetto! I campeggi non sono costosi e cercano di mantenere l'ambiente sano e pulito. Le guide non danno il diritto di arrampicare o andare ovunque; ricordate che siete sempre ospiti della comunità locale.

Arrampicare è molto pericoloso, e non sono presenti avvertimenti o avvisi di sicurezza in campagna o in mointagna! Vi consigliamo di avere assoluto riguardo della norme di sicurezza. Esiste un codice generale europeo:

gli alpinisti sono responsabili per la loro stessa incolumità
gli alpinisti devono personalmente controllare ogni misura di sicurezza
gli alpinisti devono essere in grado di riconoscere equipaggiamento o falesie non affidabili
gli alpinisti devono valutare ogni rischio, sempre, e mai smettere di farlo.

A volte la falesie possono anche cadere!!! Se avete commenti specialmente riguardanti la nostra classificazione, o pensate che una qualsiasi delle nostre informazioni non sia corretta, per favore scriveteci al nostro indirizzo che trovate sulla copertina del libro, o tramite posta elettronica all'indirizzo info@jingowobbly.com

Este libro nos ofrece una visión general de la escalada en Europa Occidental. Está dirigido a escaladores de todos los niveles, desde principiantes y aficionados de fin de semana a verdaderos fanáticos y guías profesionales. Se incluyen todo tipo de escaladas aunque se centre más en vías equipadas y boulder. Nos ofrece mucha información global, con la ventaja de estar concentrada en un solo libro, con el tamaño idóneo para poder llevarse en la tapa de la mochila. En cualquier lugar de Europa en el que te encuentres, podrás conseguir reseñas de las mejores zonas de escalada. En Internet tienes multitud de datos, casi se puede decir que demasiados y, en ocasiones, poco fiables. Por eso, EUROPA-DEPORTE VERTICAL ofrece al escalador una información clara y concisa, además de un fácil manejo y una cuidada edición, complementado con más de 350 fotos de gran calidad. Una compañera de viaje imprescindible en todas tus escapadas.

Iconos

Nuestra intención es que la guía pueda ser utilizada por personas de cualquier nacionalidad. Por eso, se ha incluido el menor texto posible. Todos los iconos referidos a la escalada son exclusivos de las guías Jingo Woobly, y han sido desarrollados a lo largo de 30 años de experiencia en este mundo. Los iconos principales se describen en varios idiomas en el interior de las cubiertas (ver también apéndice 4)

Regiones

Se ha dividido Europa Occidental en 99 regiones, agrupadas en 6 grandes bloques (ver índice en el interior de la cubierta) Cada región tiene diferente estructura y tamaño, pero lo normal es que cuente con unas 800-1000 vías, suficientes para llenar unas vacaciones de 2 semanas. Teniendo en cuenta esta idea, las regiones se han diseñado de tal forma que puedas encontrar todas las zonas de escalada en un radio de 2 horas en coche desde tu lugar de alojamiento, tomándolo como campo base para tus escapadas diarias. Esperamos poder editar 4 páginas con fotos de cada región, pero teniendo en cuenta que hay que visitar 2600 zonas, tardaremos unos cuantos años...

Esquema

En la guía hay 3 tipos de páginas diferentes: Mapas de datos, mapas de localización y páginas de información. Los mapas de datos están diseñados para que el escalador obtenga una clara impresión de las mejores zonas de cada región. Las más importantes están destacadas en color amarillo y las más populares se marcan con un punto rojo (máx. 40 por cada región) El número total de zonas y de vías en cada región se indica en la parte superior de la página y los recuadros color turquesa muestran la cobertura total de la guía. Para poder sacar el mayor partido a tu viaje puede ser una buena idea combinar estos planos con un buen mapa de carreteras o con uno específico de la zona. El funcionamiento de los iconos se explica en el interior de la cubierta. A primera vista parece complicado, pero utilizamos el mismo principio en cada vía por lo que no deberá ser difícil acostumbrarnos. En cada zona de escalada se incluyen: número de vías (codificadas en colores con el porcentaje de cada grado), orientación, altura de las vías y altitud media de la zona; tipo de roca y diferentes estilos de escalada; aproximación: dificultad y duración de la misma.

Estrellas

Se otorga a cada zona una estrella de diferente color (1-3) para indicar su calidad. Una estrella verde indica una buena escalada, en un lugar mediocre (Ej.: cantera sucia, zona próxima a carretera ruidosa, ...) Una estrella azul nos indica una buena escalada en un lugar muy agradable. La estrella roja está reservada a escaladas excepcionales dentro de un marco incomparable (ver apéndice 1 para ejemplos de cada tipo). Las estrellas se han concedido basándonos en nuestra experiencia personal al visitar cada zona.

Croquis

Cuando visites una zona por primera vez, puede ser bastante difícil conseguir una guía local, tal vez se haya agotado, ya no existe la tienda, etc. Para prevenirlo se intentan incluir, al menos, 4 croquis de alguna de las zonas de escalada. De esta forma podrás quitarte el gusanillo y conocer a otros escaladores.

Son suficientes para un primer contacto. Hemos intentado indicar los lugares de aparcamiento, los caminos correctos para las aproximaciones con referencias que nos faciliten la tarea, etc. No indican ni las prohibiciones de paso a las zonas ni las restricciones de escalada si las hubiera. Todos tienen marcado el Norte en la parte superior y muestran una escala. Existen también iconos especiales, de color blanco, que describen hasta 26 tipos de roca caliza que a su vez suponen 26 formas diferentes de escalada (ver tapa trasera) apéndice 3, photos.)

Pagina de informacion

Los mapas de datos se complementan con páginas de información; Jingo y Woobly hacen sus comentarios en Inglés y en el idioma local, si es posible. Jingo representa el punto de vista de un escalador fuerte y musculoso y Woobly hace sugerencias para los escaladores más técnicos y artistas. En Europa hay unas 500 guías de escalada diferentes. Queremos apoyar todas las guías locales, así que incluimos una foto de la portada junto con algunos detalles de interés: autor, fecha de publicación, páginas, tamaño y una lista de comercios donde puedas comprarla (con días de apertura) Se califican con estrellas dividas en 5 categorías: Información general, croquis a las vías, información de cada vía, facilidad de uso para quienes no hablen el idioma local, fotografías. Puesto que cada guía cuesta mucho trabajo y esfuerzo realizarla, hemos procurado calificarlas de manera muy cuidadosa. Jingo y Woobly han tenido la amabilidad de indicarnos, al menos, un buen lugar de acampada, bien localizado; como ocurre con los grados, el amarillo corresponde a un camping sencillo y el púrpura a uno exótico.

Información sobre Europa

La "deportiva" es el estilo de escalada más popular de Europa. La cuerda más utilizada es la cuerda simple, de 10'5mm. y de unos 70 metros, junto con unas 12 cintas exprés. El casco es una protección bastante útil, aunque sin olvidarnos de avisar cuando caiga algo de la pared. De noviembre a febrero es mala época para la escalada, aunque son buenas fechas para visitar algunas regiones de España, Italia, Grecia, etc;

de marzo a mayo, junto con octubre es mejor escalar a baja altitud; una altitud media (sobre 1000m) es recomendable para los meses de junio y septiembre; mientras que en julio y agosto decántate por vías cercanas a los 2000m de altitud. Ladrones: que te abran el coche suele ser común en muchas regiones, así que déjalo vacío, abierto e inmovilizado. La escalada se está volviendo muy popular, así que, por favor, no acampes por libre. Los camping no son caros y ayudan a mantener la zona limpia y saneada. Ninguna guía de escalada te da derecho a escalar o atravesar cualquier lugar. Recuerda que eres un invitado de la localidad en la que te encuentres.

Escalar es potencialmente peligroso y no hay avisos ni advertencias en el monte. En ocasiones no nos acordamos de tomar las debidas medidas de seguridad. Aquí tienes un código general:

Cada escalador es responsable de su propia seguridad. Cada escalador debe comprobar personalmente cualquier medida de seguridad. Cada escalador debe ser capaz de reconocer vías y equipamientos poco fiables. Cada escalador debe evaluar los riesgos en cada momento y en cada situación.

Puede ocurrir que las vías sufran cambios inesperados. Si tienes algún comentario al respecto, sobre nuestra graduación, morfología de la vía, o piensas que alguna de nuestra información ya está desfasada, puedes escribirnos a nuestra dirección (ver detalles en la portada de la guía) o mándanos un e-mail a info@jingowobbly.com

Ayerbe, Riglos, Huesca (18)

Tato kniha je vyčerpávajícím přehledem lezeckých oblastí v západní Evropě. Je napsána pro lezce všech kategorií, pro začátečníky a víkendové nadšence, ale i pro odborníky a profesionální horské průvodce. Popisuje všechny druhy lezení, ale zaměřuje se převáž ně na zajištěné sportovní cesty a bouldrování. Je to průvodce, který předkládá znalosti o evropském lezení na encyklopedické úrovni. At jste v Evropě kdekoliv, můžete zde okamžitě najít opravdu dobré lezecké oblasti. Na webových stránkách naleznete velké množství informací, ale mnoho z nich bývá nespolehlivých. Europe - Sport Vertical podává lezci okamžité, kvalitní a stručné informace, které jsou doplněny více než 350 fotografiemi. Kniha je důvěryhodným, veselým a barevným společníkem na cesty pro všechny lezce.

Ikony

Vytvořili jsme průvodce, který je použitelný pro lezce všech národností. Pro srozumitelnost je zde použ íváno co nejméně textu. Všechny naše speciální lezecké ikony jsou unikátní v průvodcích Jingo Wobbly a jsou vyvíjeny již více než 30 let z lezeckých zkušeností. Hlavní ikony jsou popsány v několika jazycích na vnitřních stranách obálky. (viz dodatek 4)

Oblasti

Rozdělili jsme západní Evropu do 96 evropských lezeckých oblastí a ty jsme seskupili do 6 hlavních regionů. Každá oblast je různé velikosti a v různém měřítku, ale všeobecně obsahují nejméně 800 - 1000 cest a nabízejí mnoho lezeckých možností pro 2-týdenní pobyt. Většina lezců potřebuje informace, jaké lezecké oblasti jsou dosažitelné 2-hodinovou jízdou autem od jejich kempu. Z toho jsme vycházeli při zobrazování většiny oblastí.

Layout

Používáme 3 druhy stránek: s hlavními oblastními mapami a daty, s místními mapovými výřezy a informační stránky. Stránky s hlavními oblastními mapami jsou vytvořeny speciálně tak, aby podaly lezcům rychlé a jasné informace o nejlepších lezeckých místech v dané oblasti. Nejdůležitější klify jsou zvýrazněny ve žlutých polích, všechny dobré a populární klify jsou označeny červenými tečkami (max. 40 v každé oblasti). Celkový počet klifů a cest v každé oblasti je uveden nahoře na stránce. Tyrkysová pole ukazují pokrytí dostupnými průvodci. Mapy nenahrazují kvalitní kartografické produkty, vždy doporučujeme obstarat si aktuální mapu. Význam ikon pro datovou část je vysvětlen na vnitřních stranách obálky.

Hvězdičky

Přiřazujeme barevné hvězdičky (1-3) na základě evropské stupnice obtížnosti, která má vysokou úroveň. Zelené hvězdičky označují dobré lezení, ale špatnou lokalitu (jako je špinavý lom nebo oblast ležící v blízkosti frekventované silnice), modré hvězdičky označují dobré lezení ve velmi příjemné lokalitě a červené hvězdičky označují vynikající lezení ve výjimečných podmínkách. Hvězdičky přidělujeme na základě našich vlastních lezeckých zkušeností - každoročně navštěvujeme přes 200 různých skalních stěn.

Výřezy map

Uvádíme přehledné a ověřené mapové výřezy, které slouží k základní orientaci v případe, že nesoženete místního dostupného průvodce.

Informační stránky

Hlavní oblastní mapy s daty doplňujeme informačními stránkami. Komentář je psaný v angličtině, kde bylo možné také v místním jazyce. Uvádíme také všechny dostupné lezecké průvodce k dané oblasti: titul, autora, datum vydání, počet stran, formát a výčet skalních stěn. Uvádíme také místa, kde je možné průvodce zakoupit (tučně = hlavní prodejní místo) a otevírací dobu (1=pondělí). Průvodcům přidělujeme hvězdičky kvality dle kategorií: všeobecné informace, obtížnost nalezení skal, informace o cestách, jazyková použitelnost průvodce, kvalita fotografií. Nejvyšší kvalitu označují hvězdičky červené, pak následují modré a zelené. Najdete zde i přehled dobrých kempů.

V případe Vašich připomínek, predevším k hvězdičkovému hodnocení nebo pokud zjistíte, že některé informace jsou zastaralé, napište nám prosím na adresu vydavatelství nebo na e-mail:
info@jingowobbly.com
nebo obchod@freytagberndt.cz.

Adršpašské Skály, Ceská (79)

はじめに

星の数ほどの岩場があり、それぞれの岩場に数え切れないほどのルートがひしめくヨーロッパ。
この本は人生の全てを賭けても周り切れない、そんな西ヨーロッパのキラ星たちを、驚くような斬新なアイデアと工夫でまとめ上げたガイドブックの決定版です。
ビギナーからウィークエンドクライマー、エキスパートからプロのガイドまで、全てのクライマーが、自分のレベル、目的、好みにあった岩場を見つけ出すために最適の1冊です。内容的には人工登攀やアルパインクライムも含んでいますが、ボルダーとスポーツクライミングが中心となっています。
合わせて本書には百科辞典並みの岩場の情報が盛り込まれています。この小さな本に盛り込まれた情報を見つけだすには、少々の慣れと根気が必要ですが、これから説明するポイントを読んでから入れば、随分手助けになると思います。
ヨーロッパのこれだけの数多くの岩場から自分の行きたい場所を見つけだすのは、非常に困難な作業です。
日本人がヨーロッパでクライミングをするケースは、クライミングツアーや海外出張の合間など、限られた時間で楽しむケースが大半ではないかと考えます。そんな時、この本は本当に役に立つと確信します。
私の場合もほぼ毎年ヨーロッパに出かけていますが、岩場探し、トポ探しに明け暮れたあげく、やっと好みの岩場にたどり着いたのは帰国2日前、ということもありました。この本をザックの雨ブタに忍ばせておけば、そんな悩みも吹き飛ぶでしょう。
さらに350枚以上のクライミングフォトが、あなたのクライミングトリップの夢を広げてくれます。
見ているだけでも、心はヨーロッパを旅してしまう、そんな素晴らしいガイドブックができあがり心より喜んでいるとともに、この翻訳のボランティア！を楽しみながら引き受けることに相成りました。

アイコン（色々なマーク）について

本書はあらゆる国、言語の人が手にとってもすぐに理解できるよう、アイコンを駆使し極力文章は少なくしています。
著者であるJingo Wobblyの30年間にわたるクライミング経験から生み出された、ユニークなアイコンについては、裏表紙部分に数か国語の訳が記されています。日本語の訳も本書後半に掲載されています。

セクター（地域分け）について

本書は対象となる西ヨーロッパの地域を便宜上、96のセクターに分けました。そしてそれらセクターが属する国（地域）は6ヶ所になります。
それぞれのセクターの大きさ、広さなどは異なりますが、どのセクターも少なくとも2週間程度のクライミングツアーで十分に楽しめる800〜1000本のルートが存在します。
通常キャンプサイトもしくは山小屋から2時間以内の運転で到着できる範囲を入れています。
ほとんどのセクターは最低4ページの記載になるよう努力していますが2600ものエリアとなり数年を要する作業でした。

本書のレイアウトについて

1. 地図のパート　セクターの中の最も重要な岩場は、黄色いテキストボックスで岩場名と場所が記されています。それ以外の良い岩場は赤い点で記されています。（1セクター40個以内に限定しています）地図の右上にはセクター内のルート数が表記されています。
また地図内の青いテキストボックスは他のセクターの重要な岩場です。隣接しているセクターの番号は、地図内の枠に青い三角印内の番号を見てください。この地図は細かい道路など詳細は記されていませんので、必ず市販の道路地図と併用して利用してください。

2. アイコン　アイコンについては最初はわかりにくいと思います。しかし全て同じパターンで使用していますので一度理解してしまえば、非常に使い勝手が良いものです。表紙裏に英語などの説明があります。全ての岩場は、ルート数、グレードの比率（黄色から紫まで8段階、本書裏表紙参照）、岩場の方位（東西南北どちらを向いているか、ルート数やグレード比率などの、長方形のアイコンの濃い黒線が下についていれば南向き、上についていれば北向き、といった具合です）、夏は日陰になるか（方位と同じパターンで濃い緑で囲ってある場合は夏は日陰という意味です）、岩場の標高、岩質、クライミングの種類、アプローチの時間や勾配、はじめて岩場にいったときの岩場の発見難易度、という情報が盛り込まれています。

スター（グレード）について

岩場などの質を表すスターグレードは3色の色を3段階で使用しています。
緑　ルートは良いのですが岩場が石切り場だったり、車の騒音がうるさいなどマイナス要因もある場合
青　ルートも良く,岩場の環境もよい場合
赤　ルートはとても素晴らしく、なおかつ環境もとても素晴らしい場合
星の数は1-3個です。大まかな目安として星1個の場合は対象ルートが100本以下、星2個は100本以上、星3個は300本以上と考えておいてください。総ルート数が500本のエリアで赤星1個であれば、500うち100本程度が素晴らしいルートである、ということです。
赤ひとつ、緑ひとつなどの違う色の星が同時についている場合は、岩場に複数のエリアがありマイナス要因があるエリアと、素晴らしいエリアが混在しているからです。細かく見ていくと基準はありますが、十分想像できる範囲です。
また星が付されていない岩場は、良くない岩場である場合と訪れていないでわからない場合があります。このため毎年200以上の新しい岩場を訪れています。スターグレードは、あくまで岩場に行った際の個人的な感覚であることをご了承下さい。

ミニマップについて

岩場によってはすぐに現地でトポを入手することが難しい場合があります。本書ではそのようなケースに備え一部のセクターで4箇所程度のミニマップを用意しました。これを見てとりあえず岩場に行けばクライミングはできるでしょうし、ローカルのクライマーに会える可能性もあります。小さな簡易図ですが、駐車位置、アプローチ、岩場の方位、目印などが記されていますので、岩場にはたどり着けると思います。地図は北が上になっており縮尺のスケールも入っています。石灰岩の岩質の詳細もアルファベットで記しています。石灰岩の更なる岩質の詳細は、本書後半で写真入で記載していますので参照下さい。

インフォメーションページについて

マップページの情報のほかに、英語(とできる限り現地の言語でも)で、セクターにおける欠かせない情報を入れました。Jingoマーク(赤い鬼)は腕に自信のあるクライマーへの情報、そしてWobblyマーク(黄色いスマイル)はエンジョイ派向けのクライマーへの情報です。ヨーロッパには何と500以上のクライミングトポが存在します。本書ではこれらのトポも写真入で紹介しています。さらに著者、発刊年度、ページ数、サイズ、岩場の方位、岩場の近くのどこでそのトポが購入できるか(その場所が休みの日まで入っている!月曜1火曜2・・・日曜7という具合に番号にて記載)、加えて5カテゴリーについてトポの出来具合も評価しています。
1. 基本的な情報　2. 岩場が見つけやすい地図、表示が入っているか　3. ルートの情報　4. トポの言語が読めなくても理解できるか
5. 写真の入り具合　の5項目です。全てのトポは作り上げるのに膨大な労力と時間を費やしていますので、この評価はとても慎重に行いました。本書はキャンピングガイドではありませんが、中心的なキャンプ場については記しています。

その他の注意事項

ヨーロッパではスポーツクライミングが、クライミングの中で最も人気があるスタイルです。
ロープは10.5mmの50m,クイックドロー(ヌンチャク)は12枚が基準となります。
ヘルメットは身を守る助けにはなりますが、常に頭上に気を配り、落下物があっても当たらないように神経を尖らせていることが重要です。
どこに、いつ行くかは、その地域の気候や天気も影響します。表記されている標高、岩場の方位が良い判断材料になります。
夏であれば日陰の岩場や120度以上の傾斜の強い岩場を、冬なら標高が低く南面の岩場を選ぶと良いでしょう。
泥棒もいます。南仏は特に要注意です。車上荒らしは日常茶飯事なので、車内は空っぽにしておくのが懸命です。
ダッシュボードも空にして、見えるように開けておく人もいます。中には何もないよ、という意思表示です。ガラスを割られるだけでも大損害ですから念には念を。
クライミングは年々ポピュラーになっています。無作法なキャンプ、野宿などは絶対にやめてください。安価なキャンプ場が快適で安全な寝床を提供してくれます。
もしトポがてにはいらなくとも、がっかりしないでください。きっと他のクライマーが助けてくれます。
クライミングツアー中はあなたはいつもお客様なのです。

クライミングは潜在的に大きな危険を含んでいます。たとえ危険な要素があっても、安全の呼びかけや注意書きなどは期待できません。
身の安全はご自身で守っていただくほかありません。

クライマーは自己の責任において安全を確保する
クライマーはあらゆる事柄について自分自身で安全確認を行う
岩場や道具などは常に危険な要素をはらんでいると強く認識する
クライマーは潜在的な危険を常に認識し、想定し、それを回避する努力を怠らない

おわりに

時には岩場が崩壊することもあります、もしグレーディングや、本文中のことで感じたことなどのご意見があれば、本文中の住所に手紙をいただくか、以下にe-mailを頂けると幸いです。
info@jingowobbly.com

日本語でのご意見などがありましたらお聞かせ下さい。
また国内で海外のより詳しい岩場の情報が得たい場合は、国内に4箇所あるスポーツクライミングセンターパンプへおいでください。
世界中のクライミングトポや雑誌、そして海外で実際にクライミングをしている多くにスタッフがあなたをお持ちしております。
電話代表 042-324-6762 e-mail pump@yk.rim.or.jp　東京都国分寺市東元町2-20-10　クライミングショップB-pump内

(有)フロンティアスピリッツ　クライミングジムパンプ　代表　内藤直也

Spider

IRS 2002

IRS (Integral Rand System): The biggest revolution since sticky rubber

- Sole, rand and heel in one piece!!
- Natural and anatomical fit of the heel, arch and forefoot
- Different thicknesses and shapes across the toe, rand and heel
- Anatomical hole in the front part of the IRS sole
- Revolutionary heel for extreme climbs
- Different thincknesses depending on the size
- No deformable y de gran durabilidad
- Eliminates the sole delamination and deformation
- Increase the durability of the sole

Boreal UK
Phone 0114 209 5220
borealuksouth@hotmail.com
borealmiduk@hotmail.com

 BOREAL

www.e-boreal.com/spider.htm

32

ESPAÑA

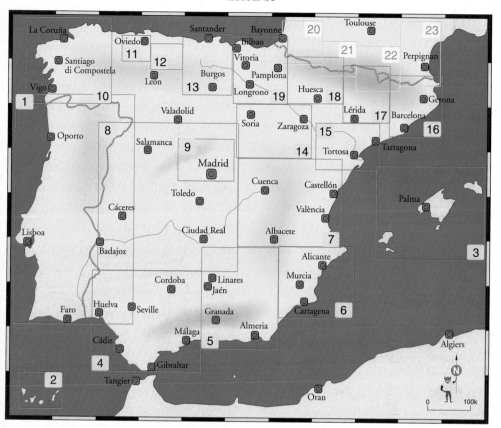

1: Portugal
2: Canaries
3: Baleares (Mallorca)
4: Sevilla - Málaga
5: Granada - Almeria
6: Alicante - Murcia
7: Cuenca - València

8: Toledo - Salamanca
9: Madrid
10: Santiago de Compostela
11: Oviedo
12: León (Picos)
13: Burgos - Santander
14: Zaragoza - Soria

15: Tortosa - Tarragona
16: Barcelona - Pedraforca
17: Lleida
18: Huesca - Mascun
19: Vitoria - Pamplona
20: Bayonne - Pau
23: Perpignan

Portugal, é um País maravilhoso na Primavera e Outono, um sítio calmo e relaxante, com muitas vias prontas a explorar. Portugal is great fun in the spring and autumn, a relaxed and quiet location, with plenty of power hungry routes. A good reason also to visit Lisboa, eat seafood and drink Port.

 Sintra caracteriza-se pelas suas vias tipicamente de granito, sem praticamente pontos onde se segurar! As falésias de Sagres e Cascais são calmas e simplesmente idílicas. Sintra slabs have that typical granite quality of no holds! The seacliffs of Sagres and Cascais are quiet and simply idyllic.

Topo: T1-1
Portugal
D. Atchison-Jones;
192 pp. 210mm x 150mm
New 2003/4

5a-7a Info

12-27+ España.
www.urbanrock.com
In production

Louriçal - Costa de Parta (1/1-31/12)
O Tamanco, Cassas Brancas 11

Orbitur Guincho (1/1-31/12)
Lugar da Areia, Guincho, Cascais

Parque de Campismo do Outào (1/1-31/12)
Estrada da Figuerinha, Setúbal

Parque de Campismo de Sagres (1/1-31/12)
Cerro das Moitas

Orbitur Quateira (1/1-31/12)
Ave. Sá Carneiro, Quarteira, Faro

OVOMALTINE 6a+, Farol da Guia; Jingo

#	Type						Name
1	Gra	A		100	10		Peneda-Bico do Patelo
2	Gra	A		100	10		Nédia
3	Gra	A		100	10		Torre Pequena
4	Gra	A		100	10		Gerês
5				3	56		Santo Tirso Bloc*
6	Gra	A		?	?		Trás os Montes
7	Gra	A		?	?		Valongo
8	Gra	A		?	?		Salto-Capela
9	Gra	A		?	?		Suaves Prestaçoes
10	Gra	A		?	?		Fraga do Cavalo
11	Gra	A		250	30		Serra da Estrela
12	1			18	67		Redhina-N. Senhora. d. Estrela*
13	Cal			?	?		Cagimil
14	16			26	29		Vale de Poios*
15	3			16	55		Reguengo do Fetal*
16	1			25	26		Montejunto Novo*
17	5			29	25		Montejunto Vehlô ⊘ 1.3 - 31.8
18	15			50	38		Castello Dos Mouros-Sintra**
19	3			4	36		Convento Bloc*
20	48			26	83		Farol da Guia**
21	Cal			100	0		Sesimbra
22	Cal			70	0		Fojo dos Morcegos
23	10			35	76		Portinho da Arrábida**
24	10			26	30		Castelejo
25	10	A/S		45	116		Cabo de S. Vicente*
26	16	A/S		45	77		Ponta de Sagres*
27	Cal			20	29		Rocca Peña*
28	Cal			30	110		Nuestra Señora de la Peña
29	Cal			?	<100>		El Castellar**

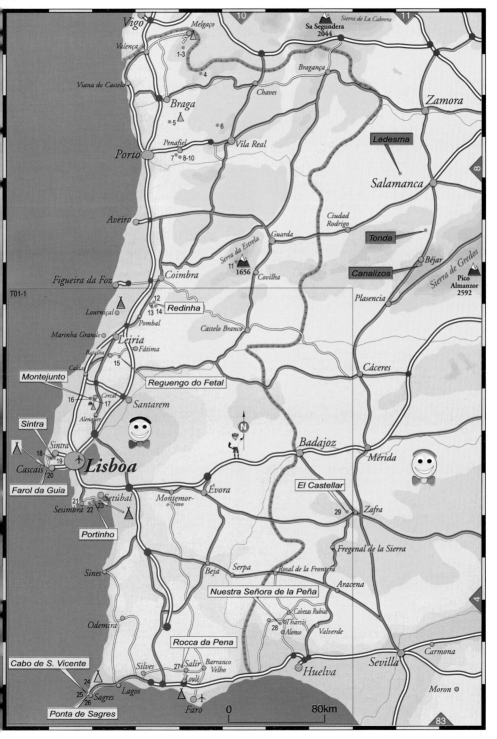

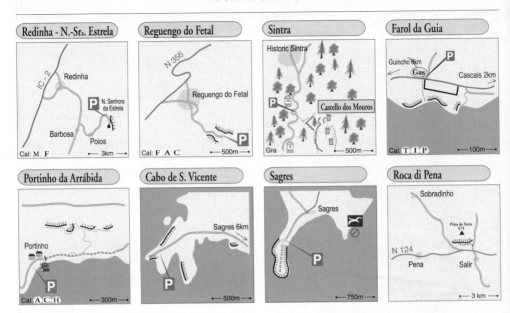

Redinha - N.-Sra. Estrela

IC-2
Redinha
N. Senhora da Estrela
Barbosa
Poios
Cal: **M F**
3km

Reguengo do Fetal

N 356
Reguengo do Fetal
500m

Sintra

Historic Sintra
Castello dos Mouros
Gra
500m

Farol da Guia

Guincho 6km
Gas
Cascais 2km
Cal: **T I P**
100m

Portinho da Arrábida

Portinho
BAR
Cal: **A C H**
300m

Cabo de S. Vicente

Sagres 6km
500m

Sagres

Sagres
P
750m

Roca di Pena

Sobradinho
Péna de Serra 474
N 124
Pena
Salir
3 km

PORTINHO DA ARRÁBIDA

NEW WAVE 6a, Castelo dos Mouros, Sintra; José Teixeira

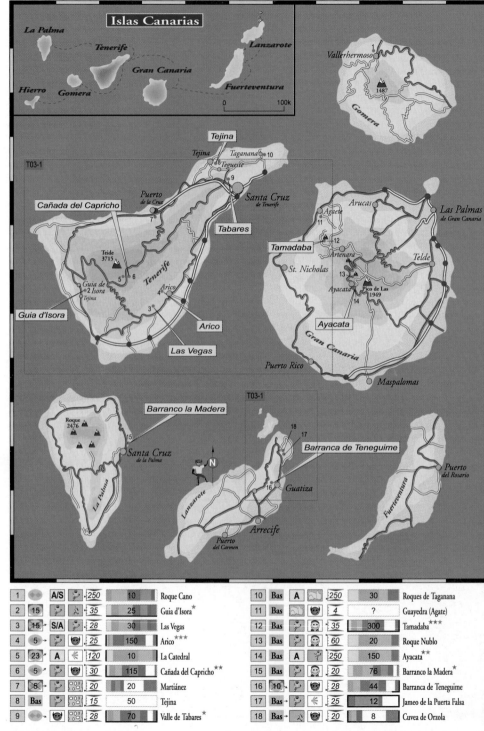

1		A/S		250	10		Roque Cano
2	15			35	25		Guia d'Isora*
3	15	S/A		28	30		Las Vegas
4	5			25	150		Arico***
5	23	A		120	10		La Catedral
6	5			30	115		Cañada del Capricho**
7	5			20	20		Martiánez
8	Bas			15	50		Tejina
9				28	70		Valle de Tabares*
10	Bas	A		250	30		Roques de Taganana
11	Bas			4	?		Guayedra (Agate)
12	Bas			35	300		Tamadaba***
13	Bas			60	20		Roque Nublo
14	Bas	A		250	150		Ayacata**
15	Bas			20	76		Barranco la Madera*
16	10			28	44		Barranca de Teneguime
17	Bas			25	12		Jameo de la Puerta Falsa
18	Bas			20	8		Cueva de Orzola

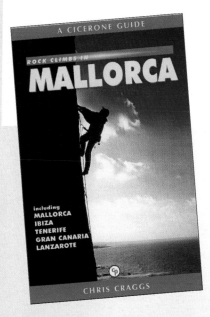

This is the genuine island in the Sun. Plenty of cheap flights from most European airports and good weather. Regarded as the tufa capital of the world. For the 7b/c climber, there is huge potential to transform into a fully grown Gorilla.

 The climbing here is well away from the major holiday beaches and crowds. The mountains offer wonderful scenery, and are very quiet. A lot of well protected routes in all grades.

Topo: T3-1
Mallorca
Chris Craggs; 2000
286pp. 174mm x 115mm

T | I | ? | 5a-7a Info | 🌐 | 📷
🌳 | ★ | ★★★ | ★★★ | ★ | ★

△ 2,3,5-14,16-18,20-22, 24,27,28.

🌐 **www.cicerone.co.uk**
www.urbanrock.com

Topo: T6-1
Costa Blanca, Mallorca, El Chorro
Alan James, Mark Glaister; 2000
360pp (69pp-Mall). 210mm x 150mm

T | I | ? | 5a-7a Info | 🌐 | 📷
🌳 | ★★ | ★★★ | ★★★ | ★★★ | ★★★

△ 2,4-8,10-12,14-15,17,19,23.

🌐 **www.rockfax.com**

△ Sun club Picafort, (1/1-31/12) Platja de Muro, Mallorca

△ S'Atalaia (1/6-30/9) Ferreries, Menorca

△ Son Bou, (1/4-12/10) Alaior, Menorca

△ San Antonio (1/4-30/9) Sant Antoni de Portmany

SOSTRE DEN BUROT 6c+, Valldemosa; Henry Nottage

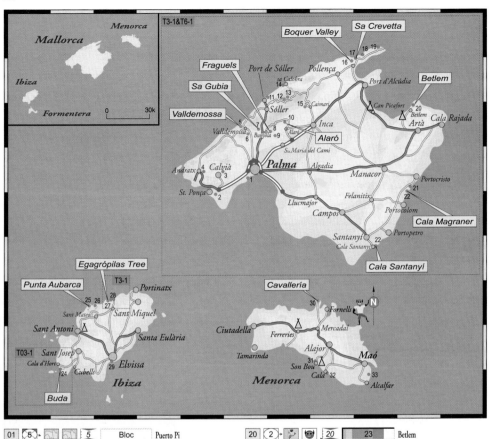

01	5			5	Bloc	Puerto Pi
02	2			20	7	Santa Ponça
03	Cal			25	21	Calviá
04	15			20	17	Andratx
05	1		60db	12	44	Valldemossa*
06	5			25	11 22	S'estret
07	20			60	108	Sa Gubia**
08	20			30	53	Fraguels**
09	Cal			30	23	Ca'n Torrat*
10	20			30	50	Alaró**
11	5			30	25	Port de Sóller*
12	10			30	11	Ca'n Nylc
13		A/S		200	4	El Paradon - Puig Major
14	⊠			20	12	Es Queixal
15	10			25	20	Las Perxes
15a	1			20	11	Hairpin Wall
16	10			20	32	Boquer Valley*
17	20			30	37	Sa Creveta*
18	15	∞		65	2	Punta la Nao
19	10			25	20	Son Xante*

20	2			20	23	Betlem
21	10			35	17	El Cuenco*
22	10			20	61	Cala Magraner*
23	5			20	35	Cala Santanyí - Tijuana*
24	Cal			30	61	Buda*
24	Cal	A/S		120	3	Buda(Vidas)
25	25			35	20	Punta Aubarca*
26	25			25	16	Jolibut
27	30			20	23	Egagrópilas Tree
28	?	∞		22	10	Sol Y Sombre
29	?			8	10	El Soto
30	Cal	S/A		70	56	Caballeria*
33	Cal			20	20	Son Bou y Llucalari
34	Cal	S/A		50	8	Cales Coves
35	Cal	S/A		25	13	Es Sotil

A truly great area for the strong climber. El Chorro is full of really steep cliffs, and the gorge offers cooler climbing when the sun starts cooking the other cliffs. Desplomilania and Archidona are ridiculously overhanging.

 This whole area offers a lot of climbing in the lower grades, but be prepared to travel around. A trip to El Torcal is very well worth it, even just for a picnic - climbing is sometimes not allowed, so bring plenty of wine.

Topo: T4-1
Escalar en Cádiz
David Munilla; 2001
72pp. 210mm x 150mm

⚠ 13,14,15,16, 23.

℮ **Pandoras, Centro Tarifa,** ¢-?
Saltamontes, C/Francos 18, Jerez de
la Frontera ¢-7; Refugio-El Chorro

Topo: T4-2
Andalusian Rock Climbs
Chris Craggs; 1992
160pp. 176mm x 117mm

⚠ 9,21,33-39.

℮ **www.Cicerone.co.uk**
www.urbanrock.com

Topo: T6-1
Costa Blanca, Mallorca, **El Chorro**
A. James, M. Glaister; 2000
360pp (73pp Cho). 210mm x 150mm

⚠ 6,9, 30 - 39.

℮ **www.rockfax.com**
www.urbanrock.com
refugio, El Chorro ¢-1(Monday)

Ⓣ	**El Chorro**
Mini Topo	Refugio; 2000
	40pp

⚠ 33-39.   ✂ **200**

℮ **Refugio-El Chorro,** ¢-1

⚠ Camping El Chorro (1/1-31/12)
Estación del Chorro, Alora, ES.
Tel: 952 11 26 96
Fax: 952 49 87 86

⚠ Tarifa 1,2,3,4 etc.. (1/1-31/12)
Tarifa
Tel:

⚠ Chullera II (1/1-31/12)
Sabinillas/Manvilla
Tel: 952 89 01 96

⚠ El Sur (1/1-31/12)
Carretera Algeciras
(1.5km-N) Ronda
Tel: 952 87 59 39
Fax: 952 87 70 54

6b+, EL TORCAL; Sabreen Qureshi

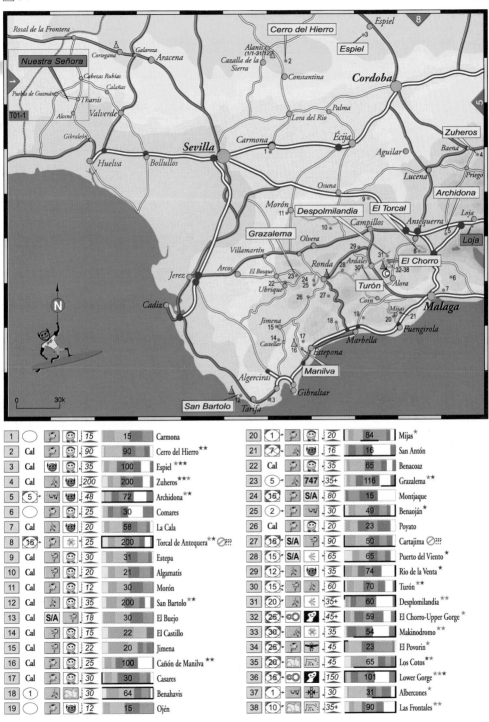

1				15	15	Carmona
2	Cal			90	90	Cerro del Hierro**
3	Cal			35	100	Espiel***
4	Cal			200	200	Zuheros***
5	5			48	72	Archidona**
6				25	30	Comares
7	Cal			20	58	La Cala
8	16			25	200	Torcal de Antequera** ⊘???
9	Cal			30	31	Estepa
10	Cal			20	21	Algamitas
11	Cal			12	30	Morón
12	Cal			35	200	San Bartolo**
13	Cal	S/A		18	30	El Buejo
14	Cal			15	22	El Castillo
15	Cal			22	20	Jimena
16	Cal			25	100	Cañón de Manilva**
17	Cal			30	30	Casares
18	1			30	64	Benahavis
19				12	15	Ojén

20	1			20	84	Mijas*
21	7			16	16	San Antón
22	Cal			35	65	Benacoaz
23	5		747	35+	116	Grazalema**
24	16		S/A	80	15	Montjaque
25	2			30	49	Benaoján*
26	Cal			20	23	Poyato
27	16	S/A		90	50	Cartajima ⊘???
28	15	S/A		65	65	Puerto del Viento*
29	12			35	74	Rio de la Venta*
30	15			60	70	Turón**
31	20			35+	60	Desplomilandia**
32	26	∞		45+	59	El Chorro-Upper Gorge*
33	30			35	54	Makinodromo**
34	25			45	23	El Povorin*
35	20			45	65	Los Cotos**
36	16	∞		150	101	Lower Gorge***
37	1			30	31	Albercones*
38	10			35+	90	Las Frontales**

Grazalema

Cal: H T C — 2km →

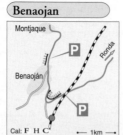

Benaojan

Montjaque

Benaoján

Cal: F H C — 1km →

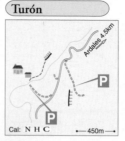

Turón

Ardales 4.5km

Cal: N H C — 450m →

Rio de la Venta

Rio de la Venta

Teba 591▲

Cal: H T — 3km →

BENAOJÁN

RIO DE LA VENTA

JULAY LAMA 5b, Túron: Birgit Darda-Memgel

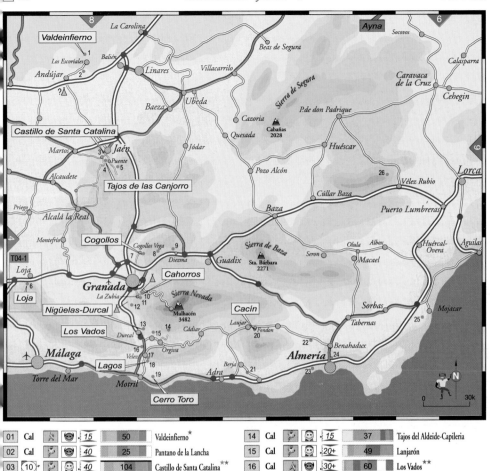

01	Cal			15	50	Valdeinfierno*		14	Cal			15	37	Tajos del Aldeide-Capileria
02	Cal			40	25	Pantano de la Lancha		15	Cal			20+	49	Lanjarón
03	Cal	(10)		40	104	Castillo de Santa Catalina**		16	Cal			30+	60	Los Vados**
04	Cal			55	56	Tajos de las Canjorro-Los Cañones		17	Cal			18	21	Los Caracolillos
05	Cal	A/S	A/S	160	15	Tajos de las Alcandoras		18	Cal			20	33	Lagos
06	Cal	(5)		30	54	Loja**		18	Cal			18	64	Cerro Toro
07	Cal			12	60	Cogollos*		20	Cal			30+	110	Cacín
08	Cal	A/S	A/S	18	<? 8 ?>	Sierra Arana		21				?	?	Dalias
09	Cal			50	42	Peña Cabrera		22				?	?	Barranco el Fuerte
10	Cal		A/S	35+	252	Los Cahorros**		23				?	?	Aguadulce
11	Cal			15	8	Cueva del Moro		24				?	?	Salto de Gallo
12	Cal			12	19	Rambla Seca - Dilar		25				?	?	Sierra de Cabrera-Almeria
13	Cal			18	48	Nigüelas Durcal		26				?	?	Sierra de Maria

⚠ Ruta del Purche (1/1-31/12)
Monachil, Granada

⚠ El Juncal (1/1-31/12)
Otura, Granada

<< GENERACION SPONTANEA 6c, El Polvorin, El Chorro; Jindrich Sainer
< REVUELTA EN EL FRENOPATICO 6c+, El Polvorin, El Chorro; Robert Marcek

This area must be one of the most well developed in Spain, and it is fortunate to have such a high density of really good cliffs. There really is a good range of short sport routes, to the traditional longer mountain routes.

 A lot of Spain is at quite a high altitude, but here there are a lot of low altitude cliffs, which make it one of the most popular winter destinations. Don't even think about coming to climb in summer - it really is toooo hot.

Topo: T6-1
Costa Blanca
A. James, M. Glaister; 2001
360pp (215p-CB). 210mm x 150mm

△ 1-7, 9-11, 14-18, 21-26, 28

Ⓔ **www.rockfax.com**
Urban rock, London
The Edge Wall, Sheffield

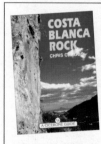

Topo: T66-2
Costa Blanca Rock
Chris Craggs; 1997
256pp. 210mm x 150mm

△ 1-6, 9-12, 14-16,19, 21-28, 34, 37

Ⓔ **www.cicerone.co.uk**
www.urbanrock.com
The Edge Wall, Sheffield

Topo: T06-3
Guia Valle de Leiva
F. Avilés, M. Cánovas; 1995
60pp. 210mm x 150mm

△ 34
Ⓔ **??**

Ⓣ *Bar, Croquis-Topo*
Bar La Cueva, Ayna
△ 37

BOREAL

PEÑON D'IFACH

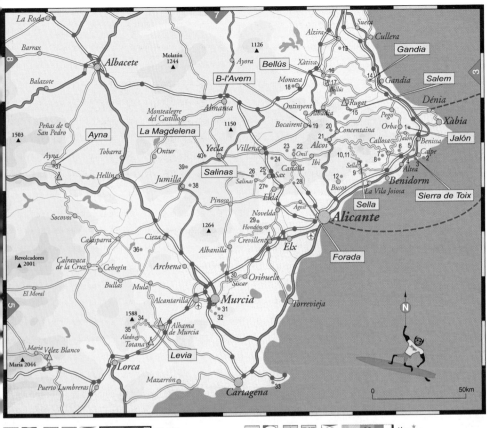

1	5+			30	79	Jalón Valley
2	20	A/S		300	23	Peñón de Ifach [*]
3	2+			30+	146	Sierra de Toix [**]
4	10	S/A	90db	250	31	Mascarat Gorge
5	20			30	20	Olta
6	5	S/A		30	25	Bernia
7	5+	A/S	Zzz	160	96	Los Echos Valley [*]
8	Cal	S/A		600	<61>	Ponoig [*]
9	60	A/S		400	<55>	Puig Campana [**]
10	5			35	215	Sella [***]
11	40	A/S		230	<30>	Peñón Divino [*]
12	15	A/S		300	<35>	Cabezón de Oro [*]
13	Cal			12	<57>	Corbera
14	10			25	155	Gandia & Bovedón [**]
15	1+			30	114	Salem [**]
16	10			45	70	Aventador [*]
17	5			18	113	Bellús [*]
18	3			20	46	Montesa [*]
19	Cal			?	<180>	Barranc de L'Avern
20	Cal			35	<25>	Concentaina

21	3		747	25	32	Alcoy [*]
22	5			20	33	Agujas Rojas [*]
23	20			45	30	Reconco [*]
24	10			25	70	Peña Rubia
25	Cal		S/A	70	71	Cabreras [*] 1/2-1/6: 50%
26	15			20	74	Salinas [**] 1/2-1/6
27	Cal			60	34	Peñas de Marin [*]
28	10			35	91	Forada [**]
29	Cal			20	<30>	Sierra de Enmedio
30	Cal	A/S		180	<20>	Pared de Siscar
31	Con	S/A		70	<40>	Los Lages
32	Con			70	<90>	La Panocha
33	Cal		S/A	80	<45>	Pico del Aguila
34	15		S/A	35+	<120>	Levia [***]
35	Cal	A/S		150	<22>	Morrón de España y Agujas
36	Cal	A/S		300	<60>	Almorchón
37	5			60	<100>	Ayna [**]
38	Cal			30+	<60>	El Buey [*]
39	Cal	S/A		150	<30>	La Graja
40	Cal			20	<70>	La Magdalena [*]

There is virtually nothing easy at Cuenca, and the bolts are well spaced, so bring a good clip stick and a strong rope. Montanejos has around 2000 routes and is great for just about all grades, and is handy if you don't have a car.

 Ciudad Entacada is like being on top of the World, and a very beautiful day out. If you want to get away from it all, Organo de Montoro is quiet beyond belief during midweek. A big area to get around though.

Topo: T7-1
Cuenca
José Manuel Hernández; 1996
144pp. 165mm x 120mm

△ 2,3,4,5.

€ *Aguaiti, C/Alicante 3, Cuenca, ₡-7*

Topo: T7-2
Montanejos
P. Llatas, "Ernesto" López; 1997
110pp. 210mm x 150mm

△ 10,11,12. (500)

€ *Refugio - Montanejos ₡-15/1-30/3 ???*

Chuilla
Ligorio; 1997
Mini Topo ?
△ 7. ⚒ 300
€ *Refugio-Chuilla*

Jerica-Croquis
?; 2000
Mini Topo 14pp - A4 ph-copie
△ 9. ⚒ 200
€ *Bar-Oasis, Jerica*

R *Refugio de Escaladores & Camping*
Crt.de Tales No 27, 12.448
Montanejos ₡-15/1-30/3
Tel: 964 13 13 17
email: erlopsas@teleline.es

Camping Cuenca (?)
Ctra. Ciudad Entacada
16147 Cuenca
Tel: 969 23 16 56
Fax:
email:

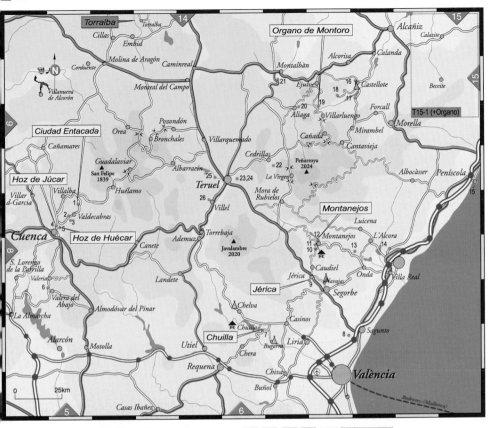

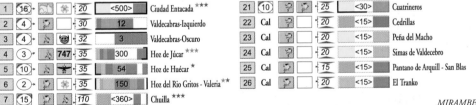

1	15		☀	20	<500>		Ciudad Entacada ★★★
2	4			30	12		Valdecabras-Izquierdo
3	4		◉	32	3		Valdecabras-Oscuro
4	3		747	35	300		Hoz de Júcar ★★★
5	10			35	54		Hoz de Huécar ★
6	2		☀	35	150		Hoz del Rio Gritos - Valeria ★★
7	15			110	<360>		Chuilla ★★★
8	Cal	A/S		30	<34>		Peñas de Güaita
9	46		☀	35	<200>		Jérica ★★
10	15		☀	30	<62>		Montanejos-Montan ★★
11	10			35	<270>		Barranco de la Maimona ★★★
12	45		☀	100	<700>		Montanejos-Mijares ★★★
13	Cal			30	<30>		Ribesalbes
14	Cal			60	<60>		Castellet
15	Cal			35	<40>		Castillo de Peñiscola ★
16	3	A		45	<5>		Castellote
17	10		☀	35	<35>		Embalse de Santolea ★
18	Cal			50	<50>		Ladroñán
19	10	A/S		250	<25>		Organo de Montoro ★★
20	5		◉	35	<20>		Aliaga

21	10			25	<30>		Cuatrineros
22	Cal			20	<15>		Cedrillas
23	Cal			20	<15>		Peña del Macho
24	Cal			20	<15>		Simas de Valdecebro
25	Cal			15	<15>		Pantano de Arquill - San Blas
26	Cal			20	<15>		El Tranko

MIRAMBEL

Ciudad Entacada
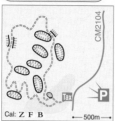
Cal: Z F B — 500m

Hoz de Júcar
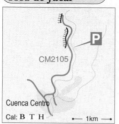
CM2105
Cuenca Centro
Cal: B T H — 1km

Hoz de Huécar

Cuenca Tourist
Cuenca Centro
Cal: F H J — 500m

Hoz de Rio Gritos
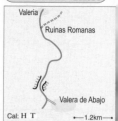
Valeria
Ruinas Romanas
Valera de Abajo
Cal: H T — 1.2km

Jérica

Oasis
Jerica
N234
Cal: F U H — 400m

Barranco de la Maimona

Refugio de Escalordes
Montanejos
CV20
Cal: F C H — 300m

Embalse de Santolea

Castellote
Pantano
Embalse de Santolea
Cal: F — 3km

Organo de Montoro
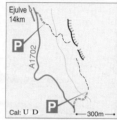
Ejulve 14km
A1702
Cal: U D — 300m

CIUDAD ENTACADA; Josune Legrand ▼

▲ *HOZ DE JÚCAR*

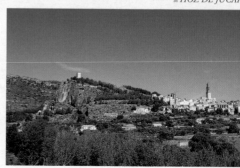

ESTRECHO DEL MIJARES, Montanejos

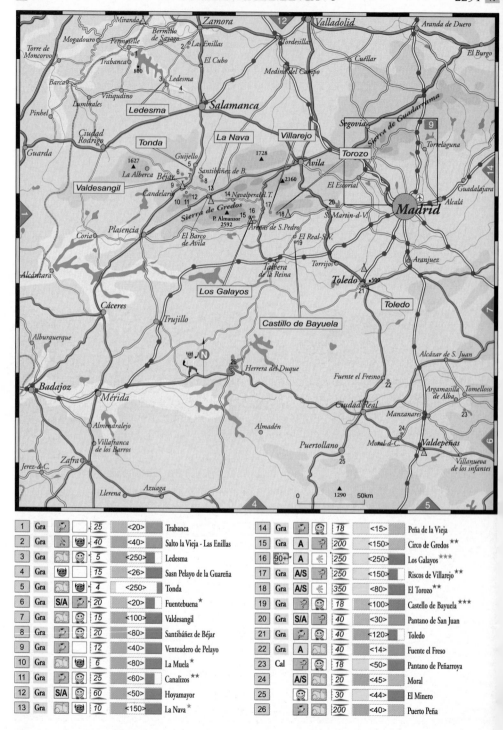

1	Gra			25	<20>		Trabanca		
2	Gra			40	<40>		Salto la Vieja - Las Enillas		
3	Gra			5	<250>		Ledesma		
4	Gra			15	<26>		Sasn Pelayo de la Guareña		
5	Gra			4	<250>		Tonda		
6	Gra	S/A		20	<20>		Fuentebuena *		
7	Gra			15	<100>		Valdesangil		
8	Gra			20	<80>		Santibáñez de Béjar		
9	Gra			12	<40>		Venteadero de Pelayo		
10	Gra			6	<80>		La Muela *		
11	Gra			25	<60>		Canalizos **		
12	Gra	S/A		60	<50>		Hoyamayor		
13	Gra			10	<150>		La Nava *		

14	Gra			18	<15>		Peña de la Vieja		
15	Gra	A		200	<150>		Circo de Gredos **		
16	90+	A		250	<250>		Los Galayos ***		
17	Gra	A/S		250	<150>		Riscos de Villarejo **		
18	Gra	A/S		350	<80>		El Torozo **		
19	Gra			18	<100>		Castello de Bayuela ***		
20	Gra	S/A		40	<30>		Pantano de San Juan		
21	Gra			40	<120>		Toledo		
22	Gra	A		40	<14>		Fuente el Freso		
23	Cal			18	<50>		Pantano de Peñarroya		
24		A/S		20	<45>		Moral		
25				30	<44>		El Minero		
26				200	<40>		Puerto Peña		

A very traditional area, plenty of long granite cracks and open corners, bring plenty of cams and some tape.

 In the summer, the high Sierra de Gredos offers plenty of long mountain routes in superb scenery.

Topo: T8-1
La Sierra de Gredos
Gabriel Martin; 1994
200pp. 165mm x 120mm

5a-7a
Info

16, 17, 18.
www.desnivel.es
Librería Desnivel, Plaza Matute, 6
Madrid 28012(Metro Antón Martin)

PEDRIZA

EL YELMO, Pedriza (9)

If you are looking for the nearest thing in Spain to Buoux, go to Patones, very good and powerful.

 The walk up to El Yelmo is best in the early shade, and the view is teriffic, pity there are no holds though!

Topo: T9-1
La Pedriza de Manzanares
Federación; 1998
94pp. 210mm x 140mm

⚠ 13, + Cancho de los Brezos

🌐 **www.desnivel.es**
Libreria Desnivel, Pza Matute, 6,
Madrid, 9.30-21.30; ¢-7

Topo: T9-2
Escaladas en La Pedriza
D. Rodríguez, J. Luján; 1992
286pp. 170mm x 120mm

⚠ 12 - 13.

🌐 **www.desnivel.es**
Libreria Desnivel, Pza Matute, 6,
Madrid, 9.30-21.30; ¢-7

Topo: T9-3
La Sierra de la Cabrera
Federación; 1999
110pp. 210mm x 140mm

⚠ 14

🌐 **www.desnivel.es**
Libreria Desnivel, Pza Matute, 6,
Madrid, 9.30-21.30; ¢-7

Topo: T9-4
Patones
Desnivel "amigos"; 1990
124pp. 170mm x 120mm

⚠ 15, 16, 17.

🌐 **www.desnivel.es**
Libreria Desnivel, Pza Matute, 6,
Madrid, 9.30-21.30; ¢-7

⚠ *Camping Pico de la Miel, (📠 ☎) (1.1-31.12)*
28751 La Cabrera, Madrid.
Tel: 91 868 80 82   Fax: 91 868 85 41

PATONES

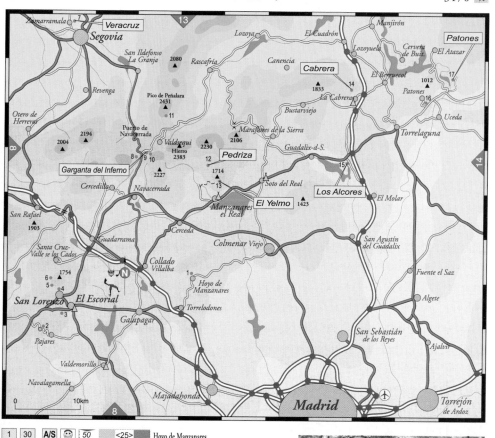

1	30	A/S	🙂	50	<25>	Hoyo de Manzanares
2	Gra	A/S	🙂	50	<20>	Zaralejo
3	Gra	S/A	🙂	15	<25>	Silla de Felipe II
4	Gra	A/S	🙂	50	<15>	Albantos
5	Gra	A/S	🙂	20	<15>	Pinares Llanos
6	Gra	A/S	🙂	40	<25>	Peña Blanca
7	Gra	🙂	🙂	7	<70>	Piedras de la Veracruz
8	25	S/A	🙂	35	<35>	Alto de Telégrafo
9	30	S/A	🙂	50	<60>	Garganta del Inferno
10	60+	A/S	🙂	150	<50>	Maliciosa
11	45	S/A	🙂	55	<150>	Peñalara
12	20	🙂	747	200	<1500>	La Pedriza **
13	90	✳	747	200	<100>	El Yelmo ***
14	45	A/S	⬅	180	<350>	La Cabrera **
15	15	🙂	🙂	20	<150>	Los Alcores - El Vellon **
16	8	🙂	🙂	20	<30>	Patones - Pueblo *
17	5	⬅	🙂	35	<550>	Patones - Hercules, Ponton ***

LOS ALCORES

GIMIE SHELTER 6a, Patones

ZIGGI STARDUST 6a, El Yelmo; Wobbly

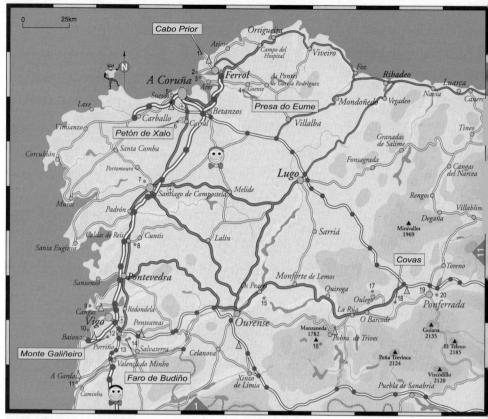

#							Name
1	10		☀	30		<60>	Cabo Prior *
2	5			15		<10>	Cabo Prioiño *
3	5+		☀	20		<55>	Acantilados de Chanteiro
4	10			35+		<50>	Presa do Eume *
5	5		☀	15		<50>	Acantilados de Suevos
6	2			25		<75>	Petón de Xalo *
7	1			16		<40>	Figueiras
8	2		☀	20		<20>	Segad
9	2			20		<13>	Hío
10	6			16		<36>	Monteferro
11	5	☀		20		<53>	Baixo Miño *
12	15+			16		<174>	Monte Galiñeiro **
13	5+	S/A		35+		<150>	Faro de Budiño ***
14	1			15		<15>	San Cibrán *
15	2			20		<35>	Cañon del Sil
16	35			50		<20>	Manzaneda *
17	10			26		<40>	Penedos de Oulego *
18	20	☀		35		<95>	Covas **
19	Gra			15		<30>	Fragas de Sil
20	Gra			40		<50>	Fragas del Boeza

A lot of brutal Granite, but don't be put off by the walk to Manzaneda, the view is worth it.

The climbing is short, but there are some lovely locations on the rugged coastline, cool winds too.

GUIA DE ESCALADA

GALICIA VERTICAL

Miguel Seoane
Javier Carreras

Topo: T10-1
Galicia Vertical
M. Seoane, J. Carreras; 1997
284pp. 200mm x 130mm

T   I   ?   5a-7a Info   🇬🇧   📷

⛰ 1-18.

€ **?? Nortrek, C/Inés de Castro,
7 Bajo, 15005 La Coruña ,** ✆-7
Toribio, C/Hórreo, 5. Santiago-d-C.

There are bears in this lovely National Park, and they don't have a problem with the 7c's.

 Quiros is one of the most perfect climbing centres, quiet, relaxed, not too hard, and a great refugio.

Topo: T11-1
Escalada en Asturias
Federación - Asturias; 1995
242pp. 165mm x 110mm

T I ? 5a-7a Info

★ ★ ★ ★ ★ E GB ★★ ★

⚠ 1 - 7 (+ 12: Bollu, Pelúgano)

© ***??? - Problem diplomatique ?***

Topo: T11-2
Quiros
Eduardo Velasco; 1992
160pp. 220mm x 140mm

T I ? 5a-7a Info

★ ★ ★ ★ ★★

⚠ 7.

© **Refugio Llana, Quiros,** ¢-7
Oxigeno, Manuel Pedregal 4
Oviedo-Centro. ¢-7

🏠 Refugio El Llano (1/1-31/12)
El Llano n 6, 33118 Quiros,
Aciera, Las Agüeras, Asturias.

Villamejín, Rio Truba, Asturias

Ermita, Teverga: & EL BORDILLO !!!!! (12)

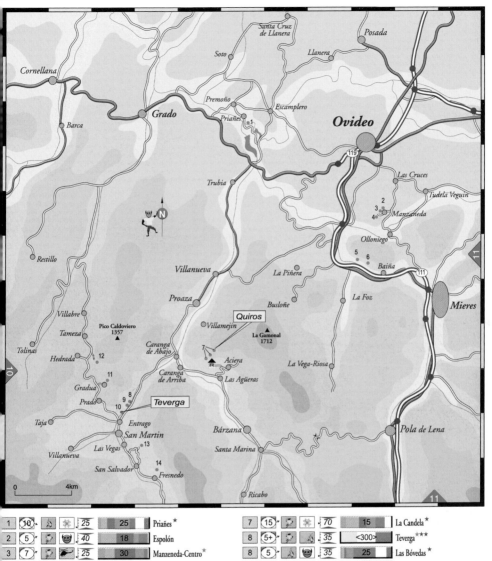

#						Name
1	10			25	25	Priañes *
2	5			40	18	Espolón
3	7			25	30	Manzeneda-Centro *
4	10			25	20	Arnea
5	Cal			30	30	Peñamiel - Les Abelles *
6	Cal			30	21	Peñamiel - Baiña
7	17			70	<300>	Quiros ***
7	25		Zzz	35	18	Rosa de Mayo *
7	15			60	25	El Escalon *
7	15			70	15	La Candela *
8	5+			35	<300>	Teverga ***
8	5			35	25	Las Bóvedas *
9	5			30	9	Pingalagua
10	10			30+	30	Entecampos **
11	10			30+	<?>	Gradura
12	7	Zzz		30	42	Tarzán - Bordilo *
13	17	A/S		120	<10>	Aguja de Sobia *
14	Cal →			?	<?>	Bóveda de Fresnedo

QUIROS

LA CALANDRIA 7a, Alimoches, Bordillo, Teverga; Jingo

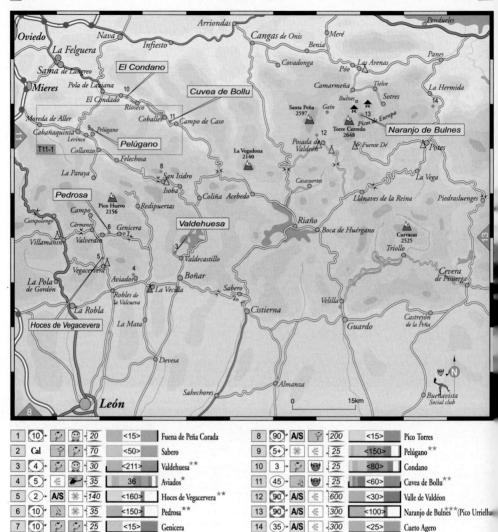

1	(10)			20	<15>		Fuena de Peña Corada
2	Cal			70	<50>		Sabero
3	(4)			30	<211>		Valdehuesa ★★
4	(5)			35	36		Aviados ★
5	(2)	A/S		140	<160>		Hoces de Vegacervera ★★
6	(10)			35	<150>		Pedrosa ★★
7	(10)			25	<15>		Genicera

8	(90)	A/S		200	<15>		Pico Torres
9	(5+)			25	<150>		Pelúgano ★★
10	3			25	<80>		Condano
11	(45)			25	<60>		Cuvea de Bollu ★★
12	(90)	A/S		600	<30>		Valle de Valdéon
13	(90)	A/S		300	<100>		Naranjo de Bulnes ★★★ (Pico Urriellu
14	(35)	A/S		300	<25>		Cueto Agero

BOREAL

The rock at Valdehuesa is some of the best Limestone around, even the slabs offer great little routes.

 The slabs at Hoches de Vegceverea offer almost nothing in the shape of holds - good or bad, hmmm.

Topo: T12-1
Cordillera Cantabrica
Miguel Angel Adrados; 1996
318pp. 210mm x 150mm

T I ? 5a-7a Info 🔷 📷

◉◉◉ ⭐⭐ ⭐ ⭐ Ⓔ ⭐⭐

⚠ 3, 5, 6, 8, 12, 13, 14.

€ **Oxigeno, Oviedo (Centro),** ¢-7
www.urbanrock.com

Topo: T12-2
Picos de Europa
Robin Walker; 1993
214pp. 170mm x 115mm

T I ? 5a-7a Info 🔷 📷

◉◉◉ ⭐⭐⭐ ⭐⭐ ⭐⭐ GB 🗑 ⭐⭐

⚠ 12,13,14 +++ Mountains

€ **www.cicerone.co.uk**
www.urbanrock.com

🔵 *Bar, Croquis-Topo*

Hostal las Rocas, Vegacervera
⚠ 5.

VALDEHUESA

5+, AVIADOS: Wobbly

5b+, PEDROSA; Atze-Cees de Vries

A warm and humid area in summer. Tourism is on the improvement, and the coast is handy for hot days.

 Aguilar de Campóo is nice and scenic, with lots of climbing and bouldering nearby, good for all year.

Peñahorada Guia
Burgos ?; 1998
28pp
Mini Topo
△ 1,2 +++.   ⚡ 80
€ ??

Escaladas en Recuvas
Escaladores; 1994
20pp
Mini Topo
△ 4.   ⚡ 150
€ ???

Escalada en Ramales
Ramales; 2000
30pp
Mini Topo
△ 8,9,10.   ⚡ 170
€ Off-d-Toursim, Ramales

△ *La Barguilla Ramales.*

🍺 **Bar, Croquis-Topo**
Bar Marcos, Ramales
△ 7,8,9,10 +.

LIERGANES

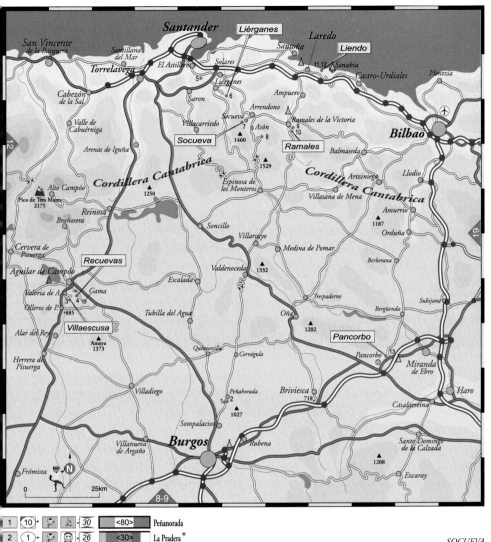

1	10			30	<80>	Peñanorada
2	1			26	<30>	La Pradera*
3	25			5	<1000>	Villaescusa - Las Tuerces*
4	12			35	<140>	Recuevas**
5	Cal			20	<15>	Peña Cabarga
6	15		Zzz	35	<25>	Liérganes*
7	18			35	<30>	Socueva*
8	16			25	<30>	Asón*
9	10+			35+	<140>	Ramales de la Victoria**
9	12			35	<50>	Pyrámide-Escaleras*
10	12			35+	40	Pared del Eco**
11	8			35+	15	Liendo Grotto*
12	6		747	35	<50>	Liendo*
13	5		90db	35+	<115>	Pancorbo**

VILLAESCUSA

VILLAESCUSA

RECUEVAS

This is one of the driest parts of Spain, and in summer you are going to get completely fried, good hard routes.

 This area is truly Spanish, shorter climbs which pack a good punch, and are generally well equipped .

Topo: T14-1
Escalando por Zaragoza
Felipe Guinda Polo; 1993
200pp. 210mm x 150mm

4, 5, 7, 8,++ 9, 10, 13, 17, 18-21.

Zaragoza ??, ∅-7

Morata de Jalón-new guide 2002

Camping Calatayud (1/6-31/9)
Carretera Nacional II, KM 239
50300 Calatayud, Zaragoza

Camping Lago Park
Nuevalos, Calatayud, Zaragoza

New guide published for Morata - 2003

JARABA

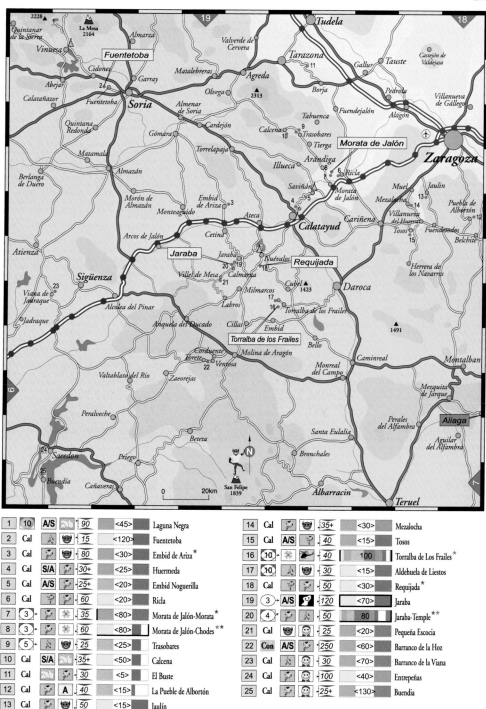

1	10	A/S		90	<45>		Laguna Negra
2	Cal			15	<120>		Fuentetoba
3	Cal			80	<30>		Embid de Ariza*
4	Cal	S/A		30+	<25>		Huermeda
5	Cal	A/S		25+	<20>		Embid Noguerilla
6	Cal			60	<20>		Ricla
7	3			35	<80>		Morata de Jalón-Morata*
8	3			60	<80>		Morata de Jalón-Chodes**
9	5			25	<25>		Trasobares
10	Cal	S/A		35+	<50>		Calcena
11	Cal			30	<5>		El Buste
12	Cal		A	40	<15>		La Pueble de Albortón
13	Cal			50	<15>		Jaulín
14	Cal			35+	<30>		Mezalocha
15	Cal	A/S		40	<15>		Tosos
16	10			40	100		Torralba de Los Frailes*
17	10			30	<15>		Aldehuela de Liestos
18	Cal			50	<30>		Requijada*
19	3	A/S		120	<70>		Jaraba
20	4			50	80		Jaraba-Temple**
21	Cal			25	<20>		Pequeña Escocia
22	Con	A/S		250	<60>		Barranco de la Hoz
23	Cal			30	<70>		Barranco de la Viana
24	Cal			100	<40>		Entrepeñas
25	Cal			25+	<130>		Buendia

ELEKTRA 7a, Puente de Roca, Morata de Jalón; Jingo

MORATA DE JALÓN

6b, TORRALBA DE LOS FRAILES

TEMPLE, Jaraba

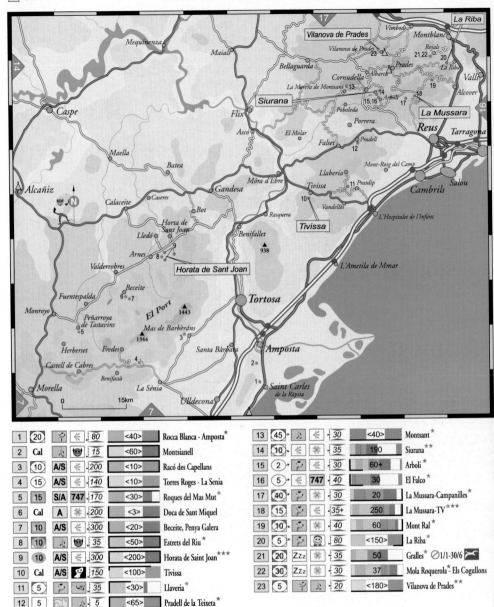

1	20	🏃	←	80	<40>	Rocca Blanca - Amposta*
2	Cal	🔧	🐵	15	<60>	Montsianell
3	10	A/S	←	200	<10>	Racó des Capellans
4	15	A/S	←	140	<10>	Torres Roges - La Senia
5	15	S/A	747	170	<30>	Roques del Mas Mut*
6	Cal	A	☀	200	<3>	Doca de Sant Miquel
7	10	A/S	←	300	<20>	Beceite, Penya Galera
8	10	🔧	🐵	35	<50>	Estrets del Riu*
9	10	A/S	←	300	<200>	Horata de Saint Joan***
10	Cal	A/S	🐾	150	<100>	Tivissa
11	5	🔧		35	<30>	Llaberia*
12	5		🔧	5	<65>	Pradell de la Teixeta*
13	45	🔧	←	30	<40>	Montsant*
14	10	🔧	☀	35	190	Siurana**
15	2	🔧	←	30	60+	Arboli*
16	5	🔧	747	40	30	El Falco*
17	40	🔧	☀	30	20	La Mussara-Campanilles*
18	15	🔧	←	35+	250	La Mussara-TV***
19	10	🔧	←	40	60	Mont Ral*
20	5	🔧	😊	80	<150>	La Riba*
21	20	Zzz	☀	35	50	Gralles* ⊘1/1-30/6
22	30	Zzz	☀	30	37	Mola Roquerola - Els Cogullons
23	5	🔧	🔧	20	<180>	Vilanova de Prades**

Sector El Pati in the valley at Siurana, now that is what I call proper Jingo climbing, take your pick 8c+ or 9a.

 The whole Prades area has become well know over the recent years, and is well deserved, not to be missed.

Topo: T15-1
Ports, Guia de Escaladas
L Alfonso, X. Buxó; 1996
220pp. 170mm x 120mm

5a-7a Info

1-15.

© *Uka Uka, Lleida,* ¢-7

Topo: T15-2
Costa Daurada
Mark Glaister, Emma Medara; 2002
176pp. 210mm x 150mm

5a-7a Info

15-23.

© *www.rockfax.com*
Climbing shops - UK.

SIURANA

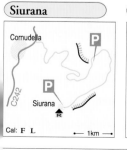

Siurana

Cornudella

Siurana

C242

Cal: F L — 1km —

La Mussara TV

La Mussara

Mont Ral

Vilaplana

Cal: H T F — 1.2km —

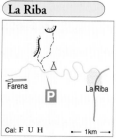

La Riba

Farena

La Riba

Cal: F U H — 1km —

Vilanova de Prades

Vimbodi

TV7004

Vilanova de Prades

Cal: B A P — 500m —

SIURANA

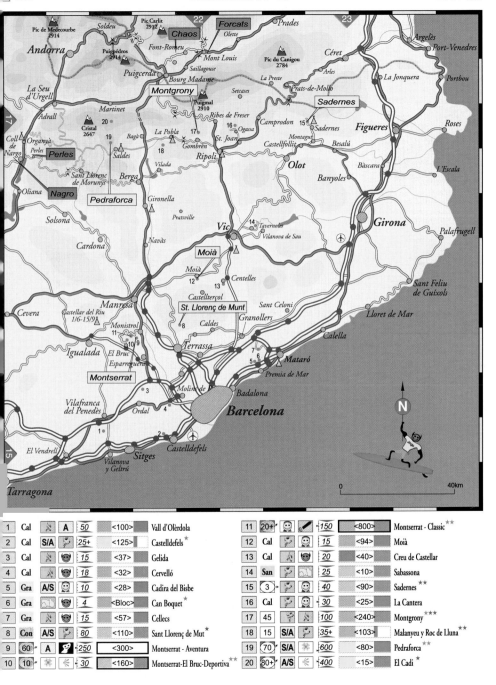

1	Cal	✗	A	50	<100>	Vall d'Olèrdola
2	Cal	S/A	✗	25+	<125>	Castelldefels*
3	Cal	✗	☺	15	<37>	Gelida
4	Cal	✗	☺	18	<32>	Cervelló
5	Gra	A/S	☺	10	<28>	Cadira del Bisbe
6	Gra		☺	4	<Bloc>	Can Boquet*
7	Gra	✗	☺	15	<57>	Cellecs
8	Con	A/S	✗	80	<110>	Sant Llorenç de Mut*
9	60		A	250	<300>	Montserrat - Aventura
10	10	✳	≪	30	<160>	Montserrat-El Bruc-Deportiva**

11	20+	☺	✗	150	<800>	Montserrat - Classic**
12	Cal	✗	☺	15	<94>	Moià
13	Cal	✗	☺	20	<40>	Creu de Castellar
14	San	✗		25	<10>	Sabassona
15	3	✗	☺	40	<90>	Sadernes**
16	Cal	✗	☺	30	<25>	La Cantera
17	45	✗	✗	100	<240>	Montgrony***
18	15	S/A	✗	35+	<103>	Malanyeu y Roc de Lluna**
19	70	S/A	≪	600	<80>	Pedraforca**
20	80+	A/S	≪	400	<15>	El Cadi*

A lot of the climbing here is old traditional mountian long routes, but there are now some great steep areas.

 There are some really good smaller climbing areas, don't miss out on Cavallers, its cool in summer and lovely.

Topo: T17-1
Roca Caliente en los Pirineos
Luis Alfonso, Xavier Buxó; 1994
337pp. 170mm x 120mm

5a-7a
Info

⚠ 7 - 15; 33,34,35,36.

✉ **Librairie; Pont de Suert**, ¢-7

Topo: T17-2
Alt Urgell
J. Gracia Coca, A. Olmeda; 1996
144pp. 165mm x 120mm

5a-7a
Info

⚠ 16,17,18,19.

✉ **Uka Uka: Lleida**, ¢-7
www.desnivel.es

Topo: T17-3
Escaladas en la Noguera
J. Marmolejo, J. Escuer; 1997
174pp. 210mm x 150mm

5a-7a
Info

⚠ 21 - 25.

✉ **Uka Uka: Lleida, Alcalde Costa 4, 25002, Lleida (Centro)** ¢-7

Topo: T17-4
Montsec Oeste
Luis Alfonso, Xavier Buxó; 1998
262pp. 170mm x 120mm

5a-7a
Info

⚠ 29, 37, 38.

✉ **Uka Uka: Lleida**, ¢-7

Vilanova de Meia
Alfonso-Buxó; 1993
Mini Topo *106pp* ★★
⚠ 27,28. ✗ **300**

Terradets
Alfonso-Buxó; 1992
Mini Topo *76pp* ★★
⚠ 30. ✗ **100+**

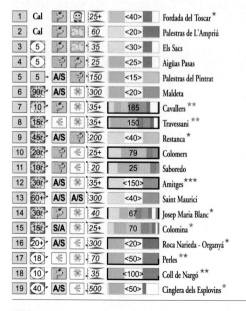

1	Cal			25+	<40>	Fordada del Toscar *
2	Cal			60	<20>	Palestres de L'Ampriú
3	5			35	<30>	Els Sacs
4	5			25	<25>	Aigüas Pasas
5	5	A/S		150	<15>	Palestres del Pintrat
6	90	A/S		300	<20>	Maldeta
7	10			35+	185	Cavallers ★★
8	15			35+	150	Travessani ★★
9	45	A/S		200	<40>	Restanca *
10	20			25+	79	Colomers
11	10			20	25	Saboredo
12	30	A/S		35+	<150>	Amitges ★★★
13	60+	A/S	A/S	300	<40>	Saint Maurici
14	30			40	67	Josep Maria Blanc *
15	15	S/A		25+	70	Colomina *
16	20+	A/S		300	<20>	Roca Narieda - Organyá *
17	18			70	<50>	Perles ★★
18	10			35	<100>	Coll de Nargó ★★
19	40	A/S		500	<50>	Cinglera dels Esplovins *
20	Cal			25	<50>	Serra de Mania *
21	5			35	<40>	Camarasa-Kuestelon *
22	5			60	46	Camarasa-Cresta *
23	1			35	<130>	Sant Llorenç de Montgai *
24	15			35	<42>	Barranc Fondo *
25	Cal	A/S		150	<65>	Mont Roig
26	Cal			40	<25>	La Pauta
27	20	S/A		250	<300>	Vilanova de Meia ★★
28	5			60	<70>	Vilanova - Cúpula ★★
29	Cal	A/S		400	<40>	Parets d'Ager
30	5	S/A		35+	<150>	Terradets ★★
31	5			30	<30>	Abella de la Conca
32	4	S/A		35+	<250>	Collegats ★★★
33	2			25	<8>	Viuet
34	5			35	<25>	Escales - Arriba *
35	5		60db	30	<10>	Escales - Pressa
36	60	A		600	<20>	Serra de Sant Gervás *
37	25	A/S		600	<100>	Montrebei ★★★
38	4	S/A		35+	<210>	Baldellou ★★★

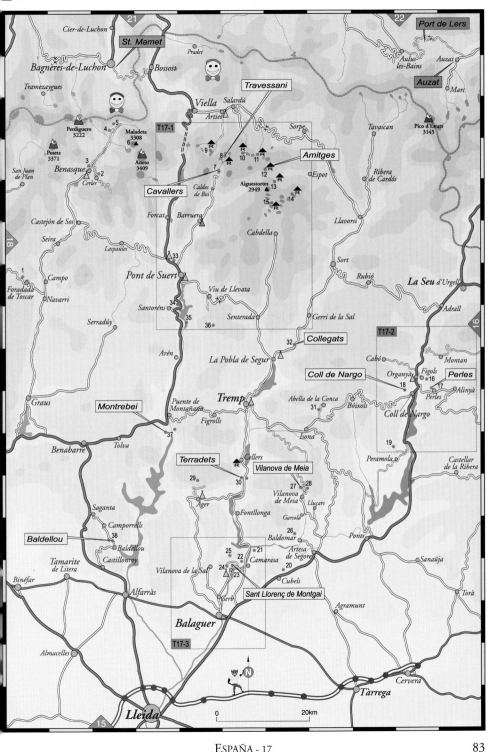

VIA DEL SOSTRET 6b, Sector Agulles Cara N; Coll de Nargo,

EL REY DE MAMBO 7b, La Cupula, Villanova de Meia; Jing

L'ENRIC 6b, Roc d'en Solà, Perles; Wobbly

The Mascun Gorge at Rodellar is one of the best Jingo habitats in Europe, 2 pitch roofs! Wow, cool man!!!

 If you want a really good wobble - eekk, try out Riglos, 8 pitches of potato fields, and tricky too.

Topo: T18-1
Rock Climbs in the Pyrenees
Derek Walker; 1990
136pp. 170mm x 115mm

⚠ 10, 28-Adv, + Pic Midi d'Ossau

€ *www.cicerone.co.uk*
www.urbanrock.com

Topo: T18-2
Rodellar - Mascún
D. Ascaso, Carlos Longroño; 2000
126pp. 210mm x 150mm

⚠ 18 - 21.

€ *Cámping Mascún*
www.guara-mascun.com

Topo: T18-3
Sierra de Guara
J. Dieste, Jose Cavero; 1993
96pp. 210mm x 150mm

⚠ 23 - 26.

€ *Librairie - Ayerbe*, ₵-7
Camping Mascún ?

Topo: T18-4 *New guide 2002*
Escaladas
Philipe Guinda Polo; 1994
214pp. 190mm x 105mm

⚠ 28-31.

€ *????*
Riglos info- Refugio Riglos
Riglos & Loarre info- Camping Banera

⅄ *Cámping Mascún (1/1-31/12)*
400m SE - Rodellar

⅄ *Campìng La Banera (1/1-31/12)*
2km NE - Ayerbe (dir Loarre)

6b, Loarre, Ayebre; Wobb

1	Cal			15	<50>	Rapún *
2	Cal			15	<12>	Embún
3	Cal			90	<25>	Coll de Ladrones
4	Cal			40	<15>	Candanchú
5	Cal			80	<50>	Forronias - Panticosa *
6	Cal			25	<20>	Escarilla
7	Cal	A/S		200	<20>	Balaitus
8	Cal			30	<20>	Balneario de Panticosa
9	Cal			15	<20>	Bujaruelo
10	Cal	A/S		400	<150>	Ordessa *
11	Cal			25	<20>	Biesla
12	Cal	A/S		300	<15>	Peña de Sin
13	Cal			30	<20>	Las Devotas
14	Cal			30	<30>	Ligüerre de Cinca *
15	③			45	<60>	Olvena *
16	Cal			30	<30>	Valcheladas
17	⑮			90	<50>	Alquézar *

18	15+			35+	<175>	Rodellar - Mascún ***
19	18			17	<23>	Camino *
20	15			40	<26>	Gran Bóveda **
21	22			35	<17>	Ventanas del Mascún *
22	Con	A/S		140	<20>	Predicadera
23	10			80	<100>	Elefante & Embalse **
24	5			250	<20>	Mallos de Ligüerri *
25	①			90	<90>	Valdiello - Pared del Entrenamiento **
26	①			40	<15>	Pared del Muerto *
27	12			29	<15>	Loarre
28	4+			300	200	Riglos ***
28	4			60	<80>	Riglos - Sport **
28	4+	747		300	<120>	Riglos - Pisón, Fire, Puro, Visera ***
29	10	A/S		200	<20>	Agüero
30	③			60	<36>	Foz de Escalete **
31				140	<10>	Aguja de Escalete *

CAMPING MASCUN
22144 RODELLAR (HUESCA),
SPAIN
Tf/fax: 974318367
www.guara-mascun.com
guara@guara-mascun.com

Campsite for canyoning and
climbing in Mascun canyon
(Sierra de Guara)
Informations & guidebooks

MASCÚN GORGE, Rodellar

MALLOS DE RIGLOS

MALLOS DE LIGUERRI, Valdiello, Sierra de Guara

There is a lot of excellent hard climbing at Oñati, very steep caves and plenty of 8's, don't miss Convento either.

 A lovely climate here, but south of Logroño gets into super high temperatures in summer, plenty of quiet spots too.

ARNEDILLO

1	15		☀	30		<50>		Apellániz*
2	15			30		<65>		Atauri**
3	15			20		<20>		Los Piñones
4	Cal			20		<20>		Aguake
5	5		❄	30		<35>		El Convento*
6	Cal			40		<60>		San Fausto
7	Cal	S/A		100		<140>		Peñartea Carrascal*
8	5+	S/A	❄	130		<450>		Etxauri***
9	Cal	S/A		250		<12>		Don Hermanas
10	Cal			20		<70>		Santa Bárbara*
11	Cal			40		<30>		Gentilbarzarta
12	15	❄	☀	200		<180>		Eguino**
13	5		☀	35		<200>		Aratoz - Oñati***
14	Cal			200		<300>		Atxarte**
15	Cal			120		<35>		Mugarra*
16	Cal			40		<40>		Baltzola*
17	Cal			20		<70>		Lamindano
18	Cal	A/S		250		<20>		Cabo Ogoño
19	Cal			20		<25>		Urduliz
20	Cal			20		<40>		Pagasarri
21	Cal			25		<66>		Oro
22	Cal			30		<25>		Subijana
23	Cal			30		<40>		Agujeros - Rioja
24	Cal			100		<30>		Nieva de Cameros
25	1		❄	60		<120>		Clavijo**
26	Cal			30		<12>		Jubera
27	15	☀		100		<80>		Arnedillo**
28	Cal	A/S		40		<40>		Isasa
29	Cal			80		<20>		Autol

APPELLÁNIZ

IL CONVENTO

APPELLÁNIZ; ZZZzzzz

CLAVIJO

WHAT TO WEAR TO THE ENDS OF THE EARTH.

THE NORTH FACE

Tekware® from The North Face. Rugged enough for climbing, ideal for global exploration, but with enough panache for the occasional brush with civilisation. Tekware® features innovative, synthetic fabrics, utilizing exclusive technologies, like our quick-drying VaporWick®. Every Tekware® piece is engineered to emphasize fit and function. You'll enjoy unsurpassed freedom of movement, exceptional durability and easy care. Packs fast and light, too, for those last-minute getaways to wherever. **Athlete-tested equipment, footwear, and apparel for men and women. From The North Face. Never stop exploring.**

NEVER STOP EXPLORING™
www.thenorthface.com

For more information and your nearest stockist, call: 01539 738882 - e-mail: uksales@vfc.com

Equipment   A5 Series™   Footwear   **Tekware®**   Outerwear   Snowsports

94

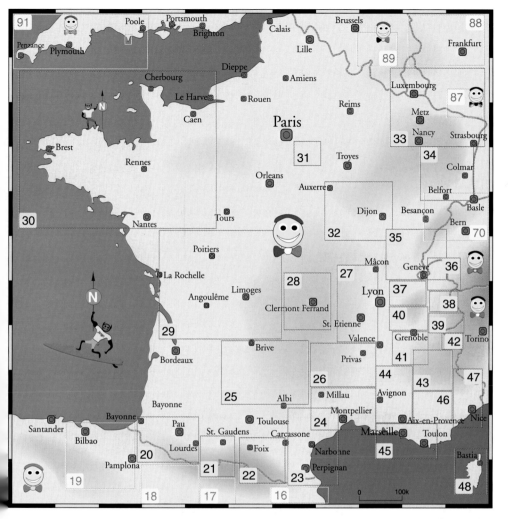

20: Bayonne - Pau
21: Saint Gaudens
22: Foix - Andorre
23: Perpignan - Narbonne
24: Montpellier - Millau
25: Cahors
26: Privas - Ardèche
27: Saint Etienne - Macon
28: Clermont Ferrand - M.Dore
29: Angoulême - Poitiers

30: Rennes
31: Fontainebleau
32: Auxerre - Dijon
33: Nancy - Metz
34: Colmar
35: Genève - (Jura-Sud)
36: Cluses - Chamonix
37: Annecy - Aix-le-Bains
38: Bourg-Saint-Maurice
39: St. Jean-de-Maurienne

40: Grenoble
41: Die
42: Briançon
43: Gap - Céüse
44: Avignon - Provence
45: Marseille - Calanques
46: Castellane - Verdon
47: Nice - Monaco
48: Corse

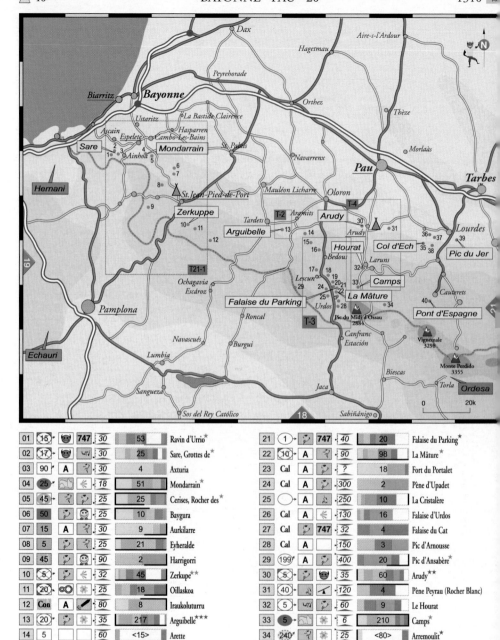

01	15		747	30	53	Ravin d'Urrio*
02	17			30	25	Sare, Grottes de*
03	90	A		30	4	Axturia
04	25			18	51	Mondarrain*
05	45			25	25	Cerises, Rocher des*
06	50			25	10	Baygura
07	15	A		30	9	Aurkilarre
08	5			25	21	Eyheralde
09	45			90	2	Harrigorri
10	5			32	45	Zerkupe**
11	20	∞		25	18	Oillaskoa
12	Con	A		80	8	Iraukoluturru
13	20			35	217	Arguibelle***
14	5			60	<15>	Arette
15	5			60	15	Lourdois, Falaise du
16	Cal			20	3	Pont d'Escot
17	Cal			35	2	Dalle d'Esquit
18	1	90db		35	15	Dalle d'Eygun
19	Cal			95	1	Caillou de Borce
20	10	A		70	3	Dent de Martain

21	1		747	40	20	Falaise du Parking*
22	10	A		90	98	La Mâture*
23	Cal	A		?	18	Fort du Portalet
24	Cal	A		300	2	Pène d'Upadet
25		A		250	10	La Cristalère
26	Cal	A		130	16	Falaise d'Urdos
27	Cal		747	32	4	Falaise du Cat
28	Cal	A		150	3	Pic d'Arnousse
29	199	A		400	20	Pic d'Ansabère*
30	5			35	60	Arudy**
31	40			120	4	Pène Peyrau (Rocher Blanc)
32	5			60	9	Le Hourat
33	5			6	210	Camps*
34	240			25	<80>	Arremoulit*
35	20			30	<30>	Col d'Ech
36	1			30	20	Bois de Lourdes
37	17		A	6	5	Béout
38	Cal			100	<50>	Pibeste* ⊘ 1.11-1.1 ⊘
39	20			35	<80>	Pic du Jer***
40	Gra			45	<30>	Pont d'Espagne

Not a lot of good overhanging rock here, but there are some fantastic harder routes which are vertical.

Pas beaucoup de dévers, mais des voies difficiles qui sont fantastiques.

 Arguibelle is a technical delight; Zerkupe, a technical treasure, and La Mâture - is very worrying! And if you really want to get scared, try out Pic Midi d'Ossau, big loose blocs, like a pyramid! - but an incredible setting.

Topo: T20-1
Escalade au Pays Basque
A. Etchepare; 1998
80pp. 210mm x 150mm

⚠ 1 - 12.

€ *Libraire des Pyrénées*
14, rue Saint Louis, 64000 Pau. ¢-7

Topo: T20-2
Arguibelle
C.Piechaud,J-M. Larricq; 2000
80pp. 210mm x 150mm

⚠ 13.

€ *Bar Le Troquet @ Aramits,*
Bar La Paloumère @ Lanne,
Mur @ Oloron

Topo: T20-3
Escalade en Vallée d'Aspe
C. Ravier, P. Puiseaux; 1990
165pp. 186mm x 130mm

⚠ 15 - 28.

€ *Libraire des Pyrénées*
14, rue Saint Louis, 64000 Pau. ¢-7

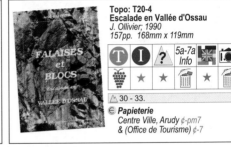

Topo: T20-4
Escalade en Vallée d'Ossau
J. Ollivier; 1990
157pp. 168mm x 119mm

⚠ 30 - 33.

€ *Papeterie*
Centre Ville, Arudy ¢-pm7
& (Office de Tourisme) ¢-7

⚠ *Europ Camping (20/4-30/9)*
Saint Jean-Pied-de-Port.
Route D918, 1km Nord.

⚠ *Camping Le Rey (1/2-30/9)*
Louvie-Juzon (Arudy 2km) 64260
0.5km, D35 rte Lourdes.

LA MÂTURE

TAFONI 6a+, Arguibelle; Malcolm McPherso

FOUFOUNE 6b+, Zerkuppe; Jingo

ARUDY 6c; Annette Sinclair

Mondarrain

Espelette
D249
Itxassou
D918
Col de Legarre
▲749m
Gneiss:
←— 1.5km —→

Arguibelle

Montory
D918
Lanne en-Barétous
D632
P
Barlanes
Cal: U
←— 2km —→

Arudy

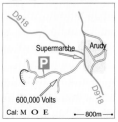

D918
Supermarche
Arudy
P
600,000 Volts
D918
Cal: M O E
←— 800m —→

Pic du Jer

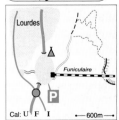

Lourdes
Funiculaire
P
Cal: U F I
←— 600m —→

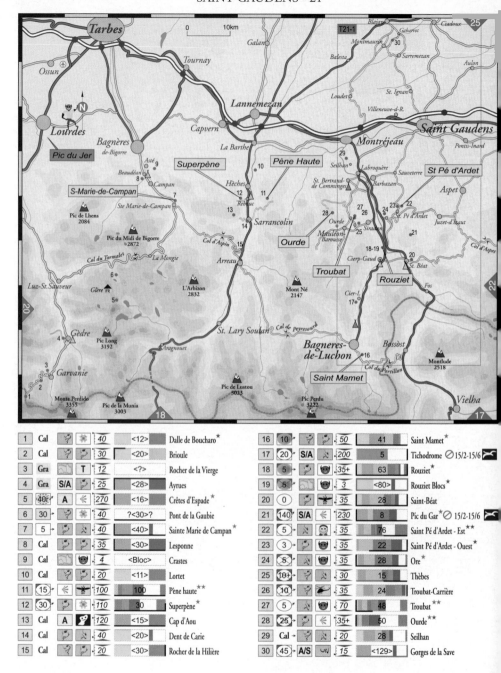

1	Cal			40	<12>			Dalle de Boucharo*
2	Cal			30	<20>			Brioule
3	Gra		T	12	<?>			Rocher de la Vierge
4	Gra	S/A		25	<28>			Ayrues
5	40r	A		270	<16>			Crêtes d'Espade*
6	30			40	?<30>?			Pont de la Gaubie
7	5			40	<40>			Sainte Marie de Campan*
8	Cal			35	<30>			Lesponne
9	Cal			4	<Bloc>			Crastes
10	Cal			20	<11>			Lortet
11	15			100	100			Pène haute**
12	30			110	30			Superpène*
13	Cal	A		120	<15>			Cap d'Aou
14	Cal			40	<20>			Dent de Carie
15	Cal			20	<30>			Rocher de la Hilière

16	10			50	41			Saint Mamet*
17	20	S/A		200	5			Tichodrome ⊘ 15/2-15/6
18	5			35+	63			Rouziet*
19	5			3	<80>			Rouziet Blocs*
20	0			35	28			Saint-Béat
21	140	S/A		230	8			Pic du Gar* ⊘ 15/2-15/6
22	5			35	76			Saint Pé d'Ardet - Est**
23	3			35	22			Saint Pé d'Ardet - Ouest*
24	5			35	28			Ore*
25	10+			30	15			Thèbes
26	10			35	24			Troubat-Carrière
27	5			70	48			Troubat**
28	25			35+	50			Ourde**
29	Cal			20	28			Seilhan
30	45	A/S		15	<129>			Gorges de la Save

Don't miss a visit to Troubat, excellent 2 pitch power climbing, and bring a 100 meter rope if you have one.
N'oubliez pas de visiter Troubat, voies excellentes de 2 longeures, une corde de 100 mètres peut-être utile.

A very nice area for the family, still with a feel of the mountains and plenty of variety.
Un endroit très sympa pour la famille, avec beaucoup de diversité et la sensation d'être à la montagne.

Topo: T21-1
Escalade en Pyrénées Centrales
Pascal, Serge et les 9b amis; 1997
154pp. 170mm x 120mm

5a-7a
Info

★ ★★ ★ ★ ★ ★ ★

16 - 27, 30.

Café, St. Pé d'Ardet
Presse, Cierp Gaud & Boulangerie!!

Sarrancolin
??; 1997
Mini Topo A4 42pp

11-12   44

Sarrancolin ???

6a+, OURDE: Jingo

Pène Haute

Ourde

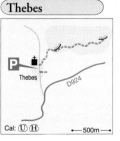

Thebes

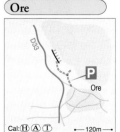

Ore

SAINT-BÉAT   *SAINT-BÉAT*

MARILOU 6c+, Troubat; Jingo

BLOCS, ROUZIET; Wobbly

Tremendous variety, technical Carol, airy Roquefixade, and blunt hard mountain bouldering of Targassone
Beaucoup de choix: la technicité à Carol, l'expo à Roquefixade et l'escalade à bloc à Targassone

 Tarascon offers the beautiful high crag of Quie, the technicality of Calmes, and the abrasiveness of Auzat.
Tarascon offre le très beau site élevé de Quie, la technicité de Calmes, et l'abrasivité d'Auzat.

Mini Topo	Auzat
T	??; 1998
	68pp
⛰ 7.	150

€ O-de-Tourisme, Tarascon, ⌀-7

Mini Topo	Sinsat-Quie
T	??; 1998
	120pp
⛰ 21-23	250

€ O-de-Tourisme, Tarascon, ⌀-7

Mini Topo	Roquefixade
T	??; 1998
	24pp
⛰ 15	150

€ Refuge, Roquefixade

La Serre Camping (1/1-31/12)
09600 Aigues-Vives (Carol)
+ camping chalets.

Pays de Tarascon ❶
avenue des Pyrénées. 09400
Tarascon. www.paysdetarascon.com

6b CALAMÈS; Jingo

Port de Lers

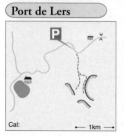

Cal: |— 1km —|

Carol

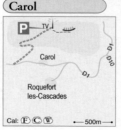

Cal: Ⓕ Ⓒ Ⓦ |— 500m —|

Calamès

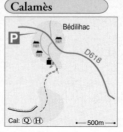

Cal: Ⓠ Ⓗ |— 500m —|

Saint Pierre-dels-Forcats

Gra: |— 2km —|

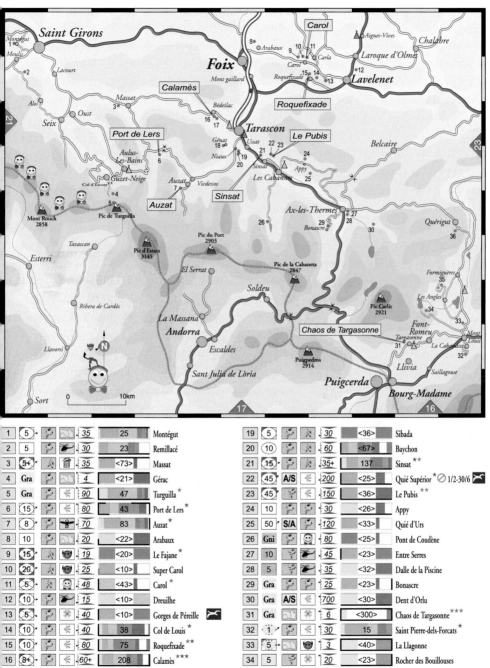

1	(5)			35	25	Montégut
2	5			30	23	Remillacé
3	(5+)			35	<73>	Massat
4	Gra			4	<21>	Gérac
5	Gra			90	47	Turguilla*
6	(15)			80	43	Port de Lers*
7	(8)			70	83	Auzat*
8	10			20	<22>	Arabaux
9	(15)			19	<20>	Le Fajane*
10	(20)			25	<10>	Super Carol
11	(5)			48	<43>	Carol*
12	(10)			15	<10>	Dreuilhe
13	(5)			40	<10>	Gorges de Péreille
14	(10)			40	38	Col de Louis*
15	(10)			80	75	Roquefixade**
16	(8+)			60+	208	Calamès***
17	(10)			30	<23>	Roc à Steph
18	(3)			35+	<41>	Génat*
19	(5)			30	<36>	Sibada
20	(10)			60	<67>	Baychon
21	(15)			35+	137	Sinsat**
22	(45)	A/S		200	<25>	Quié Supérior* ⊘ 1/2-30/6
23	(45)			150	<36>	Le Pubis**
24	10			30	<26>	Appy
25	50	S/A		120	<33>	Quié d'Urs
26	Gni			80	<25>	Pont de Coudène
27	10			45	<23>	Entre Serres
28	5			35	<32>	Dalle de la Piscine
29	Gra			25	<23>	Bonascre
30	Gra	A/S		700	<30>	Dent d'Orlu
31	Gra			6	<300>	Chaos de Targasonne***
32	1			30	15	Saint Pierre-dels-Forcats*
33	(5)			3	<40>	La Llagonne
34	5			20	<23>	Rocher des Bouillouses
35	Gra			30	<30>	Roc dels Moros (Balcère)
36	Gra			17	<17>	Quérigut

6b+, Roquefixade; Wobbly

7c+, Carol; Jingo

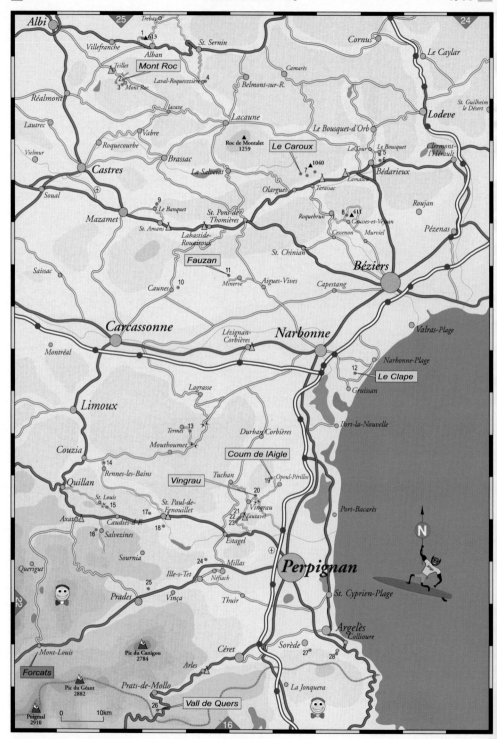

Vingrau is a lot less crowded than in the 1980's, but when it rains in the mountains, we all love to come back.
Vingrau est moins populaire que dans les années 80, mais lorsqu'il pleut en montagne on aime y retourner.

 It you want to get away from the crowds, then a trip to Carroux in the Autumn is simply beautiful.
Si vous voulez vous éloigner de la foule, alors une visite à Carroux an automne est simplement merveilleux.

Vingrau — Bruno Colla; 1997 — 124pp — Mini Topo — 20. — 200 — Vingrau-Presse, ¢-pm.7

Le Clape — A. Berché; 1996 — 150+pp ed-Mimosa. — Mini Topo — 12. — 400 — Gruissan ?,

Caroux Escalades — CAF Béziers; 1991 — ? — Mini Topo — 7. — 200 — ?,

HORTUS (24.15) - am!

1	15	15	<14>	Roc Saint-Michel
2	10	15	<65>	Mont Roc (Le Calvaire)*
3	Qua	20	<15>	Le Castellas-Le Dadounet
4	Qua	20	<20>	Laval-Roquecezière
5	Cal	20	<20>	Bosquet de la Balme
6	Cal	15	<30>	Roc Rouge
7	Vol	A/S	300	<300>	Le Caroux**
8	8	40	<50>	Landeyran
9	Vol	40	<40>	Le Banquet
10	Cal	35+	<70>	Notre Dame du Cros
11	Cal	25	<60>	Gorges de la Cesse - Fauzan*
12	15	S/A	20	<400>	Le Clape**
13	Cal	S/A	100	<35>	Laroque de Fa
14	15	?	<60>	Cardou
15	Cal	40	<100>	Col de Saint Louis**
16	Cal	60	<20>	Champ du Mouréau
17	Cal	30	<25>	La Tirounère
18	Cal	S/A	100	<30>	Clue-de-la-Fou (Fenouillèdes)
19	Cal	40	<60>	Coum de l'Aigle-Périllos*
20	10	80	300	Vingrau***
21	Cal	40	<25>	Saint Martin
22	Cal	45	<40>	Alzine*
23	Cal	20	<12>	Alentou
24	Gra	20	<20>	Néfiach
25	Gra	?	Bloc	Eus
26	Cal	60	<35>	Vall de Quers
27	Vol	70	<30>	Puig Naud-Château d'Ultrera
28	Gni	12	<20>	Rimbaut

La Jonte is the place for good air time. Seynes is full of steep flared tufas, very hard to clip from.!!!!
La Jonte est idéal pour un bol d'air frais. Seynes est rempli de colonnes ce qui rend plus dur le mousquetonnage.

 A lovely - low altitude area for the spring and Autumn, just nice to get on rock in the warm sun.
Un lieu sympa en basse altitude pour le printemps e t l'automne, parfait pour grimper sous le soleil chaud.

Topo: T24-1
La Jonte
CAF; 1997
104pp. 210mm x 125mm

5a-7a
Info

★ ★★★ ★ ★★

⚠ 4.
€ *Millau ?, ¢-7*

Topo: T24-2
Escalades au Thaurac
F. Roumanille, J-L. Fabre; 2002
120pp. 210mm x 150mm

5a-7a
Info

★ ★★★★★ ★★

⚠ 10,11,12,13.
€ *Café Glacier, St.Bauzille-de-Putois*

Topo: T24-3
Claret
Rasta Boy - H. Beauzille; 1998?
63pp. 170mm x 140mm

5a-7a
Info

★ ★★

⚠ 1-3, 5-6, 8-9,16-19, 25
€ *Café-Claret*

Topo: T24-4
Les Falaises de Seynes
Serge Imbert; 1999
98pp. 210mm x 150mm

5a-7a
Info

★★ ★ ★ ★

⚠ 22,23,24,25,26.
€ *?, ¢-7*

Hortus
P.Auguste; 1980's
40pp
Mini Topo
⚠ 15.
€ ?
🪝 60

S-B-de-Montmel
?; 1999
64pp
Mini Topo
⚠ 17.
€ *Café du Puech, SB-Montmel*
🪝 100

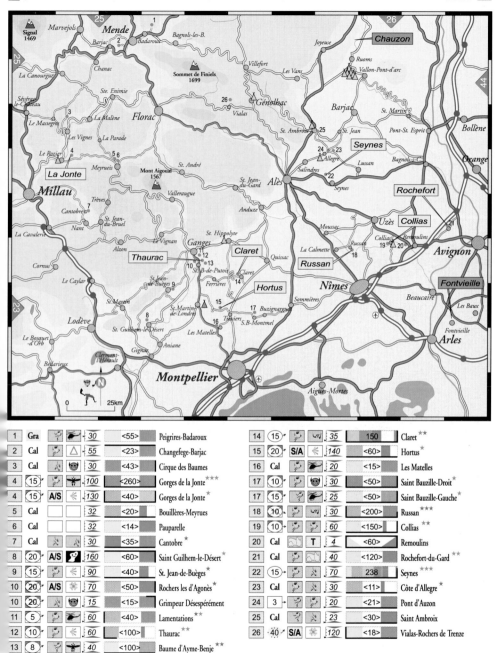

1	Gra			30	<55>		Peigrires-Badaroux
2	Cal			55	<23>		Changefege-Barjac
3	Cal			30	<43>		Cirque des Baumes
4	(15)			100	<260>		Gorges de la Jonte ***
4	(15)	A/S		130	<40>		Gorges de la Jonte *
5	Cal			32	<20>		Bouillères-Meyrues
6	Cal			32	<14>		Pauparelle
7	Cal			30	<35>		Cantobre *
8	20	A/S		160	<60>		Saint Guilhem-le-Désert *
9	(15)			90	<40>		St. Jean-de-Buèges *
10	20	A/S		70	<50>		Rochers les d'Agonès *
10	20			15	<15>		Grimpeur Désespérément
11	(5)			60	<40>		Lamentations **
12	10			60	<100>		Thaurac **
13	8			40	<100>		Baume d'Ayme-Benje **

14	(15)			35	150		Claret **
15	20	S/A		140	<60>		Hortus *
16	Cal			20	<15>		Les Matelles
17	10			30	<50>		Saint Bauzille-Droit *
17	15			25	<50>		Saint Bauzille-Gauche *
18	10			30	<200>		Russan ***
19	10			60	<150>		Collias **
20	Cal		T	4	<60>		Remoulins
21	Cal			40	<120>		Rochefort-du-Gard **
22	(15)			70	238		Seynes ***
23	Cal			30	<11>		Côte d'Allegre *
24	3			20	<21>		Pont d'Auzon
25	Cal			23	<30>		Saint Ambroix
26	40	S/A		120	<18>		Vialas-Rochers de Trenze

ecteur Escalator 6b+, Claret; Michael Posch

◄◄ *SAINT GUILHEM-LE-DÉSERT*

AYESHA 6a, Baume d'Ayme, Thaurac; Wobbl

113

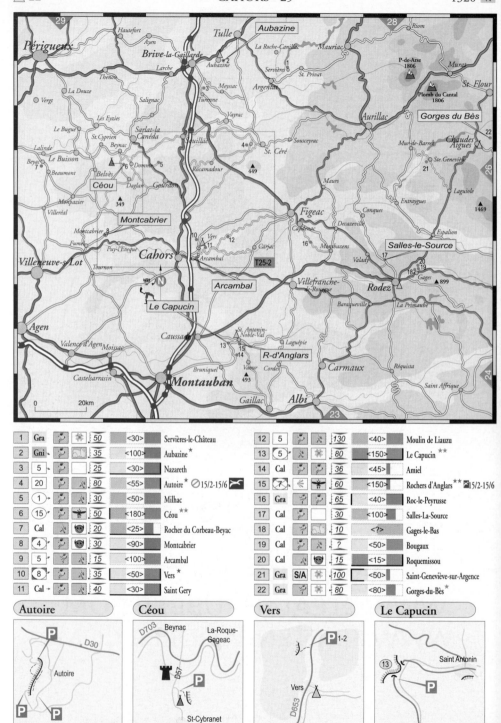

1	Gra		❄	50	<30>		Servières-le-Château		12	5	⚔	130	<40>		Moulin de Liauzu
2	Gni			35	<100>		Aubazine *		13	(5)	❄	80	<150>		Le Capucin **
3	5			25	<30>		Nazareth		14	Cal		36	<45>		Amiel
4	20		⚔	80	<55>	⊘15/2-15/6 🏊	Autoire *		15	(7)	❄	60	<150>	🏊15/2-15/6	Rochers d'Anglars **
5	(1)			30	<50>		Milhac		16	Gra		65	<40>		Roc-le-Peyrusse
6	(15)			50	<180>		Céou **		17	Cal		30	<100>		Salles-La-Source
7	Cal			20	<25>		Rocher du Corbeau-Beyac		18	Cal		10	<?>		Gages-le-Bas
8	(4)			30	<90>		Montcabrier		19	Cal	⚔	?	<50>		Bougaux
9	5		⚔	15	<100>		Arcambal		20	Cal		15	<15>		Roquemissou
10	(8)		⚔	35	<50>		Vers *		21	Gra	S/A	100	<50>		Saint-Geneviève-sur-Argence
11	Cal		⚔	40	<30>		Saint Gery		22	Gra	❄	80	<80>		Gorges-du-Bès *

Autoire

P — D30
Autoire
P   P
Cal: ← 1km →

Céou

D703   Beynac   La-Roque-Gageac
D57
P
▲
St-Cybranet
Cal: Ⓑ Ⓗ Ⓞ   ← 3km →

Vers

P 1-2
Vers
D653
▲
Cal: Ⓤ Ⓒ Ⓐ   ← 2.6km →

Le Capucin

(13)   Saint Antonin
P
Cal: Ⓗ Ⓔ Ⓐ   ← 3km →

Le Capucin is the place to be when you are feeling strong, Céou is for those not feeling so strong!!!
Le Capucin est l'endroit ou aller losque vous vous sentez fort, Céou est pour ceux qui ne se sentent pas si fort!!!

 The Dordogne and Lot river valleys give some idyllic scenery, with lovely technical climbing on quiet cliffs.
Les vallées de la Dordogne et du Lot offrent de belles vues et de très bonne voies sur des falaises tranquilles.

Topo: T25-1
Ecaclades au Ceou
F. Thibaudeau; 1997
38pp. 210mm x 150mm

5a-7a
Info

6.
Camping Maisonneuve, Ceou.
¢1/11-31/3

Topo: T25-2
L'Escalades dans le Lot
FFME; 2000
160pp. 210mm x 150mm

5a-7a
Info

4,5,- - ,8,9,10,11,12.
Presse-Saint-Antoinin,
¢-pm.7

Saint-Antonin
?; 1996
? (80-ish) pp
Mini Topo
13,15.   200
Office-Tourisme, ¢-6,7

Aubazine
?; 1986
?
Mini Topo
2   100
Rest-Le Saut de la Bergère

LE CAPUCIN

Rochers d'Anglars, Tarn-et-Garonne
Le Marie, Saint-Antonin-Noble-Val.

Le Camping a Céou, Wow!

Daglan, Dordogne

E FLEURS DU MALE, 7a, Céou;

The Ardèche is a bigger area than you realise, but the hard routes are polished, so bring your extra sticky boots.
L'Ardèche est une grande région pour l'escalade, mais les voies difficiles sont patinées.

 'You will never climb alone' is the motto of the Ardeche. Well bolted climbing and wet canoeing.
'Vous ne grimperez jamais seul' est la devise de l'Ardèche. Voies bien équipées.

Topo: T26-1
Ardèche
CDFFME; 2000
192pp. 210mm x 150mm

€ **Presse-Libraire** ¢-7
Aubenas, Ruoms:
Privas

5a-7a
Info

1-29.

GORGES DE L'ARDÈCHE

1	5		△	23	<18>		Saint Sauveur-Champer
2	5			45	<110>		Mazet Plage **
3	5			35	<40>		Les Actinidias *
4	7			35	<180>		Chaulet ***
5	8			35	<105>		Salavas-Fontgarnide **
6	12			35	<25>		Les Branches *
7	20	A/S		150	<80>		Gorges de l'Ardèche **
8	8			22	<50>		Saint Montan - Sainte Beaume *
9	12			35	<300>		Chauzon-Cirque les Gens ***
10	5			35	<45>		Balazac - Audon
11	5			20	<35>		Lanas
12	5			16	<20>		Vogüé
13	5			20	<150>		Chabanne-Lussas *
14	10			30	<100>		Courpatas-Saint Laurent *
15	15			23	<40>		St. Michel de Boulogne
16	3			18	<90>		Chomérac *
17	5			25	<85>		La Payre *
18	15			20	<135>		Rompon *
19	5			25	<32>		Châteaubourg - La Goule
20	8			30	<30>		Dunière -sur-Eyrieux
21	8			25	<90>		Les Cabannes - Saint Maurice *
22	10			25	<42>		Beauvene
23	3			20	<65>		Mariac
24	15			35	<33>		Le Lac d'Issariès *
25	5			25	<15>		Les Combes - Géorand
26	20	S/A		20	<23>		Les Coux - Sainte Eulalie *
27	20			20	<27>		Valgorge
28	10			55	<10>		Borne
29	10	S/A		35+	<57>		Montseluges

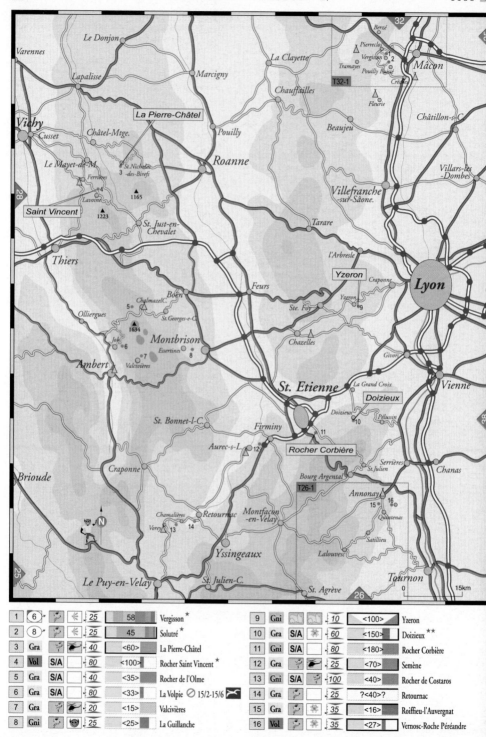

Go straight to Le Capucin, because in summer, it is often high enough to be at the perfect temperature.
En été allez directement au site Le Capucin car il est situé assez haut pour être à la température idéale.

 Dent de Rancune, is just one of those lumps of rock, that you have to climb - yes it's brilliant.
Dent de Rancune est une de ces roches ou vous devez absolument grimper - tout simplement excellent.

Topo: T28-1
Le Massif du Sancy
D.Collangettes-G.Monneron-M.Chalier
1996; 74pp. 210mm x 150mm

(T) (I) ? | 5a-7a Info | 🏴 📷

🍇 ★ ★ ★★★ ★

⚠ 4,6,7,8,9,10.
€ *Librarie-Mont-Dore, ¢-7*

DENT DE RANCUNE

1	Vol	S/A	🐾 60		<75>		Châteauneuf-les-Bains
2	Vol		8		<60>		Gour de Tazanet
3	Gra		20		<25>		Ceyrat
4	15	A/S	60		<24>		La Roche Tuilière
5	Gra		80		<22>		Saint-Sauves
6	15		80		<70>		Le Capucin **
7	10		31		<45>		Le Verrou
8	45	S/A	80		<25>		La Crête du Coq *
9	45		80		<40>		La Dent de la Rancune ***
10	Vol		25		<25>		Lac Pavin *
11	15		60db 60		<60>		Rivalet
12	10		25		<12>		Saurier
13	Vol		40		<25>		Grotte de Bort
14	Vol		70		<10>		Bort-Belevèdère
15	Vol		90		<?>		Rocher d'Urlande
16	Vol		25		<10>		Auteroche
17	25		20		<60>		Riom-ès-Montagne *
18	10		35		<25>		Marchastel
19	Vol		30		<24>		Cascade de Salins
20	Vol	A/S	250		<80>		Roc d'Hozières ⊘ 15/2-15/6
21	25		25		<20>		Pas de Peyrol - Tourte
22	Vol		25		<20>		Saint-Flour

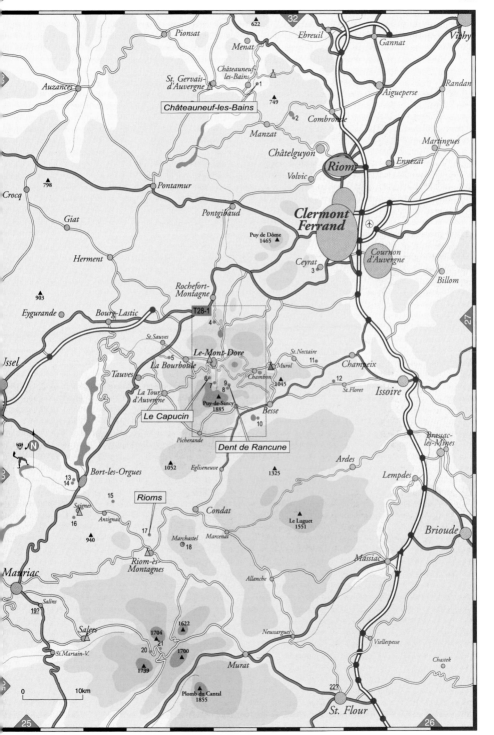

Hard and uncompromising, with bolts well apart! The quality of Guignoterie and La Forge, is a gem.
Difficile et intransigeant avec des broches espacées mais la qualité de la Guignoterie et de La Forge est un plus.

 Shorter climbing than most, in lovely countryside which makes this a real fun place for groups of mixed standards.
Des voies plus courtes que d'habitude mais le joli paysage fait de ce lieu qu'il est parfait pour les groupes.

Topo: T29-1
Escalade en Charente
F. Chabelard; 1992
90pp. 150mm x 210mm

New Topo 2002

€ **O-de Tourisme:**
Châteauneuf ¢-7
Restaraunt-Tabac:
Puyomen

T I ? 5a-7a Info

★★★★ ★★

⚠ 10,11.

Topo: T29-2
Esc-dans le Val-d-Dronne, Perigord
Michel Bertrand; 1997
112pp. 210mm x 150mm

T I ? 5a-7a Info

★★★★★★★★ ★

⚠ 12,13,14,15,16,17.

€ **Le relais de l'Ecalade (Bar),**
Paussac. ¢-pm-3

Mini Topo

Guignoterie
CAF; 1992
48pp

⚠ 7. (8&9?)
€ **Café, Anglin**

120

Camping du Nizour (1/4-31/10)
Sireuil, 16440 Roullet St. Estephe
(10km Angoulême)

5b, CHIRON DU FOUR; Wobbly

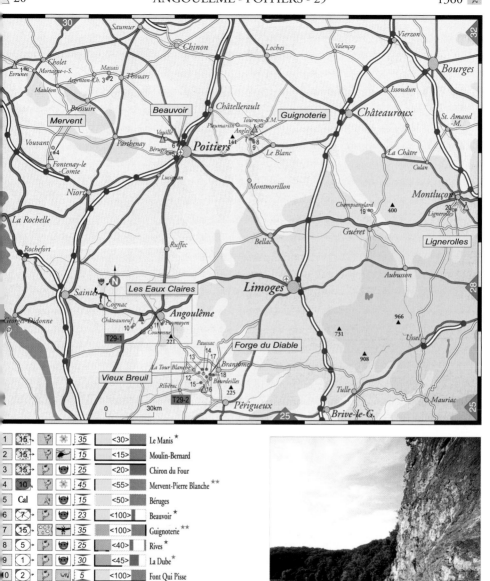

#						name
1	15			35	<30>	Le Manis *
2	15			15	<15>	Moulin-Bernard
3	15			25	<20>	Chiron du Four
4	10			45	<55>	Mervent-Pierre Blanche **
5	Cal			15	<50>	Béruges
6	7			23	<100>	Beauvoir *
7	15			35	<100>	Guignoterie **
8	5			25	<40>	Rives *
9	1			30	<45>	La Dube *
10	2			5	<100>	Font Qui Pisse
11	10			20	<300>	Les Eaux Claires ***
12	3			18	<90>	Le Vieux Breuil **
13	3			15	<50>	Les Clos
14	Cal			20	<10>	La Tabaterie
15	1			25	<42>	Moulin de Rochereuil *
16	5			25	<80>	Forge du Boulou **
17	2			25	<35>	Forge du Diable *
18	Cal			4	<100>	Blocs des Bourdeilles *
19	Gra	A/S		60	<60>	Jupile
20	10			35	<40>	Lignerolles *

MERVENT

MOULIN DE ROCHEREUIL

LE FORGE DU DIABLE

BOURDEILLES

CAUCHEMAR EN 4 DIMENSIONS *7c+, Licorne, Les Eaux Claires; Jingo*

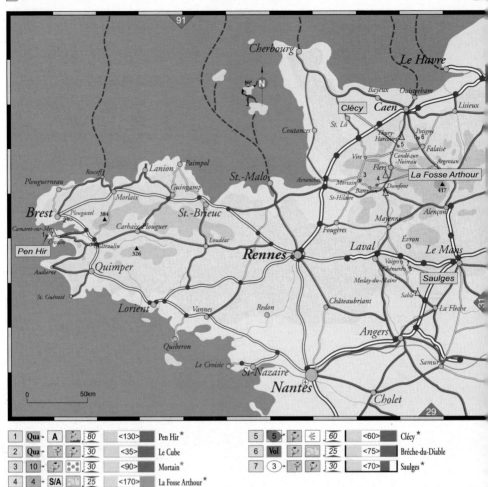

1	Qua→	A	🪨	80	<130>	Pen Hir*
2	Qua→			30	<35>	Le Cube
3	10→			30	<90>	Mortain*
4	4→	S/A		25	<170>	La Fosse Arthour*

5	5→			60	<60>	Clécy*
6	Vol			25	<75>	Brèche-du-Diable
7	3→			30	<70>	Saulges*

 It's all soft climbing around here, but the Sea cliffs of Pen Hir can give some worrying moments.
De bonnes voies mais les falaises de Pen Hir peuvent procurer quelques moments effrayants.

 Clecy offers a great range of climbs, camping and bars, and has almost a mountain feel to the climbing.
Clécy offre une large gamme de voies, de campings et de bars et la presque sensation d'être à la montagne.

Topo: T30-1
Escalade à Clécy
CAF Basse Normandy; 2001
42pp. 210mm x 140mm

T I ?   5a-7a Info

⛰ 5.

€ **Tabac, Clécy,**
Camping (Le Vey), Clécy.

Topo: T30-2
French Rock
Bill Birkett; 1993
304pp. 208mm x 145mm

T I ?   5a-7a Info

⛰ 1, 2, 3, 5. (++++40 ⛰ in France)

€ **www.cicerone.co.uk**
www.urbanrock.com

129

Strength alone is not enough for Font, you need applied strength with technique.
La force n'est pas seulement suffisante pour Font, vous devez associer à cette force une bonne technique.

 You need a good map to even find the boulders in the forest and don't miss out on the circuits - they are fun.
Une bonne carte est nécessaire pour trouver les sites. N'oubliez pas de suivre les circuits qui sont divertissants.

Topo: T31-1
Escalade à Fontainebleau
J&F Montchausse, J Godoffe; 1999
240pp. 220mm x 120mm

T **I** **?** **5a-7a** **Info**

★★ ★ ★★★★ ★★

⚠ 1-2,-,4-7,-,8-10,-,12-24,-,25?

€ **Presse-Milly-la-Forêt**, ¢-pm.7
Libraire-Fontainebleau, ¢-7

Topo: T31-2
Les Trois Pignons
Cosiroc; 1998
176pp. 210mm x 150mm

T **I** **?** **5a-7a** **Info**

★★ ★ ★ ★★★★

⚠ 16-21

€ **Decathlon-Villiers-en-Bière**, ¢-pm.7

Topo: T31-1a
Fontainebleau Climbs
J&F Montchausse
J Godoffe; 1999
256pp; 220mm x 120mm
Full English translation
by Sue Harper
€ **www.urbanrock.com**

Circuit Orange, Mont Aigu (9),
Fontainebleau;
Gordon Stainforth

⚠ 300   8000

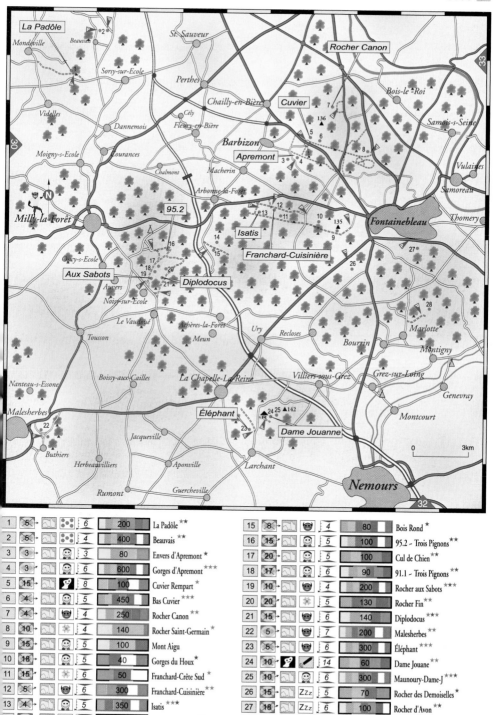

1	5			6	200		La Padôle **
2	5			4	400		Beauvais **
3	3			3	80		Envers d'Apremont *
4	3			6	600		Gorges d'Apremont ***
5	15			8	100		Cuvier Rempart *
6	4			5	450		Bas Cuvier ***
7	4			4	250		Rocher Canon **
8	10			4	140		Rocher Saint-Germain *
9	15			5	100		Mont Aigu
10	18			5	40		Gorges du Houx *
11	15			6	50		Franchard-Crête Sud *
12	5			6	300		Franchard-Cuisinière **
13	4			5	350		Isatis ***
14	5			5	80		Rocher de la Reine *
15	8			4	80		Bois Rond *
16	15			5	100		95.2 ~ Trois Pignons **
17	20			5	100		Cul de Chien **
18	17			6	90		91.1 ~ Trois Pignons **
19	10			4	200		Rocher aux Sabots ***
20	20			5	130		Rocher Fin **
21	5			6	140		Diplodocus ***
22	5			7	200		Malesherbes **
23	5			6	300		Éléphant ***
24	10			14	60		Dame Jouane **
25	10			6	300		Maunoury-Dame-J ***
26	15		Zzz	5	70		Rocher des Demoiselles *
27	18		Zzz	6	100		Rocher d'Avon **
28	15			5	100		Restant du Long Rocher *

LE BILBOQUET, Cul de Chien, Trois Pignons; Jamie Ogilvie

Franchard - Crête Sud

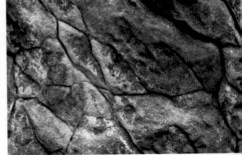

Grés, Diplodocu

Le rosbeef dans LA CHARCUTERIE 6c, Bas Cuvier; Jingo

LE CIRCUIT BLEU, La Roche aux Sabots, Trois Pignons; Graeme Hughes

Éléphant

Bas Cuvier

Cuvier Rempart

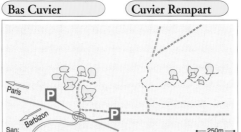

Apremont

SILVA *Multinavigator*

MILLY-LA-FÔRET

BLEU - ROCHER FIN, Trois Pignons; Jamie Ogilvie

BARBIZON

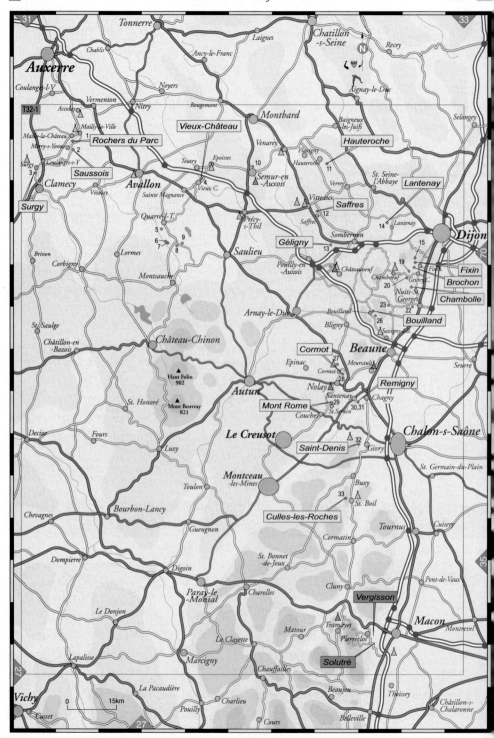

The Vieux Combe is magnificent, and so is Bouilland, but please remember the bird restrictions.
Le Vieux Combe et Bouilland sont magnifiques, mais n'oubliez pas de respecter les restrictions pour les oiseaux.

 Fixin is really technical, and so is Hauteroche, lots of climbing on not a lot of rock.
Fixin et Hauteroche sont très technique, beaucoup de voies sur très peu de rochers.

Topo: T32-1
Bourgogne
Jingo Wobbly; 2003
336pp. 210mm x 150mm

5a-7a Info

★★★★★★★

⚠ 1-4,11-14, 16, 18, 21, 23, 24-33

€ Office-de-Tourisme; Vitteaux
O-d-T; Gevrey Chambertain (Fixin)
Camping: Nolay, Mailly-Le-Château
www.urbanrock.com

Topo: T32-2
Surgy
Denier, Paulevé et amis; 1999
132pp. 210mm x 140mm

5a-7a Info

★★★★★★★★ ★

⚠ 3

€ Office-de-Tourisme; Clamecy

Topo: T32-3
Hauteroche
Alain Finet; 1992
104pp. 210mm x 140mm

5a-7a Info

★ ★★ ★ ★★

⚠ 11

€ Office-de-Tourisme: Venarey-I-L.

Topo: T32-4
Saffres
J-Y. Gerbet, J. Wiedmer; 1993
168pp. 210mm x 140mm

5a-7a Info

★★★★★★ ★ ★

⚠ 12

€ Office-de-Toursime-Vitteaux
Presse, Vitteaux

	Saussois & Parc Flageat; 1994 128pp	Escalade - Morvan J-L Scola; 1997 71pp	Escal-Grand Crus P.Gleizes; 1998 160pp	Cormot CAF; 1999 68pp??
Topo		Mini Topo	Mini Topo	Mini Topo
⚠ 1&2.	400	⚠ 4 - 10 — 189	⚠ 17-21. — 186	⚠ 27. — 150
€ Rest.-Les Roches (Saussois)		€ Presse-Epoisses	€ O-D-T; Gevrey Chambertin	€ Lib- Charlet, Nolay, ¢pm1&pm7

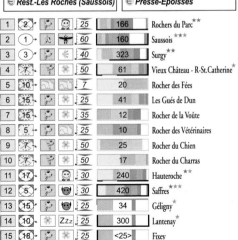

1	2	😊	25	166	Rochers du Parc**		
2	1	🦅	60	160	Saussois***		
3	3	40	323	Surgy**			
4	50	61	Vieux Château - R-St.Catherine*				
5	10	7	20	Rocher des Fées			
6	15	25	41	Les Gués de Dun			
7	15	35	12	Rocher de la Voûte			
8	5	25	10	Rocher des Vétérinaires			
9	50	25	Rocher du Chien				
10	50	17	Rocher du Charras				
11	17	😊	30	240	Hauteroche**		
12	5	●	30	420	Saffres***		
13	15	●	25	34	Géligny*		
14	10	Zzz	25	300	Lantenay*		
15	18	25	<25>	Fixey			
16	15	😊	35	255	Fixin***		
17	3	△	20	<40>	Brochon-Nord ⊘ Rockfall!		
18	20	Zzz	25	32	Brochon-Sud		
19	15	Zzz	15	18	Combe de la Bossière		
20	7	●	40	8	Bed of Judry		
21	15	●	25	56	Chambolle-Musigny*		
22	15	Zzz	3	<15>	Grottes de Nuits		
23	10	25	70	Arcenant			
24	5	35	90	Bouilland**			
25	25	45	<60>	Bouilland-Sauvage ⊘ 15/2-15/6			
26	15	35	<100>	Vieux Combe** ⊘ 15/2-15/6			
27	15	35	<25>	Bout de Monde* ⊘ 15/2-15/6			
28	8	40	215	Cormot**			
29	3	25	47	Rome Château-St. Sernin			
30	1	25	10	Remigny-Reggae* ⊘ 9/9-1/4			
31	1	25	22	Remigny-Dalle ⊘ 9/9-1/4			
32	11	20	29	Saint-Denis-de-Vaux			
33	1	14	37	Culles-Roches			

LA FAUSSE DER 6a, Saussois: Jean-Paul Avat

Chablis

Gevrey-Chambertin

Gevrey-Chambertin

Fixin

Époisses Château

PROJECT 8c, Fixin; Pierre Duroché

GILBERT DU MOI 4b, Cormot; Rachel Chester

Sandstone powerhungry Kronthal is not to be missed, but for beauty visit the overhanging, shaded Berdorf.

 A few hours spent at Dames de Meuse will test your technical ability to use pockets.
Quequaes heures passées à Dames de Meuse testera votre capacité à utiliser des trous.

Topo: T33-1
Berdorf
Jacques Welter; 1998
48pp. 210mm x 150mm

| T | I | ? | 5a-7a Info | | 📷 |
| 🌳 | ★ | ★★★ | ★★ | ★★ | |

⚠ 1.
€ **Camping Belle Vue-Berdorf,** ¢-7
Café ?

Ch.de Windstein

T Mini Topo	
⚠ 8.	⚔ 80

€ **Restaurant-Aux deux Chât.**

Kronthal

€ Marlenheim

T Mini Topo	
⚠ 13.	⚔ 100

€ **Relais de la route de Vins**

⚠ Belle-Vue-2000 (1/1-31/12)
29, rue de Consdorf, L-6551 Berdorf

DAMES DE MEUSE

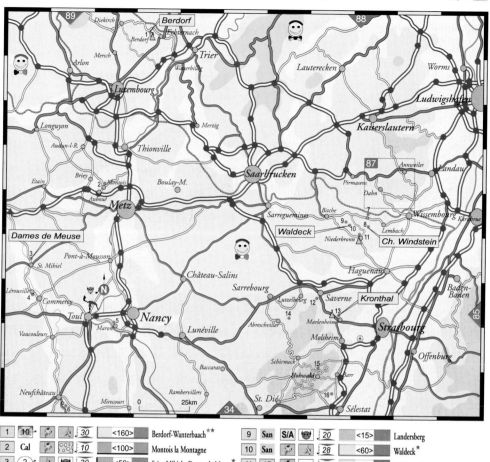

1	10			30	<160>	Berdorf-Wanterbaach**
2	Cal			10	<100>	Montois la Montagne
3	2			30	<50>	Saint Mihiel - Dames de Meuse*
4	Cal			35	<80>	La Chartelle - Lérouville
5	Cal			15	<80>	Maron - Nancy
6	Cal	S/A		25	<20>	Rebeuville
7	San	S/A		20	<20>	Obersteinbach
8	5	S/A		25	<80>	Château de Windstein*

9	San	S/A		20	<15>	Landersberg
10	San			28	<60>	Waldeck*
11	15			20	<22>	Heidenkopf
12	San			25	<23>	Grotte de Brotsch
13	45			25	<120>	Kronthal
14	10			30	<30>	Hohwalschfels
15	San			25	<50>	Neuntelstein
16	35			50	<20>	Falkenstein

1 ⊘ Berdorf-Wanterbaach: At the moment you need a permit
to climb here. This is difficult to obtain, you need to
phone up and order one in advance - especially difficult
for climbing at weekends - too many climbers, but only
a restricted number of permits. (Jan 2003)

Rocher Hans is not strictly power hungry, but it certainly saps you energy at a good rate.
Même si Rocher Hans ne nécessite pas seulement d'être puissant, il vous fera dépenser beaucoup d'énergie.

 For those hot summer days, drive up to the top of Honeck and don't miss out on beautiful views from Martinswand.
Pour les jours d'été très chauds, allez à Honeck et ne manquez pas les vues splendides depuis Martinswand.

Topo: T34-1
Topo d'Escalades des Vosges du Sud
Jacques Dreyer; 1999
112pp. 210mm x 150mm

6-13.
Office-de-Tourisme, Munster, ✆-7

Hattstatt, Gueberschwihr

Nouveau Gueberschwihr

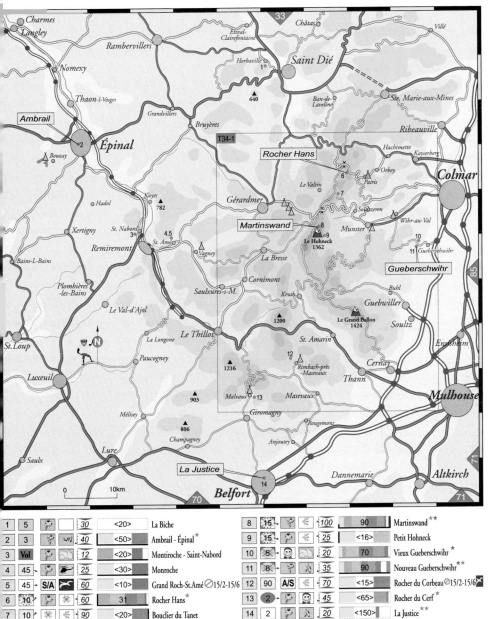

HERWOL 6a, Vieux Gueberschwihr: Rudy

LA QUITTE OU DOUBLE 5c, Martinswand

6b+, NEUVILLE-SUR-AIN

1	Cal			40	<60>		Monetier
2	(15)		⇐	200	<300>		Le Salève ***
3	Cal			27	<15>		Rocher Bataillard *
4	Cal			90	<7>		Vovray
5	Cal			40	<52>		Léaz *
6	Cal			60	<80>		Champfromier * ⊘15/2-15/6
7	45			35+	<40>		Nantua
8	(10)			15	<80>		Cerdon * ⊘15/2-15/6
9	(5)			25	<75>		Neuville-sur-Ain *
10	Cal	T		10	<36>		Cuiron
11	Cal	747		50	<120>		Jarbonnet *
12	Cal			20	<30>		Belleydoux
13	Cal			60	<45>		Le Becquet ⊘15/2-15/6
14	Cal			40	<40>		Trois Commères *
15	(3)			30	<70>		Chambly *
16	(15)			30	<70>		Mirebel
17	Cal			20	<15>		Pannessières
18	Cal			40	<34>		Poligny - Trou de la Lune
19	(10)	A/S		75	4		Le Saraz
20	(10)	A		250	<5>A3		Sarrazine *
21	(15)			55	<7>		Creux Billard * ⊘15/2-15/6
22	(1)			20	100		La Fauconniere *
23	30	S/A	⇐	60	13		Roches Blanches *
24	(10)	S/A		120	<50>		Aiguilles de Baulmes *
25	(10)			50	<130>		Saint Loup **

FRANCE - 35

6b, CERDON; Wobt

ALEVE

CHANT DU RASTA 7b, Creux Billard; Jingo

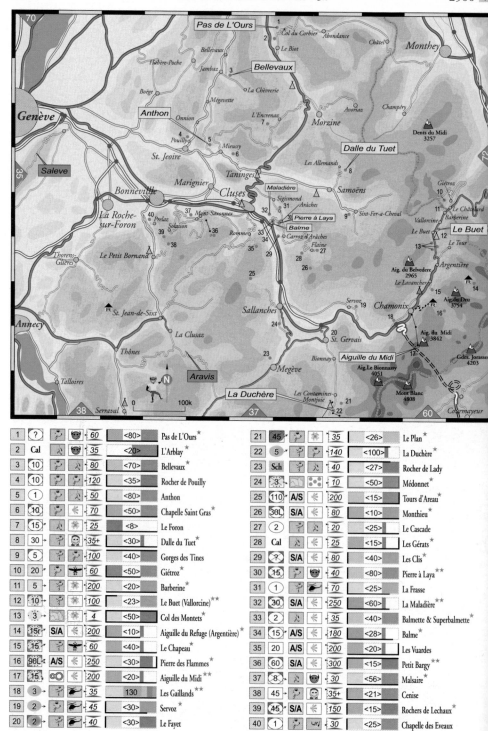

1	?			60	<80>	Pas de L'Ours*
2	Cal			35	<20>	L'Arblay*
3	10			80	<70>	Bellevaux*
4	10			120	<35>	Rocher de Pouilly
5	1			50	<80>	Anthon
6	10			70	<50>	Chapelle Saint Gras*
7	15			25	<8>	Le Foron
8	30			35+	<30>	Dalle du Tuet*
9	5			100	<40>	Gorges des Tines
10	20			60	<50>	Giétroz*
11	5			200	<20>	Barberine*
12	10			100	<23>	Le Buet (Vallorcine)**
13	3			4	<50>	Col des Montets*
14	15	S/A		200	<10>	Aiguille du Refuge (Argentière)*
15	15			60	<40>	Le Chapeau*
16	90L	A/S		250	<30>	Pierre des Flammes*
17	15			200	<20>	Aiguille du Midi**
18	3			35	130	Les Gaillands**
19	2			45	<30>	Servoz*
20	2			40	<30>	Le Fayet
21	45			35	<26>	Le Plan*
22	5			140	<100>	La Duchère*
23	Sch			40	<27>	Rocher de Lady
24	3			10	<50>	Médonnet*
25	110	A/S		200	<15>	Tours d'Areau*
26	30L	S/A		80	<10>	Monthieu*
27	2			20	<25>	Le Cascade
28	Cal			25	<15>	Les Gérats*
29	?	S/A		80	<40>	Les Clis*
30	15			40	<80>	Pierre à Laya**
31	1			70	<25>	La Frasse
32	30	S/A		250	<60>	La Maladière**
33	2			35	<40>	Balmette & Superbalmette
34	15	A/S		180	<28>	Balme*
35	20	A/S		200	<20>	Les Vuardes
36	60	S/A		300	<15>	Petit Bargy**
37	8			30	<56>	Malsaire*
38	45			35+	<21>	Cenise
39	45	S/A		150	<15>	Rochers de Lechaux*
40	1			30	<25>	Chapelle des Eveaux

For cragging, Cluses gets the better over Chamonix, an incredible area with incredible routes.
Cluses est un meilleur site que Chamonix. Un lieu incroyable avec des voies superbes.

 A lot of very impressive climbing, with fantastic exposure. Much better weather than the high mountains.
Beaucoup de voies impressionantes, très expo. Temps en général meilleur qu'en haute montagne.

Topo: T36-1 New edition 2002

Vallee de L'Arve
Eskiproc; 1997
168pp. 210mm x 150mm

⚠ 20-40.

© *Sport 2000, Cluses,* ¢-7
Vieux Campeur, Sallanches

Topo: T26-2
Crag climbs in Chamonix
F. Burnier, D. Potard; 1998
168pp. 168mm x 120mm

⚠ 10-13, 15,16,18, 20.

© *Vieux Campeur, Sallanches,*
Technicien du Sport, Chamonix

Topo: T36-3

Chamonix Cragging
Nigel Shepherd; 1995
144pp. 210mm x 150mm

⚠ 4-11,19,25,27,32-37

© *www.urbanrock.com*

Topo: T36-4
Topo guide to Mont Blanc
M. Piola; 1986
160pp. 160mm x 115mm

⚠ 16,17, + Capucin, Aig Roc, etc.

© *?????*

ES GENTIANES 4c, La Duchère

LE DRU

AIGUILLES DE GRANDS CHARMO

FLAMMES DE PIERRE - 'la vue incroyal

+, FLAMMES DE PIERRE

Most probably the best 6c-7b area in France, with the main emphasis on vertical cliffs with beautiful locations.
Probablement le meilleur endroit en France pour les 6c-7b. Bonnes falaises dans de superbes locations.

 Low crags for winter, high crags for summer, some overprotected, and some definitely under protected!
Rochers à basse altitude pour l'hiver et en haute altitude pour l'été. Equipement soit très bon ou très mauvais.

Topo: T37-1
Escalades autour du Lac Bourget
Philippe Mussatto; 1995
112pp. 210mm x 150mm

5a-7a Info

★★★★★★

8,8,10,11,12,13,14,15,16.
Aix-les-Bains ???, ¢-7

New edition-2002

Topo: T37-2
14 Falaises
Robert Durieux; 1997
80pp. 190mm x 147mm

5a-7a Info

★★★★★★ (F) ★

19-23, 26-31, 33
libraire, Annecy, ¢-7
Libraire, Thônes, ¢-7
Presse, Faverges, ¢-7

Topo: T37-3
Biclop Talabar
Robert Durieux; 1997
64pp. 190mm x 147mm

5a-7a Info

★ ★ ★★★★

32
libraire, Annecy, ¢-7
Libraire, Thônes, ¢-7
Presse, Faverges, ¢-7

Topo: T37-4
La Falaise D'Ablon
Robert Durieux; 1994
36pp. 210mm x 135mm

5a-7a Info

★ ★

34
Libraire, Thônes, ¢-7
Le Ferme-Refuge (d'Ablon),

Topo: T37-5
Massif des Aravis Escalade
Haute Savoie; 1995
138pp. 210mm x 150mm

5a-7a Info

★ ★★★★

35,37,38,40.
Libraire, Thônes, ¢-7

Topo: T37-6
Le Calcaire en Folie
Michel Piola; 1999
272pp. 210mm x 150mm

5a-7a Info

★★★★★★ (F) ★
★★

19-23, 26-31, 33
Libraire, Thônes, ¢-7
Vieux Campeur, Sallanches (Cluses)

Topo: T37-7
Roc'n Bugey
Grimpeur's; 1998
120pp. 210mm x 150mm
Tabac, Virieux le
Grand ¢-1-2 ?

5a-7a Info

★ ★★★★★★

1,2,3,4,5.

ARAV

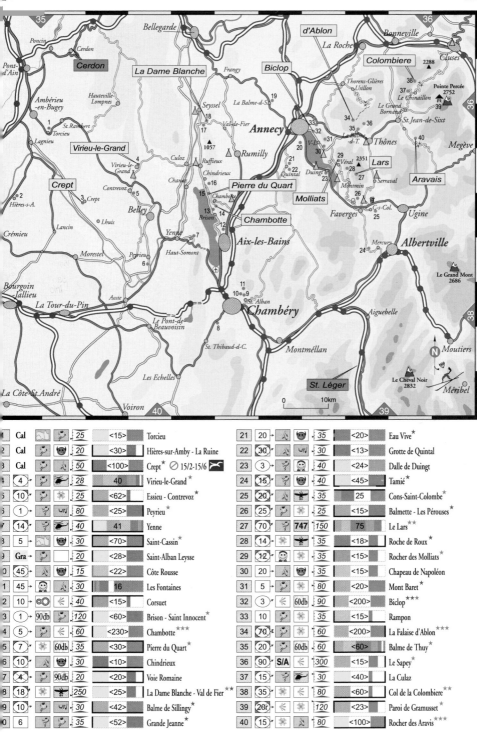
#							Name
1	Cal			25	<15>		Torcieu
2	Cal			20	<30>		Hières-sur-Amby - La Ruine
3	Cal			50	<100>	⊘ 15/2-15/6	Crept*
4	(4)			28	40		Virieu-le-Grand*
5	(10)			25	<62>		Essieu - Contrevoz*
6	(1)			80	<25>		Peyrieu*
7	(14)			40	41		Yenne
8	5			30	<70>		Saint-Cassin*
9	Gra			20	<28>		Saint-Alban Leysse
10	(45)			15	<22>		Côte Rousse
11	45			30	16		Les Fontaines
12	10			40	<15>		Corsuet
13	(1)	90db		120	<60>		Brison - Saint Innocent*
14	5			60	<230>		Chambotte***
15	(7)	60db		35	<30>		Pierre du Quart*
16	(10)			30	<10>		Chindrieux
17	(×)	90db		20	<20>		Voie Romaine
18	(18)			250	<25>		La Dame Blanche - Val de Fier**
19	(10)			30	<42>		Balme de Sillingy*
20	6			35	<52>		Grande Jeanne*
21	20			35	<20>		Eau Vive*
22	(30)			30	<13>		Grotte de Quintal
23	(3)			40	<24>		Dalle de Duingt
24	(15)			40	<45>		Tamié*
25	(20)			35	25		Cons-Saint-Colombe*
26	(25)			25	<15>		Balmette - Les Pérouses*
27	(70)		747	150	75		Le Lars**
28	(14)			35	<18>		Roche de Roux*
29	(12)			35	<15>		Rocher des Molliats*
30	20			35	<15>		Chapeau de Napoléon*
31	5			80	<20>		Mont Baret*
32	(3)	60db		90	<200>		Biclop***
33	10			35	<15>		Rampon
34	(70)			60	<200>		La Falaise d'Ablon***
35	(20)	60db		60	<60>		Balme de Thuy*
36	(90)	S/A		300	<15>		Le Sapey*
37	(15)			30	<40>		La Culaz*
38	(35)			80	<60>		Col de la Colombiere**
39	(20c)			120	<23>		Paroi de Gramusset*
40	(15)			80	<100>		Rocher des Aravis***

TOUT FEU TOUT FLAMME 5b, Yenne; Frédéric Gros

6b+ Contrevoz; Jing

XERCISE 6a+, Chambotte; Christophe Peccoud

ABLON

CHAUD QUI PEUT 6c+, Ablon; Frederic Ponsa

THÔNES

LAC ANNECY

LES FORCATS 6a, Falaise de la Colombiere; Gerard Ferlin

A very beautiful area in Summer, Super Vanoise comes up with the arm pumping, body pumping, workouts! Un endroit magnifique en été, Super Vanoise vous gonflera les muscles des bras!

 The slabs of Séloge are a bit hollow!!! But the situation is fantastic, and the entire valley is beautiful and unspoilt. Les dalles de Séloge sont un peu creuses!!! Mais le site est fantastique et la vallée magnifique.

Topo: T38-1
Topo de la Vanoise
P. Deslandes, J. Merel; 1995
136pp. 170mm x 120mm

⬛ 1-16; 20, 23, 25.

€ *Librairie- Bourg St. Maurice*, ¢-7
Presse-Librairie; Aime, ¢-pm.7
Le Caribou-Librairie; Valloire, ¢-7

Topo: T38-2
Escalade en Haute Tarentaise
Christian Emprin, Gaby Giroud; 2000
56pp. 190mm x 136mm

⬛ 16-19, 22-27.

€ *Librairie- Bourg St. Maurice*, ¢-7
O-d-Tourisme; Val d'Isere, ¢ ?
Presse-Librairie; Aime, ¢-pm.7

AIME

 BLOCS DE CERIS

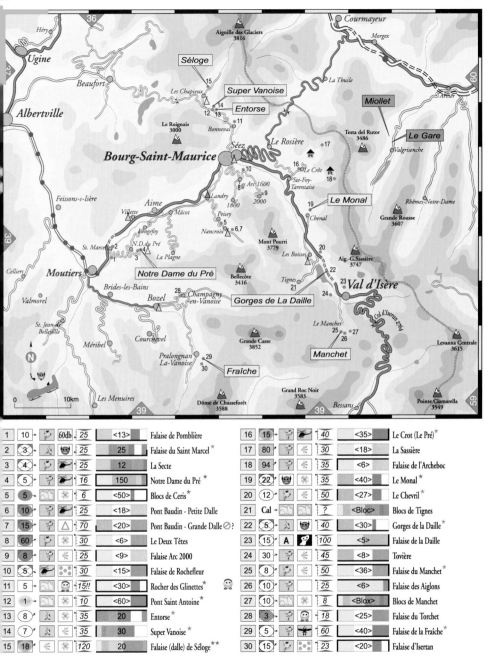

1	10			60db	25	<13>	Falaise de Pomblière
2	3			25	25		Falaise du Saint Marcel*
3	4			25	12		La Secte
4	5			16	150		Notre Dame du Pré*
5	5			6	<50>		Blocs de Ceris*
6	10			25	<18>		Pont Baudin - Petite Dalle
7	15			70	<20>		Pont Baudin - Grande Dalle ⊘?
8	60			30	<6>		Le Deux Têtes
9	8			25	<9>		Falaise Arc 2000
10	5			30	<15>		Falaise de Rochefleur
11	5			15!!	<30>		Rocher des Glinettes*
12	1			10	<60>		Pont Saint Antoine*
13	8			35	20		Entorse*
14	7			35	30		Super Vanoise*
15	18			120	20		Falaise (dalle) de Séloge**

16	15			40	<35>	Le Crot (Le Pré)*
17	80			30	<18>	La Sassière
18	94			35	<6>	Falaise de l'Archeboc
19	22			35	<40>	Le Monal*
20	12			50	<27>	Le Chevril*
21	Cal			?	<Bloc>	Blocs de Tignes
22	5			40	<30>	Gorges de la Daille*
23	15	A		100	<5>	Falaise de la Daille
24	30			45	<8>	Tovière
25	8			50	<36>	Falaise du Manchet*
26	10			25	<6>	Falaise des Aiglons
27	10			8	<Blox>	Blocs de Manchet
28	3			18	<25>	Falaise du Torchet
29	5			60	<40>	Falaise de la Fraîche*
30	15			23	<20>	Falaise d'Isertan

COMBAZ DES CHEFS 7b, Falaise du Monal; Wobbly

ECOUTE LA LUNE 6b, Falaise du Torchet; Thomas Flagel

DÉVERS TEBRE 6c, Super Vanoise; Mathilde Maurel

There are stiff competition routes at Croe and Amoureux, but these routes are more technical than thuggy.
Il y a des voies très techniques, raides et difficiles à Croe et Amoureux.

 A trip up the monolithe will certainly get you wobbling, very dodgy conglomerate, a lot of suspect rock in the area.
Un voyage en haut du monolithe vous fera trembler. Conglomérat très douteux.

Topo: T39-1
Escalades en Maurienne
Patrick Col; 1999
160pp. 170mm x 120mm

T	I	?	5a-7a Info		

★★★★★★★★★

⚠ 1-27.

€ **Bureau des Guides-Aussois,**
Le Caribou-Librairie; Valloire- ✆-7

AUSSOIS

ROCHER SAINT PIERRE, VALLOIRE

ROCHER DES AMOUREUX-NORD

FALAISE (CHAOS) DU CRO

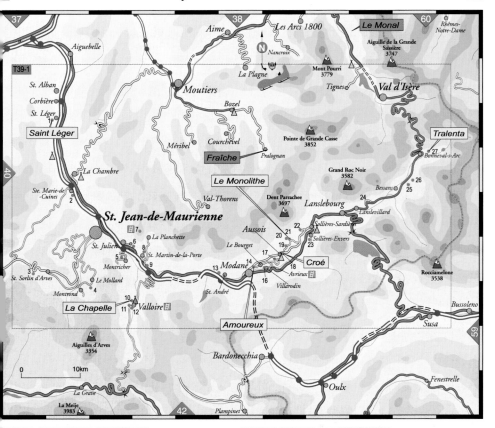

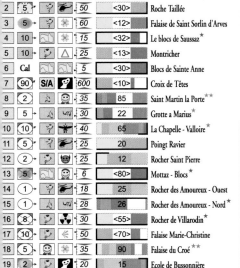

#						Name
1	5		60	<75>		Falaise de Saint Léger*
2	5		50	<30>		Roche Taillée
3	5		60	<12>		Falaise de Saint Sorlin d'Arves
4	10		15	<32>		Le blocs de Saussaz*
5	10		25	<13>		Montricher
6	Cal		5	<30>		Blocs de Sainte Anne
7	90	S/A	600	<10>		Croix de Têtes
8	2		35	85		Saint Martin la Porte**
9	5		30	22		Grotte a Marius*
10	10		40	65		La Chapelle - Valloire*
11	5		25	20		Poingt Ravier
12	2		25	12		Rocher Saint Pierre
13	5		6	<80>		Mottaz - Blocs*
14	1		18	25		Rocher des Amoureux - Ouest
15	1		28	26		Rocher des Amoureux - Nord*
16	8		30	<55>		Rocher de Villarodin*
17	10		50	<70>		Falaise Marie-Christine
18	5		35	90		Falaise du Croé**
19	2		20	15		Ecole de Bussonnière
20	15		70	<20>		Roche Qui Pisse
21	2		90	3		Le Monolithe
22	10		35	7		Falaise du Mont
23	1		12	30		Rocher Saint Claude*
24	10		12	15		Blocs de la Madeleine
25	5	A/S	70	<7>		Balme Noire
26	5		25	<20>		Drailles Blanches
27	5		5	<30>		Blocs de Tralenta*

BLOCS DE LA MADELEINE

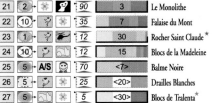

St. Pancrasse has a view, technicality, silly angle, polished holds, bolt on holds - it has simply everything!
St Pancrasse offre de belles vues, la technique, des prises patinées, en bref de tout!

 If you want a really good wobble, just look at Presles. Then climb for the wobble of your life!
Si vous voulez trembler, allez à Presles.

Topo: T40-1
Escalades autour de Grenoble
D. Duhaut, C. Vigier; 1998
184pp. 210mm x 150mm

T I ? 5a-7a Info

★ ★★★ ★★★ (F) ★★

△ 1-23. + (37.2) Hières

€ *Librairie-Grenoble*, ¢-7
Sport;Pont-en-Royans, ¢-7

Topo: T40-2
Grimper en Isère
D. Duhaut; 1998
102pp. 210mm x 150mm

T I ? 5a-7a Info

★ ★★★★ (F) ★★

△ 24-36

€ *Librairie-Grenoble*, ¢-7
Sport;Pont-en-Royans, ¢-7

Topo: T40-3
Escalades à Presles
D. Duhaut; 1998
192pp. 210mm x 150mm

T I ? 5a-7a Info

★ ★★ ★ (F)(GB) ★★

△ 34 + 32,33,35

€ *Librairie-Grenoble*, ¢-7
Sport;Pont-en-Royans, ¢-7

Saint-Pierre-de-Chartreuse
Saint-Egrève

Saint-Hilaire (St.-Pancrasse)
6b+, Gorges du Crosse

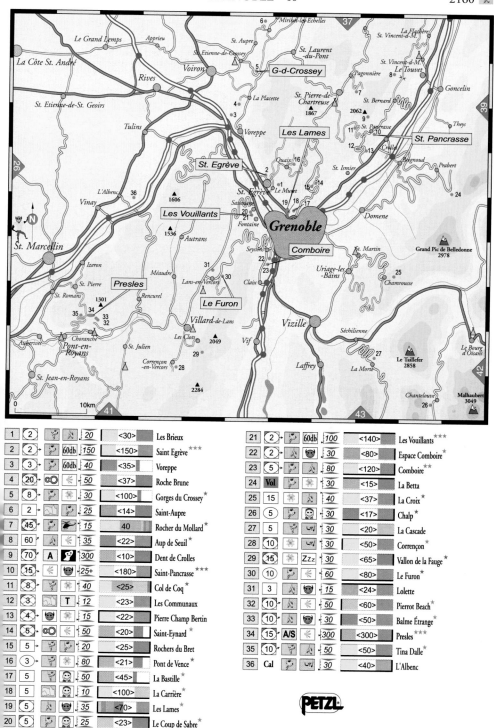

1	2			20	<30>		Les Brieux
2	2		60db	150	<150>		Saint Egrève ***
3	3		60db	40	<35>		Voreppe
4	20	∞		50	<37>		Roche Brune
5	8			30	<100>		Gorges du Crossey *
6	2			25	<14>		Saint-Aupre
7	45			15	40		Rocher du Mollard *
8	60			35	<22>		Aup de Seuil *
9	70	A		300	<10>		Dent de Crolles
10	15			25+	<180>		Saint-Pancrasse ***
11	8			40	<25>		Col de Coq *
12	3	T		12	<23>		Les Communaux
13	4			15	<22>		Pierre Champ Bertin
14	5	∞		50	<20>		Saint-Eynard *
15	5			20	<25>		Rochers du Bret
16	3			80	<21>		Pont de Vence *
17	5			50	<45>		La Bastille *
18	5			10	<100>		La Carrière *
19	5			35	<70>		Les Lames *
20	5			25	<23>		Le Coup de Sabre *

21	2		60db	100	<140>		Les Vouillants ***
22	2			30	<80>		Espace Comboire *
23	5			80	<120>		Comboire **
24	Vol			30	<15>		La Betta
25	15			40	<37>		La Croix *
26	5			30	<17>		Chalp *
27	5			30	<20>		La Cascade *
28	10			30	<50>		Corrençon *
29	15	Zzz		30	<65>		Vallon de la Fauge *
30	10			60	<80>		Le Furon *
31	3			15	<24>		Lolette
32	10			50	<60>		Pierrot Beach *
33	10			30	<50>		Balme Étrange *
34	15	A/S		300	<300>		Presles ***
35	10			50	<50>		Tina Dalle *
36	Cal			30	<40>		L'Albenc

PETZL

INTERLUDE 6a, La Plage, Saint-Pancrasse; Lu divine larThoma

DENT DE CROLLES

MEGLAOMANIE 7b+, St.-Pancrasse; Jingo

The valley of Omblèze is your trusted hideout, shady rock for shady characters, or a visit to Le Moulin le Pipe.

 The valley of Saou is a beautiful paradise, a Jazz café in town, and the comfortable crag of Graville.
La vallée de Saou est un vrai paradis, un café jazz en ville et le site sympa de Graville.

Topo: T41-1
Rochefort-Samson
CAF; 1997
52pp. 210mm x 150mm

5a-7a Info

△ 2,3,4,5.

€ Bar-Tabac-Barbières,

Topo: T41-2
Omblèze
F. Marion, P. Saury; 1997
136pp. 210mm x 150mm

Humour

5a-7a Info

△ 8,9.

€ Moulin de la Pipe-Omblèze,
O-d-Tourisme, Crest ?, ¢-7

Topo: T41-3
Saou
Jean-Marc-Belle; 1997
144pp. 210mm x 150mm

5a-7a Info

△ 10-15

€ Office-Tourisme, Saou, ¢-??????

Topo: T41-4
Diois - Escalade & Canyons
Véronique, G. Woodhouse, V. Gruart;
1996 132 pp. 210mm x 150mm

5a-7a Info

△ 21,23-29.

€ Librairie - Die, ¢-7
Office-Toursime-Die, ¢-7

Les Ecoles D'Escalade
Mini Topo 20pp

△ 6,7,++.   100

€ ?? St Jean-en Royans?, ¢-7

Gallo Romain Camping (1/5-30/9)
1km SE - Barbières,
26300 Barbières

FALAISE D'ANS

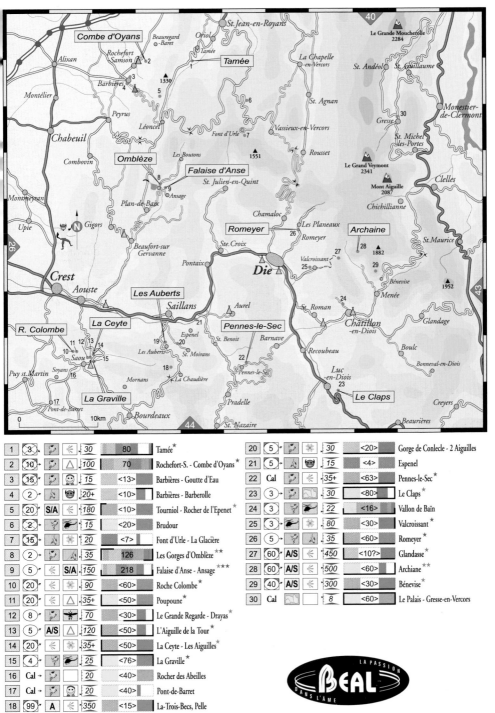

#							Name
1	(3)			30	80		Tamée*
2	(10)			100	70		Rochefort-S. - Combe d'Oyans*
3	(15)			15	<13>		Barbières - Goutte d'Eau
4	(2)			20+	<10>		Barbières - Barberolle
5	(20)	S/A		180	<10>		Tourniol - Rocher de l'Epenet*
6	(2)			15	<20>		Brudour
7	(15)			20	<7>		Font d'Urle - La Glacière
8	(2)			35	126		Les Gorges d'Ombleze**
9	(5)		S/A	150	218		Falaise d'Anse - Ansage***
10	(20)			90	<60>		Roche Colombe*
11	(20)			35+	<50>		Poupoune*
12	(8)			70	<30>		Le Grande Regarde - Drayas*
13	(5)	A/S		120	<50>		L'Aiguille de la Tour*
14	(20)			35+	<50>		La Ceyte - Les Aiguilles*
15	(4)			25	<76>		La Graville*
16	Cal →			20	<40>		Rocher des Abeilles
17	Cal →			20	<40>		Pont-de-Barret
18	(99)	A		350	<15>		La-Trois-Becs, Pelle
19	(45)			30	40		Les Auberts*
20	(5)			30	<20>		Gorge de Conlecle - 2 Aiguilles
21	(5)			15	<4>		Espenel
22	Cal			35+	<63>		Pennes-le-Sec*
23	(3)			30	<80>		Le Claps*
24	(3)			22	<16>		Vallon de Baïn
25	(3)			80	<30>		Valcroissant*
26	(5)			35	<60>		Romeyer*
27	(60)	A/S		450	<10?>		Glandasse*
28	(60)	A/S		500	<60>		Archiane**
29	(40)	A/S		300	<30>		Bénevise*
30	Cal			8	<60>		Le Palais - Gresse-en-Vercors

BEAL — LA PASSION DANS L'ÂME

ROCHE COLOMBE

"I hear Jazz, let's get outta here and have lunch"

SAOU - *"bebop & Latin"*

FONT D'URLE - LA GLACIÈR

SAOU

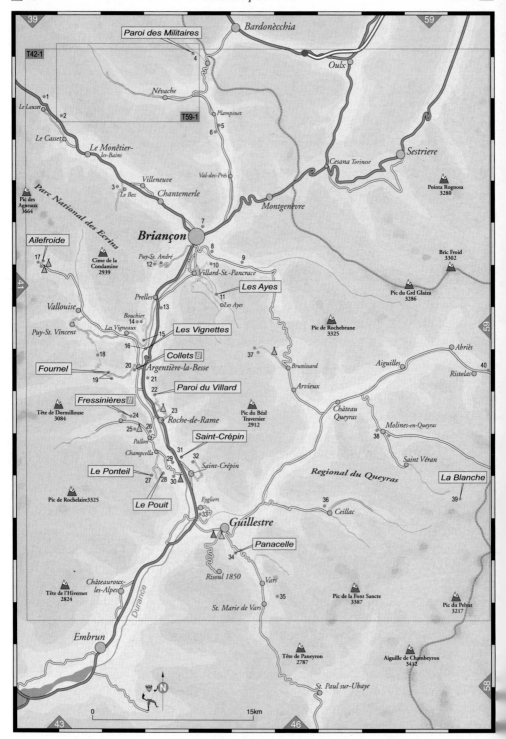

The altitude of the valley makes power climbing here, a soft summer recreation, with beer intervals.

 300 days of sunshine a year a wobbly paradise. This valley stays a lot drier than the majority of the Ecrins.
300 jours de soleil dans l'année, un paradis. Cette vallée reste plus au sec que la majorité des Ecrins.

Topo: T42-1
Grimper dans le Haut Val Durance
Y,M,J-J Roland; 2002
240pp. 220mm x 135mm

5a-7a Info

★★ ★ ★★

1 - 40 ++++

© **Alpi'mat @ Briançon**,
Camping Le Verger @ Roche - Rame,
Maison de la Presse @ Guillestre

Camping Les Verger (1/1-31/12)
Roche de Rame, Briançon, 05310

Camping Municipal de l'Ille (1/6-30/9)
Saint Crépin 05600

Camping Ailefroide (15/6-15/9)
Camping Municipal d'Ailefroide, Briançon 05340

Camping Le Saint James (1/1-31/12)
Guillestre 05600

Camping Le Planet (15/6-15/9)
Brunissard, Arvieux 05350

L'ARGENTIERRE LA BESSE - VIA FERRATA;
Jean Mangharam

No.	Code		Value	Bar	Name
01	(15)	S/A	35+	24	Chemin du Roy
02	(5)	90db	15	56	Rocher Maubert
03	Cal	S/A	120	25	Rocher du Bez
04	(5)		35+	37	Paroi des Militaires*
05	(10)		20	33	Plampinet-Rocher Qui Repond
06	(15)		30	35	Le Sapet
07	Cal		20	30	Les Salettes
08	Cal		?	63	Les Randouillet*
09	(5)		20	34	Terre Rouge*
10	(45)		30	30	Rocher Gafouille*
11	(3)		50	25+	Les Ayes*
12	(10)		20	35	Puy Saint André
13	(5)		20	27 / 6	Rocher Baron*
14	(25)		35	21	Le Bouchier*
15	(10)		20	44	Les Traverses*
16	(15)		25	59	Les Vignettes**
17	(5)		100	200	Ailefroide**
18	(15)		30	46	Tournoux*
19	(15)		35+	70	Fournel**
20	(5)		25	42	Horloge - Les Collets*
21	(5)	90db	30	9	l'Oratoire
22	(15)		30	29	Paroi du Villard*
23	(2)		20	10	Roche-de-Rame*
24	(15)		35+	152	Fressinières**
25	(25)		30	7	Bec de l'Ase*
26	(3)		20	11	Falaise du Barage
27	(15)		150	30	Le Ponteil**
28	(3)		60	76	Le Pouit**
29	(15)		35	27	Barrachin*
30	(10)		15	41	Chanteloube*
31	(10)		25	84	Saint-Crépin**
32	(10)		60	15	Le Villard - Les Guions*
33	(5)		35	100	Mont Daupin**
34	(2)		30	12 / 30	Panacelle*
35	Cal		20	17	Col de la Coulette
36	Cal		10	11	La Viste, Celliac
37	(10)		30	36	Clapeyto*
38	Cal		6	<B>	La Rua, Pierre Grosse
39	(90)		35	21	La Blanche*
40	Cal		25	<50>	La Roche Écroulée*

BTP 6b+, Montdauphin-Fort; Olivier Querbe

FRESSINIÈRES

DECENDEZ ON VOUS DEMANDE 6b; St. Crepin; Wizzard

BALIVERNE 6b, St. Crépin; Adrian Pais

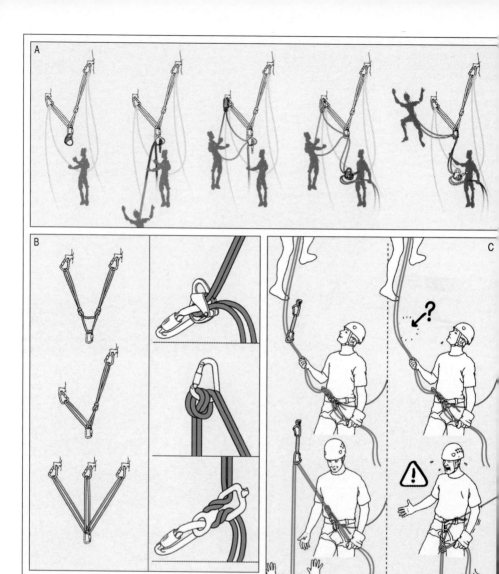

Multi-pitch climbing

The changeover manoeuvres at the belay must be simple and precise if you want to be quick and efficient (A).
The belayer is on a belay in the middle of the wall. The leader's fall could exceed factor 1. It is fundamental to know
that the belayer, depending on the device he or she is using, could have difficulty in stopping the fall: the force could
exceed 3 kN, the rope would slip in the hand, risking not only a burn but the possibility of letting go.
It could even be worse: I leave the belay without having placed a runner and then, 3 metres above the belay, I slip and
fall (C). The friction of the rope burns the belayer's hands and he doesn't manage to stop the fall before the ledge
which is several metres lower down...

Information is non-exhaustive. Refer to the other pages as well as to the
user instructions and technical manuals. Technical training is essential.

182

Cëuse is possibly the best crag in the world, with probably the worst approach in the world!
Cëuse est probablement le meilleur site du monde mais avec la pire approche au monde!

 Orpièrre is one of the most ideal climbing areas for easy climbs, which are all overgraded.
Orpièrre est l'un des meilleurs sites pour les voies faciles, qui sont dessous-cotées.

Topo: T43-1
Escalades a la Berarde
Jean-Michel Cambon; 1999
64pp. 210mm x 150mm

5a-7a Info

△ 1 - 4.

€ *L'Epicerie, La Berarde*
Grenoble ???

Topo: T43-2
Céüse, Champsaur, Dévoluy, V-von
M. Balcet et amis; 1999 ??
132pp. 210mm x 150mm

5a-7a Info

△ 5, 6, 20 - 24.

€ *Camping Les Guérins-Sigoyer*
Le Perroquet Vert, La Palud (Verdon)

△ *Camping Les Guérins (1/1-31/12)*
Sigoyer (1km NW)

SISTERO

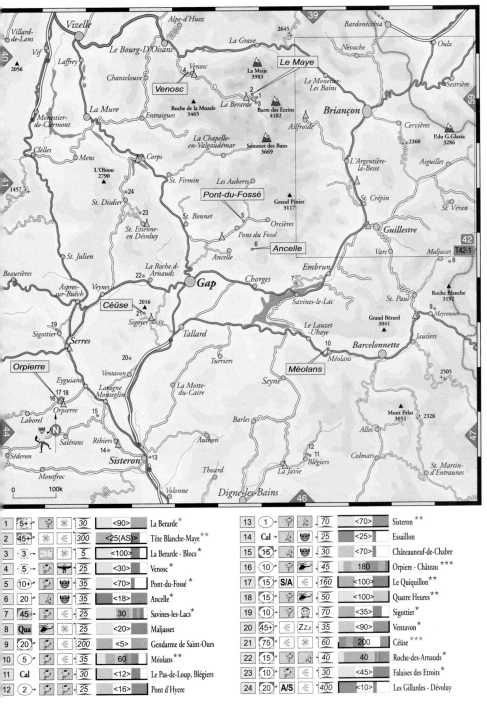

1	5+			30	<90>	La Berarde[*]
2	45+			300	<25(AS)>	Tête Blanche-Maye[**]
3	3			5	<100>	La Berarde - Blocs[*]
4	5			25	<30>	Venosc[*]
5	10+			35	<70>	Pont-du-Fossé[*]
6	20			35	<18>	Ancelle[*]
7	45			25	30	Savines-les-Lacs[*]
8	Qua			25	<20>	Maljasset
9	20			200	<5>	Gendarme de Saint-Ours
10	5			35	60	Méolans[**]
11	Cal			30	<12>	Le Pas-de-Loup, Blégiers
12	2			25	<16>	Pont d'Hyere
13	1			70	<70>	Sisteron[**]
14	Cal			25	<25>	Essaillon
15	15			30	<70>	Châteauneuf-de-Chabre
16	10			45	180	Orpiere - Château[***]
17	15	S/A		160	<100>	Le Quiquillon[**]
18	15			50	<100>	Quatre Heures[**]
19	10			70	<35>	Sigottier[*]
20	45+		Zzz	35	<90>	Ventavon[*]
21	75			60	200	Céüse[***]
22	15			40	40	Roche-des-Arnauds[*]
23	10			30	<45>	Falaises des Etroits[*]
24	20	A/S		400	<10>	Les Gillardes - Dévoluy

MONZOB SUR MER 7b, Céüse; Tom Lipp

CÉÜS

MIRAGE 7c+, Céüse;

Buoux, in case you don't know, is the Climbing mecca for aspirant Jingo's;
Buoux, si vous ne le savez pas déjà est la Mecque de la grimpe pour les aspirants Jingo.

 It is very hard to find anything wrong with Buis-les-Baroniees - yes, no night life! (especially camping!!)
Il est très difficile de reprocher quelque chose au site de Buis-les-Baronies - seulement que les soirées sont calmes

---

Topo: T44-1
Buis-Les-Baronnies
V.Isley; 1992
70pp. 210mm x 150mm

5a-7a
Info

★ ★★★★ ★★

⚠ 7,8,10.

€ *Off-Tourisme, Buis-L-B, ¢-7*

Topo: T44-2
Dentelles de Montmirail
O. Gaude, R. Leroy; 1998-9
160pp. 210mm x 150mm

5a-7a
Info

★★★★ ★ ★★ ★

⚠ 14-18.

€ *Office-Tourisme; Gigondas, ¢-7*
Office-Tourisme; Beaume-de-V, ¢-7

Topo: T44-3
Orgon
Pierre Duret; 1995
152pp. 210mm x 150mm

5a-7a
Info

★★ ★ ★★ ★

⚠ 29,30.

€ *Tabac-Presse, Orgon, ¢-7*

Topo: T44-4
Gigondas Onsight - à Vue (2004)
David Atchison-Jones
338pp. 210mm x 150mm

5a-7a
Info

★★★★★★★★ ★★

⚠ 1-24.

€ **www.urbanrock.com**

In production
due out end - 2004

⛺ *Camping Les Ephélides (?/4-31/10)*
1km Sud, Buis les Baronnies

1	10		❄	30	<30>		Pelleret*
2	15			50	<30>		Mévouillon - Est*
3	18			35	<20>		Mévouillon - Ouest*
4	10		❄	35+	37		Rocher de L'Aiguier*
5	10			35	<76>		Baume Rousse**
6	2			35	<41>		Passo d'Hannibal*
7	10			40	50		Ubrieux**
8	25		❄	90	90		Rocher Saint-Julien**
9	5		❄	30	15		Beauvoisin*
10	3		△	60	10		Plaisians*
11	15		747	35	<40>		Saint-Léger - Gorges Nord**
12	10		747	35	<40>		Saint-Léger - Gorges Sud*
13	10			35	<65>		Trois Rivières**
14	10			25	<44>		Chaîne du Grand Travers*
15	18		747	90	<70>		Chaîne du Gigondas**
16	5			35+	<30>		Rocher Saint-Christophe*
17	5			35+	<20+>		Cascade de Lafare*
18	20	S/A		130	<180>		Chaîne du Clapis***
19	15			35	80		Combe Obscure*
20	10			35	<25>		Malaval
21	15		❄	35	<20>		Archéo
22	15		❄	40	<30>		La Belvédère* - Gorges de la Nesq
23	10			25	<50>		Rocher Saint-Pierre*
24	Cal			25	<60>		Quinsan - Venasque
25	Cal			20	<50>		Pont Julien
26	10			90	<450>		Buoux***
27	10			30	<30>		Oppède-le-Vieux
28	5			40	<200>		Cavaillon**
29	2			35	<100>		Orgon Canal**
30	3			70	<300>		Orgon***
31	15		❄	50	<150>		Fontvielle**
32	Cal			35	<120>		Valampe
33	Cal			40	<40>		Mont Gaussier
34	Cal			25	<30>		Maussanne
35	10			35	<250>		Mouriès***
36	5			30	<100>		Aurielle
37	Cal			40	<90>		Mont Menu
38	Cal			18	<50>		Saint Anne-de-Goiron
39	Cal			20	<60>		Château-Virant

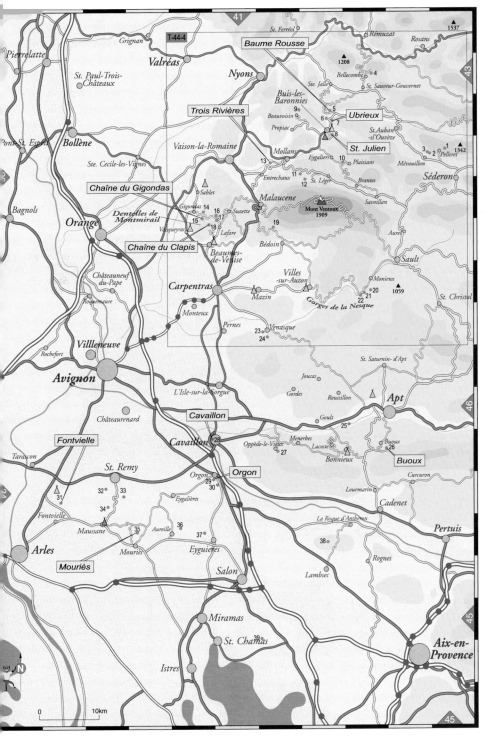

L A RAMPE 6a+; St. Julien; Mike Smi

serez-vous aussi dynamique que nos cordes ?

control

perfection

emotion

zen

spirit

energy

solution

power

summit

nature

harmony

movement

serenity

safety

UNIVERSAL LANGUAGE
BY
THE DYNAMIC COMPANY

Pour gratuitement le catalogue Beal, demandez à:
Beal - BP 235 - 38201 Vienne Cedex France

7c+, Saint-Léger; Michal Gouze

CHAÎNE DU GIGONDA

'OUATE 8a, Buoux; Jean-Baptiste Tribout

Châteauvert is most probably the best known crag in the whole world! It's good, but it isn't the best here.

Chateauvert est probablement le site le mieux connu au monde! Bon site mais pas le meilleur en ce lieu.

 The Calanqes are a range of arid Limestone hills by the azur blue sea, perfect. Car break-in's are guarranteed!

Les calanques sont des collines de calcaire très arides près de la mer bleue azur. Effractions de voitures garanties.

Calanques
??; 1997
160pp
Mini Topo

🧗 400

⛰ 6 - 12.

€ Marseille??

Châteauvert
??; 1998
150??pp
Mini Topo

🧗 200

⛰ 25

€ Châteauvert

Topo: T45-2
Escalades autour de Toulon
Garnier, Elichabe, Delpy, Lantier 1997
270pp. 210mm x 150mm

5a-7a
Info

★ ★★★★★★ ★

⛰ 15 - 24

€ **Gruarin Sport, 4 Pl- Louis Blanc Toulon**, ¢-7 Librairie - Toulon, ¢-7
Perroquet Vert, La Palud, Verdon

CALLELONGUE

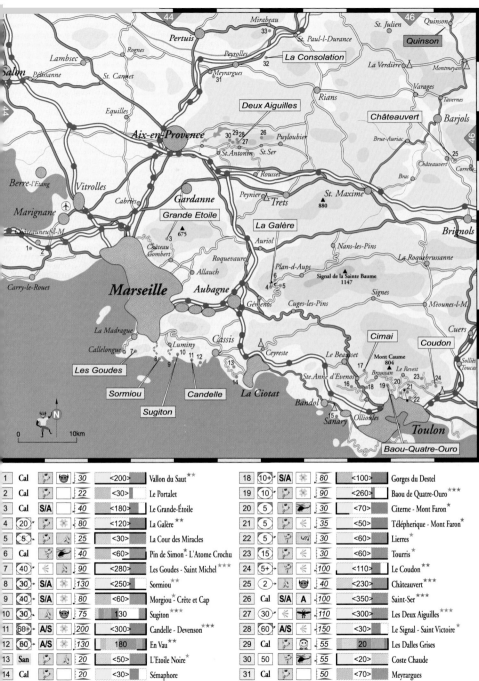

#						Name
1	Cal			30	<200>	Vallon du Saut **
2	Cal			22	<30>	Le Portalet
3	Cal	S/A		40	<180>	Le Grande-Étoile
4	20			80	<120>	La Galère **
5	5			25	<30>	La Cour des Miracles
6	Cal			40	<60>	Pin de Simon * L'Atome Crochu
7	40			90	<280>	Les Goudes - Saint Michel ***
8	30	S/A		130	<250>	Sormiou *
9	40	S/A		80	<60>	Morgiou - Crête et Cap
10	30			75	130	Sugiton ***
11	60+	A/S		200	<300>	Candelle - Devenson ***
12	60	A/S		130	180	En Vau **
13	San			20	<50>	L'Etoile Noire *
14	Cal			20	<30>	Sémaphore
15	15			30	36	Cride - Sanary
16	2			35	<41>	Gros Cerveau
17	10			80	230	Cimai ***
18	10+	S/A		80	<100>	Gorges du Destel
19	10			90	<260>	Baou de Quatre-Ouro ***
20	5			30	<70>	Citerne - Mont Faron *
21	5			35	<50>	Télépherique - Mont Faron *
22	5			30	<60>	Lierres *
23	15			30	<60>	Tourris *
24	5+			100	<110>	Le Coudon **
25	2			40	<230>	Châteauvert ***
26	Cal	S/A	A	100	<350>	Saint-Ser ***
27	30			110	<300>	Les Deux Aiguilles ***
28	60	A/S		150	<30>	Le Signal - Saint Victoire *
29	Cal			55	20	Les Dalles Grises
30	50			55	<20>	Coste Chaude
31	Cal			50	<70>	Meyrargues
32	Cal			25	<130>	Rochers de la Consolation
33	Cal			30	<30>	Pont Mirabeau

LES AUTRES ETOILES 8b, Les Goudes; Jean-Marc Trousie

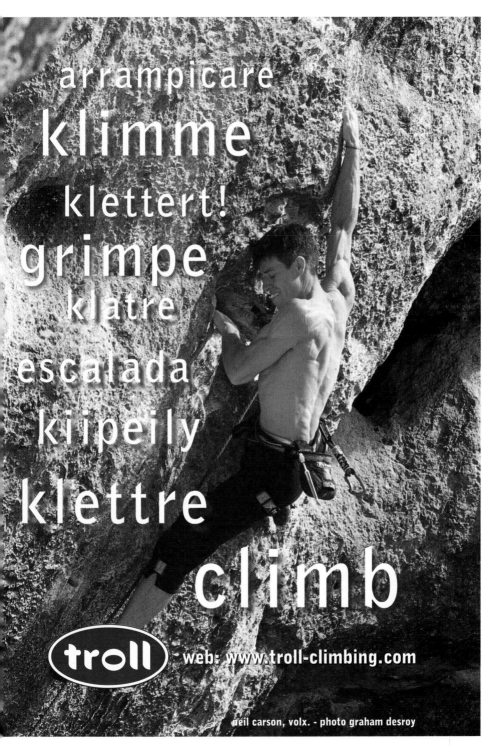

arrampicare
klimme
klettert!
grimpe
klatre
escalada
kiipeily
klettre
climb

LES ETOILES MEURENT AUSSI 7b, Les Goudes-Grotte; Matt Saunders

EN VAU

LES GOUDES

If you miss out on climbing in the Verdon Gorge, then what on earth are you playing at - tut, tut, bad show. Si vous oubliez de grimper dans les Gorges du Verdon, alors à quoi jouez-vous?

 The South side of the Verdon has a lot newer and better protected routes, how much do you want to be scared, eh!! La partie sud du Verdon a beaucoup de nouvelles et de bonnes voies, soyez prêt à avoir peur, eh!!

Topo: T46-1
Grimper au Verdon
B.Gordon, D.Taupin, S.Hermant; 1997
352pp. 210mm x 150mm

⊤ Ⅰ ? 5a-7a Info 📷

🌲 ★★ ★ ★★ ★★★

⚠ 7 - 13, +++ Adventure

€ *Le Perroquet Vert, La Palud, Verdon*
Tabac-Presse, La Palud, ¢-pm7

Topo: T46-2
Aiguines
Philippe Bugada; 1997
178pp. 210mm x 150mm

⊤ Ⅰ ? 5a-7a Info 📷

🌲 ★★ ★ ★★★ ★★

⚠ 14 - 18

€ *Aiguines.*
Le Perroquet Vert, La Palud

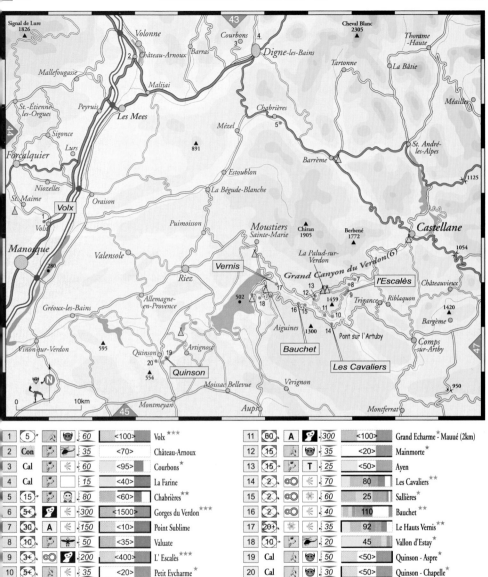

1	(5)			60	<100>		Volx ***
2	Con			35	<70>		Château-Arnoux
3	Cal			60	<95>		Courbons *
4	Cal			15	<40>		La Farine
5	(15)			80	<60>		Chabrières **
6	(5+)			300	<1500>		Gorges du Verdon ***
7	(30)	A		150	<10>		Point Sublime
8	(10)			50	<35>		Valuate
9	(3+)	oO		200	<400>		L'Escalès ***
10	(5+)			35	<20>		Petit Eycharme *

11	(80)	A		300	<100>		Grand Echarme - Mauué (2km)
12	(15)			35	<20>		Mainmorte *
13	(15)		T	25	<50>		Ayen
14	(2)	oO		70	80		Les Cavaliers **
15	(2)	oO		60	25		Sallières *
16	(2)	oO		40	110		Bauchet **
17	(20+)			35	92		Le Hauts Vernis **
18	(10)			20	45		Vallon d'Estay *
19	Cal			50	<50>		Quinson - Aspre *
20	Cal			30	<50>		Quinson - Chapelle *

LES GORGES DU VERDON

TICKET DANGER 6b+, Falasie de l'Escalès; Simona Soldati

Falasie de l'Escalès

WIDE IS LOVE 6a, Falasie de l'Escalès; Wobbly

A lot of change here, slip away to Gorges de Loup and Jurassic Park, and be prepared for Monsters!!
Allez aux Gorges du Loup et Jurassic Parc et préparez-vous pour des voies monstreuses!!

 The quality of the routes here is very high, a lot of traffic on the coast, but inland - even too quiet. Zzzzzz
La qualité des voies est incroyable, beaucoup de circulation sur la côte mais dans les terres c'est très calme.

Topo: T47-1
Alpes-Maritimes
Jean Claude Raibaud; 1996-7 ???
252pp. 210mm x 143mm

T	I	?	5a-7a Info

△ 1 - 7, 9 - 36.
€ *Presse, St. Jeannet, ¢-pm. 7*
Alticoop, Nice. ¢-7

6b, Gréolières; Matteo Gambaro

AIGLUN

1	(5)	A/S	20+	<13+12(A)>	Saint Etienne de Tinée
2	(15)	S/A	50	<80>	Col de la Cayolle
3	(15)		30	<15>	Saint-Martin d'Entraunes*
4	(20)		20	<20>	Valberg
5	(10+)		40	<30+>	Roubion*
6	10		45	<10>	Saint-Martin Vesubie*
7	(15)		35	<40>	Roquebillière*
8	5		25	<80>	Annot*
9	(10)	S/A	45	<7>	Col Saint Raphael
10	(20)	S/A	300	<20+>	Aiglun**
11	20+		60	<16>	Col du Buis*
12	(10)		35	<45>	Saint Auban*
13	(5+)		40	<40>	Seranon*
14	(10)		35	<60>	Castellaras
15	(10)	A/S	80	<5>	Les Baumons*
16	(15)		25	<70>	Gréolières**
17	5		35	<25>	Saint Pons
18	(10)		20	<46>	Le Broc*
19	5		20	<30>	Châteauneuf-de-Contes*
20	(20)	S/A	80	<7>	Peillon
21	(15)		60	<160>	Turbie-Grand Paroi***
22	(15)		40	<300>	La Loubière***
23	5		12	<40>	La Mala*
24	(3)		4	<60>	Coco Beach*
25	2		10	<60>	Gairut*
26	(25)		35	<210>	Saint-Jeannet - Ressaut**
27	(20)		35	150	Saint-Jeannet - Source**
28	(10)		20	85	La Colle-sur-Loup*
29	(8)		35	15	Pulpice Surplomb*
30	(15)		25	<40>	Courmes
31	(5)		35	<15>	Balcons, Gorges du Loup*
32	(20)	S/A	100	<10>	L'Hermitage*
33	(20)		50	20	Jurassic Park*
34	5		25	<110>	Gourdon**
35	5		20	<20>	Caussois
36	1		10	<80>	Cabris*
37	5	S/A	80	<150>	Gorges du Blavet*
38	San		6	<200>	Roquebrunne-sur-Argens
39	45		35	<60>	Roussiveau
40	Sch	S/A	30	<45>	Cap du Dramont

LE PILIER DE LA BRECHE 6b, Saint Jeannet; Corrine

DIEDRE LA REPUBLIQUE 5+, Loubière; Laurence Ricco

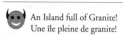 An Island full of Granite!
Une île pleine de granite!

 Even more Granite!!!

Topo: T48-1
Arrampicate Sportive in Corsica
Maurizio Oviglia - 2001
112pp. 210mm x 150mm

5a-7a Info

⚠ 1 - 19

www.urbanrock.com

SLURP

Topo: T48-2
Guide d'escalade en Corse
J-Paul Quilici, B. Vaucher; 2000
368pp. 200mm x 137mm

5a-7a Info

⚠ 17

www.urbanrock.com

Carte Nécessaire !!

#							Name
1	Gra		A/S	40		<?>	Ile-Rousse
2	Cal			25		<15>	Saint-Florent
3	5			25		<30>	Pietralba*
4	Cal			25		<15>	Francardo
5	Cal			50		<60>	Caporalinu
6	Gra	A/S	△	40		<75>	Vallée de la Restonica
7	Gra	A/S		200		<?>	Gorge de la Lonca
8	Gra	A/S		200		<?>	Capu d'Ortu
9		S/A		80		<?>	Ponte Vecchio
10	Gra	A/S		200		<5>	Christe Elison

#							Name
11	Gra			25		<50>	Bocognano - Richiusa Gorges
12	Gra	A/S		60		<35>	Monte Gozzi
13	Gra			15		<12>	La Reta
14	Gra			20		<20>	Terre Sancrée
15	10			40		41	Zicavo - Monte Rossu*
16	Gra			50		<6 ?>	Chisa
17	45+	A		300		<300>	Bavella***
18	15			40		48	Sari - Monte Santu*
19	5			60		46	Conca*

AIGLUN (47)

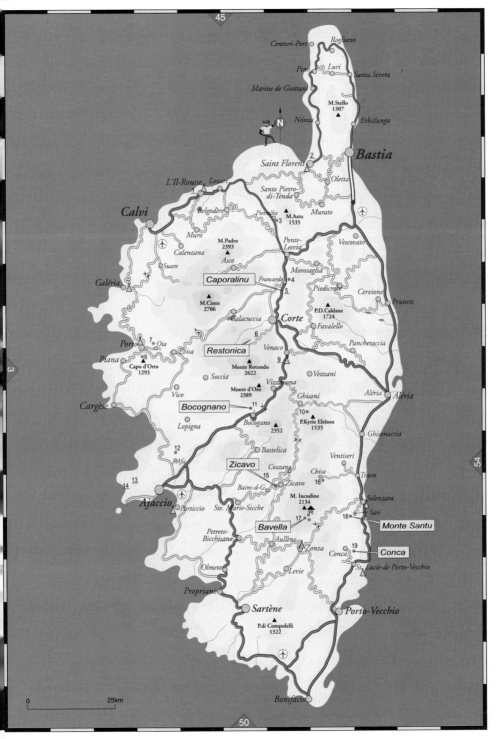

BABYMARTI 7a, Miollet Alta, Aosta(60); Gabriele Ricagno

48: Corse
49: Malta
50: Sardegna
51: Sicilia
52: Calabria
53: Napoli
54: Roma
55: L'Aquila
56: Firenze
57: Lucca

58: Cúneo
59: Torino - Susa
60: Aosta
61: Maggiore - Lecco
62: Sondrio - Mello
63: Bréscia
64: Trento - Arco
65: Ortisei - Sella
66: Corina d'Ampezzo
67: Udine

68: Trieste
69: Greece
70: Neuchâtel
71: Basel
72: Montreaux - Sion
73: Luzern
74: Chur - Rätikon
75: Innsbruck
76: Salzburg
77: Villach - Klagenfurt

Great for the strong climber, lots of afternoon shade and two main centres. More scope for development also.

 Not so great for the lower grade climber, but then again, what a great place for a sunny holiday.

Topo: T50-1
Pietra di Luna
Maurizio Oviglia; 1995
202pp. 210mm x 150mm

T | I | ? | 5a-7a Info | 📷
★★★ ★ ★ (I)(D) ★★

⛰ 1-4, 6-8, 10, 12-39

€ *Cagliari ?, ¢-7*
www.urbanrock.com

Topo: T50-2
Gennargentu Ultimp paradiso
Maurizio Oviglia; 2001
202pp. 210mm x 150mm

T | I | ? | 5a-7a Info | 📷
★ ★★ ★ ★ (I)(GB) ★★

⛰ 4-17

€ *Cagliari ?, ¢-7*
www.urbanrock.com

⛺ *Camping Cala Gonne (1/4-15/10)*
Via Collodo 1, Cala Gonne, Dorgali.

⛺ *Camping Sennisceddu (1/1-31/12)*
Pau, Sardegna

⛺ *Camping Orri (1/6-30/8)*
Tortoli, Arbatax

NATALIE 5b, Budinetto, Cala Gnome; Paul Astie (photo Mark Glaister

No	Area	Height	Rating	Name
1	Gra	30	<20>	Capo Testa*
2	Cal	25	<20>	Siniscola
3	20	30	<22>	Biddiriscottai
4	20	25+	<15>	Margheddie
5	15	35	<5>	El Chorro
6	15	30	<20>	Monte Iveri
7	10	25+	<14>	Budinetto-Flinstone
8	Cal	25+	<60>	La Poltrona*
9	5	30	<41>	Dorgali - La Pineta
10	Cal	15+	<60>	Monte Maccione*
11	Cal	35	<32>	Lanaitto*
12	45 (A/S)	120	<20(5sport)>	Surtana
13	5	35	<30>	I Tornati
14	60?	25	<50>	Cala Fuili (Strap & Placc)*
15	60 (S/A)	10	<35>	Cala Luna
16	60 (S/A)	100	<12>	Cala Goloritzé*
17	5	90	<14>	Regno dei Cieli*
18	Cal	30	<14>	Campo dei Miracoli
19	Cal	30	<40>	Il Castello*
20	Cal	25+	<25>	Isola del Tesoro*
21	Cal	30	<25>	Palazzo d'Inverno*
22	Cal	15	<50>	Pietra Filosofale
23	Cal	20	<45>	Urania - Corvo Spaziale*
24	Cal	20	<30>	Cubo Magico - Pentagramma
25	Cal	30	<7>	Conca Manna
26	Gra	15+	<10>	Ti-Mi-Ama
27	Cal	30	<60>	Cala Fighera*
28	Cal	35+	<45>	Scogliera di Masua*
29	Cal	25	<66>	San Giovanni
30	Cal	20	<16>	Ombre Rose
31	Cal	20+	<48>	Chinatown - P.S. Michelle*
32	1	35	<18>	Canneland
33	Cal	60	<26>	Ruota dei Tempo*
34	Cal	70	<45>	Punta Pilocca*
35	Gra	25	<17>	Villacidro*
36	Bas	20+	<28>	Monte Arci
37	Cal	25	<30>	Capo Caccia*
38	Cal	35	<12>	Osilo Grande*
39	Cal	12	<8>	Osilo Superpippo

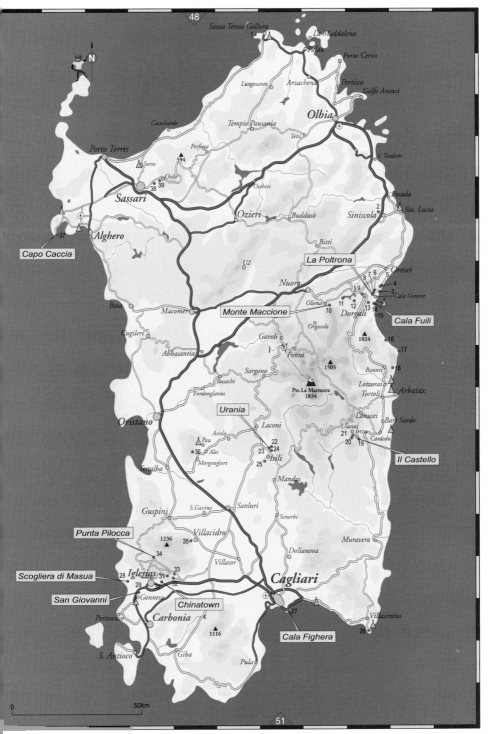

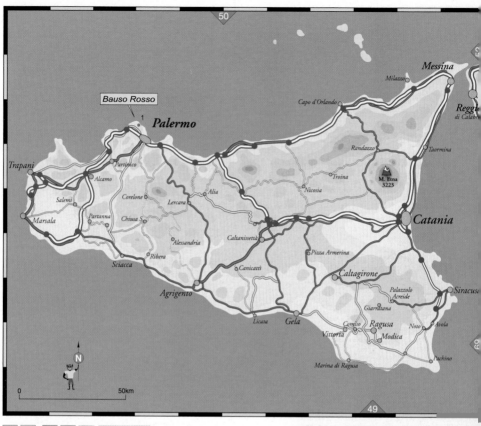

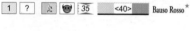

1   ?   🔺   👁   35   <40>   Bauso Rosso*

ARAJ 7a+, Cala Luna, Sardegna (50)
(photo Mark Glaister)

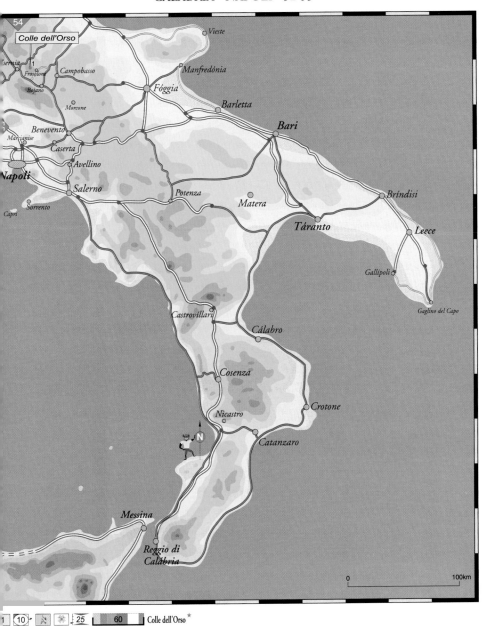

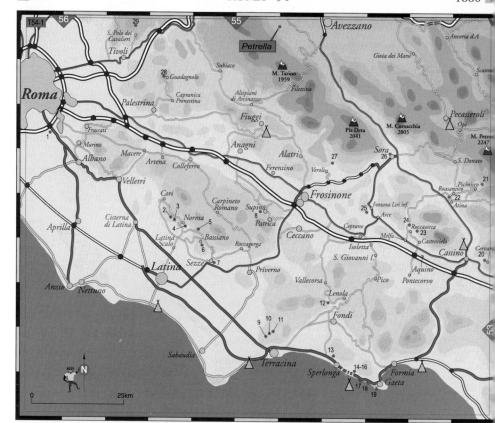

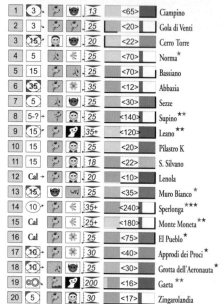

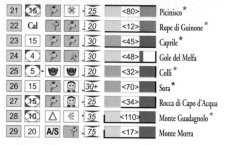

1	3			13	<65>		Ciampino
2	3			25	<20>		Gola di Venti
3	15			20	<22>		Cerro Torre
4	5			25	<70>		Norma*
5	15			25	<70>		Bassiano
6	35			35	<12>		Abbazia
7	5			25	<30>		Sezze
8	5-?			25	<140>		Supino**
9	15			35+	<120>		Leano**
10	15			25	<20>		Pilastro K
11	15			18	<22>		S. Silvano
12	Cal			20	<10>		Lenola
13	15			25	<35>		Muro Bianco*
14	10			35+	<240>		Sperlonga***
15	Cal			25+	<180>		Monte Moneta**
16	Cal			25	<75>		El Pueblo*
17	10			30	<40>		Approdi dei Proci*
18	10			25	<30>		Grotta dell'Aeronauta*
19	∞			200	<16>		Gaeta**
20	5			30	<17>		Zingarolandia

21	15			25	<80>		Picinisco*
22	Cal			20	<12>		Rupe di Guinone*
23	15			30	<45>		Caprile*
24	4			30	<48>		Gole del Melfa
25	5			20	<32>		Colli*
26	15			30+	<70>		Sora*
27	15			25	<34>		Rocca di Capo d'Acqua
28	10	△		35	<110>		Monte Guadagnolo*
29	20	A/S		75	<17>		Monte Morra

Topo: T54-1
...in cerca di guai
Piero Ledda; 1998
304pp. 180mm x 130mm

T　I　?　5a-7a Info

⚠ 1 - 29.

€ **Libreria all'Orologio,** *via del Governo Vecchio 7, 00186, Roma (2km ESE Vatican), 11-13; 16.30-19.30* ¢-pm 1

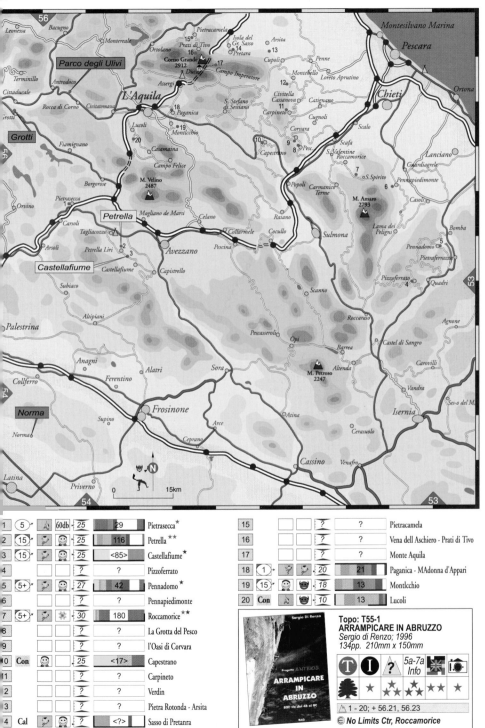

1	(5)	60db	- 25	29	Pietrasecca*
2	(15)		25	116	Petrella**
3	(15)		25	<85>	Castellafiume*
4			?	?	Pizzoferrato
5	(5+)		27	42	Pennadomo*
6			?	?	Pennapiedimonte
7	(5+)		30	180	Roccamorice**
8			?	?	La Grotta del Pesco
9			?	?	l'Oasi di Corvara
10	Con		25	<17>	Capestrano
11			?	?	Carpineto
12			?	?	Verdin
13			?	?	Pietra Rotonda - Arsita
14	Cal		?	<?>	Sasso di Pretarna

15			?	?	Pietracamela
16			?	?	Vena dell Aschiero - Prati di Tivo
17			?	?	Monte Aquila
18	(1)		20	21	Paganica - MAdonna d'Appari
19	(15)		18	13	Montlcchio
20	Con		10	13	Lucoli

Topo: T55-1
ARRAMPICARE IN ABRUZZO
Sergio di Renzo; 1996
134pp. 210mm x 150mm

T I ? 5a-7a Info

★ ★★ ★★★ ★★ ★

△ 1 - 20; + 56.21, 56.23

© No Limits Ctr, Roccamorice

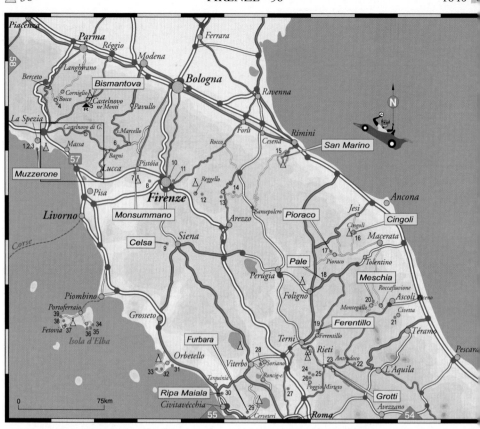

1	5				30	<60>	Muzzerone, Parete Centrale *
2	15				60	<40>	Specchio & Atlantide *
3	17	S/A			150	<10>	Parete Striata *
4	30				30	<21>	Asfodeli
5	5				30+	<120>	La Pietra di Bismantova **
6	20				35	<38>	Cocciglia *
7	2				30	<130>	Monsummano **
8	2				10	<8>	Roveta
9	5				24	<70>	Celsa *
10	5				17	<23>	Faentina
11	3				28	<60>	Maiano *
12	20				25	<15>	Massa Nera
13	15				15	<24>	Pratomagno
14	1				17	<17>	La Verna
15	5				25	<50>	San Marino *
16	15				30	<47>	Cingoli *
17	1				35	<46>	Pioraco *
18	?				25	<150>	Pale **
19	5				30	<350>	Ferentillo ***
20	5				6	<250>	Meschia ** ⊘ 1.10/31.10

21	Cal				?	13	Rocca dei Borboni
22	8				27	13	Parco degli Ulivi, Antrodoco
23	5				25	90	Grotti **
24	5				25	<32>	Roccantica
25	10				25	<10>	Eremo di S. Michele
26	5				18	<48>	Poggio Catino
27	?				25	<14>	Monte Soratte
28	?				6	<?>	Soriano - Monte Cimino
29	20				40	<50>	Sasso di Furbara *
30	10				30	<98>	Ripa Maiala * 15/2-15/7
31	3				22	<20>	Ansedonia
32	15				24+	<30>	Canne d'Organo *
33	30				30	<11>	Cape D'Uomo
34	?				23	<25>	Ginepro
35	?				15	<10>	Baia dei Pirati
36	?				9	<18>	Remaiolo
37	1				15	<33>	Fetovaia
38	30				17	<12>	Madonna del Monte
39	Gra				15	<15>	Sant'Andrea

You don't go climbing in central Italy without a visit to Ferentillo or Grotti, fingery pockets.

 A contrasting area; sea views at hot Muzzerone, and then coolness at the high and quiet area of Bismantova.

Topo: T56-1
Arrampicata sportiva nell'Italia centrale
Andrea Gennari Daneri; 1996
176pp. 200mm x 140mm

⚠ 1 - 5, 7, 16 - 19, 21 (++)
€ ????

Topo: T56-2
Bouldering a Meschia
Mauro Calibani & Amanda; 2001
48pp. 138mm x 160mm

⚠ 20.
€ Bar, Roccafluvione ??

Topo: T56-3
Toscana E Isola d'Elba
Filippo Lenzi; 1998
288pp. 210mm x 150mm

⚠ 56: 1-14, 31-36.
57: 1-21.
€ ????

MUZZERONE

PORTOVENERE, (Muzzerone-Bello-panorama), La Spézia

CORNÍGLIA, Cinque Terre - La Spézia (5

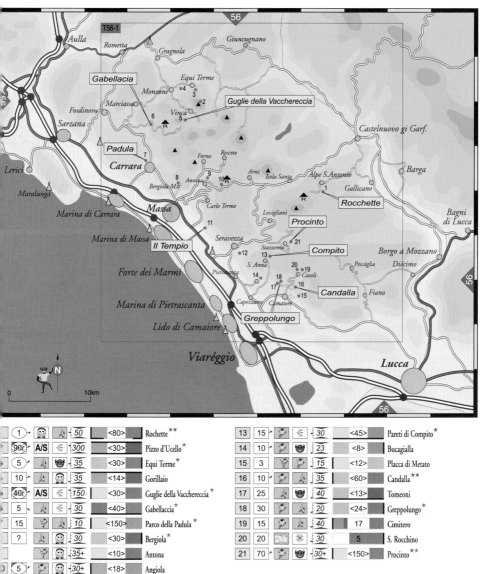

1			50		<80>		Rochette**
90r	A/S		300		<30>		Pizzo d'Ucello*
5			35		<30>		Equi Terme*
10			35		<14>		Gorillaio
40r	A/S		150		<30>		Guglie della Vacchereccia*
5			30		<40>		Gabellaccia*
15			10		<150>		Parco della Padula*
?			30		<30>		Bergiola*
			35+		<10>		Antona
5			30+		<18>		Angiola
?			30		<50>		Il Tempio*
15			25		<13>		Il Secondo*

13	15			30	<45>		Pareti di Compito*
14	10			23	<8>		Bucagialla
15	3			15	<12>		Placca di Metato
16	10			35	<60>		Candalla**
17	25			40	<13>		Tomeoni
18	30			20	<24>		Greppolungo*
19	15			40	17		Cimitero
20	20			30	5		S. Rocchino
21	70			30+	<150>		Procinto**

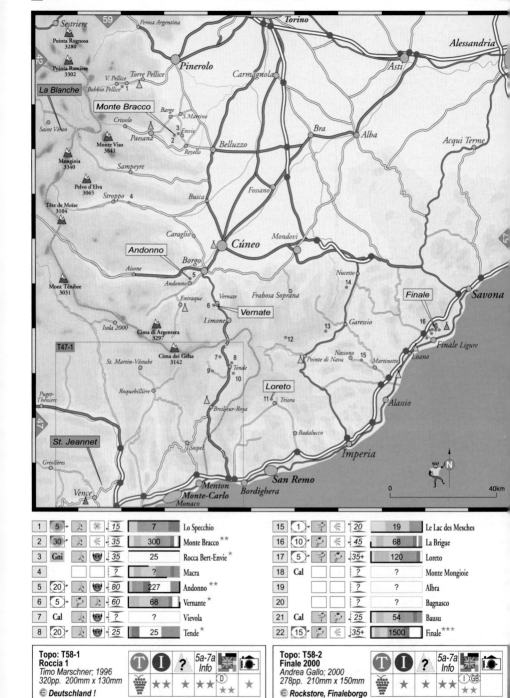

1	5	⋋	✳	15	7	Lo Specchio
2	30	⋋	⟨	35	300	Monte Bracco**
3	Gni	⋋	😎	35	25	Rocca Bert-Envie*
4				?	?	Macra
5	20	⋋	😎	80	227	Andonno**
6	5	⋋	⋋	60	68	Vernante*
7	Cal	⋋	😎	?	?	Vievola
8	20	⋋	😎	25	25	Tende*

15	1	⋋	⟨	20	19	Le Lac des Mesches
16	10	⋋	⟨	45	68	La Brigue
17	5	⋋	⋋	35+	120	Loreto
18	Cal			?	?	Monte Mongioie
19				?	?	Albra
20				?	?	Bagnasco
21	Cal	⋋	⋋	25	54	Bausu
22	15	⋋	⟨	35+	1500	Finale***

Topo: T58-1
Roccia 1
Timo Marschner; 1996
320pp. 200mm x 130mm
€ *Deutschland !*

T I ? 5a-7a Info 🇬🇧 D

🍇 ★★ | ★ | ★★★ | ★

⛰ 2, 3, 5, 6, 17, 21, 22.

Topo: T58-2
Finale 2000
Andrea Gallo; 2000
278pp. 210mm x 150mm
€ *Rockstore, Finaleborgo*

T I ? 5a-7a Info 🇬🇧 GB

🍇 ★ | ★ | ★★ | ★★

⛰ 22. (1500 Routes - wow!!)

RAINING SISTERS 6a+, Monte Cucco, Finale; Almos Hernath

ANDONNO

FINALE BORGO

FINALE LIGURE

FINALE BORGO

GORRA, Fina

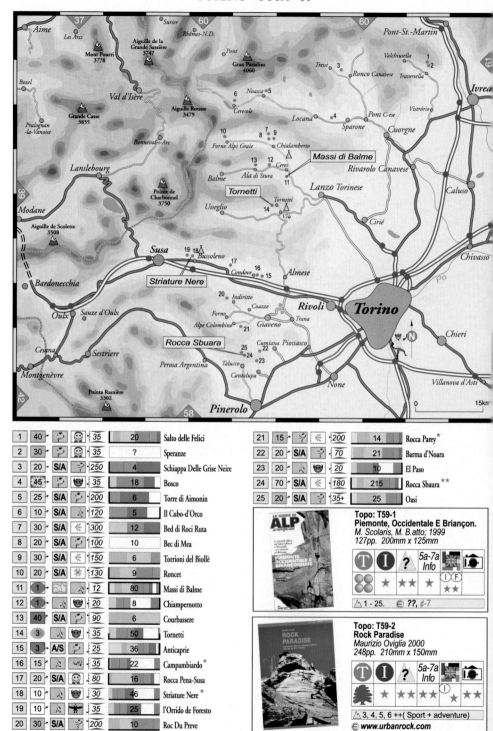

#						Crag
1	40			35	20	Salto delle Felici
2	30			35	?	Speranze
3	20	S/A		250	4	Schiappa Delle Grise Neire
4	45			35	18	Bosco
5	25	S/A		200	6	Torre di Aimonin
6	10	S/A		120	5	Il Cubo-d'Orco
7	30	S/A		300	12	Bed di Roci Ruta
8	20	S/A		100	10	Bec di Mea
9	30	S/A		150	6	Torrioni del Biollè
10	20	S/A		130	9	Roncet
11	1			12	80	Massi di Balme
12	1			20	8	Chiampernotto
13	40	S/A		90	6	Courbassere
14	3			35	50	Tornetti
15	3	A/S		25	36	Anticaprie
16	15			35	22	Campambiardo*
17	20	S/A		80	16	Rocca Pena-Susa
18	10	S/A		30	46	Striature Nere*
19	10			35	25	l'Orrido de Foresto
20	30	S/A		200	10	Roc Du Preve

#						Crag
21	15			200	14	Rocca Parey*
22	20	S/A		70	21	Barma d'Noara
23	20			20	10	El Paso
24	70	S/A		180	215	Rocca Sbaura**
25	20	S/A		35+	25	Oasi

Topo: T59-1
Piemonte, Occidentale E Briançon.
M. Scolaris, M. B.atto; 1999
127pp. 200mm x 125mm
T I ? 5a-7a Info
★ ★★ ★★
1 - 25. ??, 7

Topo: T59-2
Rock Paradise
Maurizio Oviglia 2000
248pp. 210mm x 150mm
T I ? 5a-7a Info
★ ★★★ ★★★★ ★★
3, 4, 5, 6 ++(Sport + adventure)
www.urbanrock.com

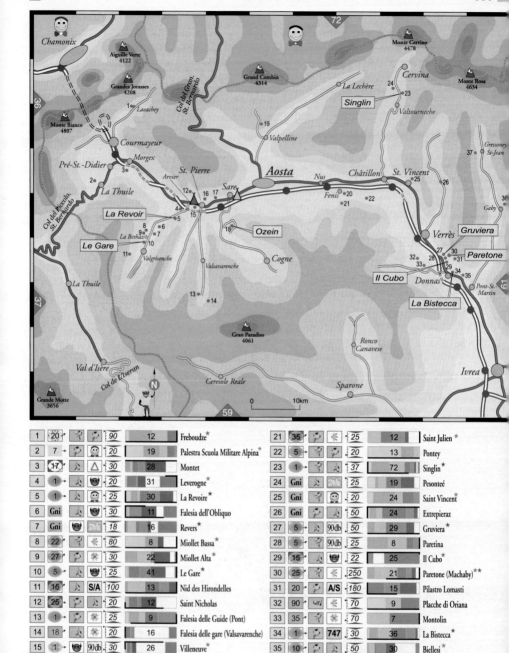

#							Name
1	20			90	12		Freboudze*
2	7			20	19		Palestra Scuola Militare Alpina*
3	17			30	28		Montet
4	1			20	31		Leverogne*
5	1			25	30		La Revoire*
6	Gni			30	11		Falesia dell'Obliquo
7	Gni			18	16		Revers*
8	22			80	8		Miollet Bassa*
9	27			30	22		Miollet Alta*
10	5			25	41		Le Gare*
11	15		S/A	100	13		Nid des Hirondelles
12	25			20	12		Saint Nicholas
13	1			25	9		Falesia delle Guide (Pont)
14	18			20	16		Falesia delle gare (Valsavarenche)
15	1		90db	30	26		Villeneuve*
16	1			40	12		Priorato
17	5		90db	30	21		Tetto di Sarre**
18	10			30	58		Oezin - Mont Ross**
19	7			20	6		Vaud
20	5			50	10		Fenis
21	35			25	12		Saint Julien*
22	5			20	13		Pontey
23	1			37	72		Singlin*
24	Gni			25	19		Pesonteé
25	Gni			20	24		Saint Vincent*
26	Gni			50	24		Extrepieraz
27	5		90db	50	29		Gruviera*
28	5		90db	25	8		Paretina
29	15			22	25		Il Cubo*
30	25			250	21		Paretone (Machaby)**
31	20		A/S	180	15		Pilastro Lomasti
32	90			70	9		Placche di Oriana
33	35			70	7		Montolin
34	1		747	30	36		La Bistecca*
35	10			50	30		Biellesi*
36	70	A/S		100	10		Parete del Pentimento
37	50	A/S		200	3		Muro del Pianto

A great choice of very steep Gneiss; don't miss out on Il Cubo and Revers, they have lovely settings.

 Val Grisenche is simply beautiful, and quiet. The routes on Miollet will certainly test your technical skill.

Topo: T60-1
Valle D'Aosta
Guides alta Monatagna; 1999
112pp. 200mm x 125mm

⚠ 1-21, 26-37.

€ *Libreria - Centre Aosta:*
Via/rue Edouard Aubert ¢-7

Topo: T60-2
Arrampicare in Valtournenche
Marcello Caccialupi; 1999
135pp. 210mm x 150mm

⚠ 22,23,24,25.

€ *Libreria - Centre Aosta::*
Via/rue Edouard Aubert ¢-7

❶ *Tourist Information Office*
Piazza Chanoux, 8
(Centre) 11100 Aosta
Tel: 0165 236 627   Fax: 0165 346 57
email: uit-aosta@regione.vda.it
www.regione.vda.it

Camping 'Monte Bianco' (1/4-30/9)
Fraz. St. Maurice 3, Sarre 11010
Dir; Sarre, 0.1km-dir Courmeyeur

Camping Arvier (15/6-31/8)
St. Antoine 6, 11011 Arvier

ROCK CLIMBING
MOUNTAINEERING
TELEMARK OFF-PISTE
SKI OFF-PISTE
SKI TOURING
HELISKI
ICE CLIMBING
CANYONING

Mountain Guide
CHRISTIAN CESA

Frazione Montan 32 11010 Sarre (Aosta) Italy
Tel. +39.0165.553960 Mobile +39.335.6951507
Web site: http://web.tiscali.it/cesa
E-mail: christian.cesa@tiscalinet.it

LEVEROGNE

CRIPTONITE 8b, Tetto di Sarre: Pietro Bagnar

T. PIERRE, AOSTA

VALGRISENCHE

EVI 92, 6a, Ozein; Alessandro Quagliolo

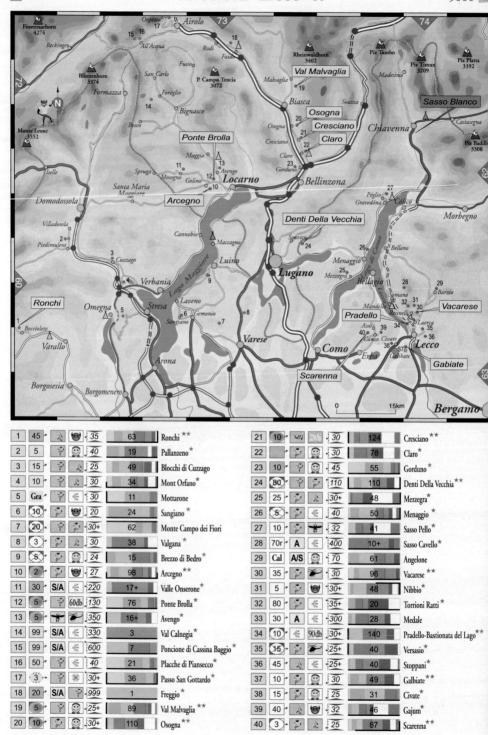

1	45			35	63	Ronchi ★★
2	5			40	19	Pallanzeno ★
3	15			25	49	Blocchi di Cuzzago
4	10			30	34	Mont Orfano ★
5	Gra			30	11	Mottarone
6	10			20	24	Sangiano ★
7	20			30+	62	Monte Campo dei Fiori
8	3			30	38	Valgana ★
9	5			24	15	Brezzo di Bedro ★
10	2			27	98	Arcegno ★★
11	30	S/A		220	17+	Valle Onserone ★
12	5		60db	130	76	Ponte Brolla ★
13	5			350	16+	Avengo ★
14	99	S/A		330	3	Val Calnegia ★
15	99	S/A		600	7	Poncione di Cassina Baggio ★
16	50			40	21	Placche di Piansecco ★
17	3			30+	36	Passo San Gottardo ★
18	20	S/A		999	1	Freggio ★
19	5			25+	89	Val Malvaglia ★★
20	10			30+	110	Osogna ★★
21	10			30	124	Cresciano ★★
22				30	78	Claro ★
23	10			45	55	Gorduno ★
24	80			110	110	Denti Della Vecchia ★★
25	25			30+	48	Mezzegra ★
26	5			40	50	Menaggio ★
27	10			32	41	Sasso Pello ★
28	70r	A		400	10+	Sasso Cavello ★
29	Cal	A/S		70	61	Angelone
30	35			30	96	Vacarese ★★
31	5			30+	48	Nibbio ★
32	80			35+	20	Torrioni Ratti ★
33	30	A		300	28	Medale
34	10		90db	30+	140	Pradello-Bastionata del Lago ★★
35	15			25+	40	Versasio ★
36	45			25+	40	Stoppani ★
37	10			30	49	Galbiate ★★
38	15			25	31	Civate ★
39	40			32	46	Gajum ★
40	3			25	87	Scarenna ★★

Lecco is the better area for the power climber, plenty of steep limestone in different settings - some very noisy!

 When the Alps has bad weather, climbing in the Locarno area will be very busy indeed, lovely climbing though.

Topo: T61-1
Varese, Canton Ticino
R. Capucciati +++ ; 1998
240pp. 210mm x 150mm

T	I	?	5a-7a Info		
🌲	★	★★★★★	① ★★	★★	

⚠ 6 - 24.

€ *Libreria dell'Angelo-Lecco, ¢-7*
Libreria Cattemeo-Lecco, ¢-7

Topo: T61-2
Arrampicate Sportiva Lecco E Como
Pietro Corti +++; 1997 (2001 reprint)
336pp. 210mm x 150mm

T	I	?	5a-7a Info		
🌲	★	★★★★★	① ★★	★★	

⚠ 25 - 40. +++

€ *Libreria dell'Angelo-Lecco, ¢-7*
Libreria Cattemeo-Lecco, ¢-7

Topo: T61-3 *3a-6b yummy*
Plaisir Sud - Schweiz-Italien
Jürg von Känel; 1998
246pp. 185mm x 120mm

T	I	?	5a-7a Info		
⚇	★	★★★★★	Ⓓ Ⓕ ★★ ①	★	

⚠ 2,4,5,12,13,16,18,23,24,30,35,37,38,

€ *Suisse, ¢-7*
www.urbanrock.com

LAGO MAGGIORE

OPERA IN NERO 6b+, Brezzo di Bedero; Wobbi

Fantastic Granite, some of the best in Europe, and certainly the most varied - some scenic and some Ugly.

 The routes at Val di Mello are 3 star, but bring you nuts and cams, and a pilots license.

Topo: T62-1
Valtellina, Valchiavenna Engadina
Guido Lisignoli +++; 1999
280pp. 210mm x 150mm

5a-7a Info

1 - 40.

€ **Libreria dell'Angelo-Lecco,** ¢-7
Libreria Cattemeo-Lecco, ¢-7
Camping Acquafraggia-Chiavenna

 Camping Acquafraggia (1/1-31/12)
1km NE - Chiavenna (dir CH)
23020 Borgonuovo di Piuro (SO)
Tel: 0343 36755

VADO A MANGIARE
DALLA MAMMA 7a,
Sasso del Drago; Guido Lisignoli

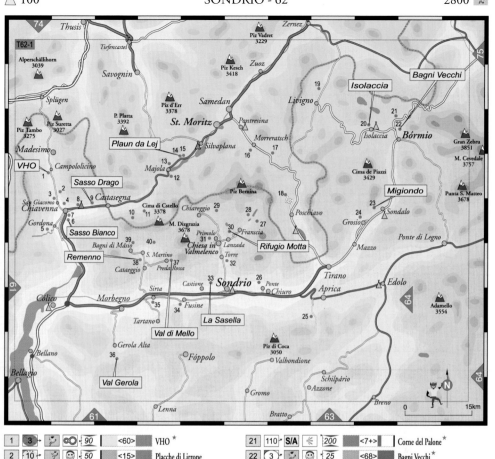

1	3			90	<60>		VHO *
2	10			50	<15>		Placche di Lirrone
3	10	S/A		300	<9+>		Il Castello *
4	20			400	<8>		Placche de Bette *
5	5	A/S		240	<4>		Paradiscan
6	10			50	<30>		Sasso Bianco *
7	45			30	<19>		Uschione *
8	15			200	<15>		Acquafraggia *
9	5			25	<37>		Sasso del Drago *
10	60r	A/S		270	<10+>		Sciora **
11	10L	A/S		250	<25+>		Albigna *
12	5			20	<16>		Maloja
13	20			20	<10>		Spluga
14	10			25	<41>		Plaun da Lej *
15	2			18	<22>		Polveriera *
16	10			20	<29>		Morteratsch
17	5			30	<32>		Lagalb *
18	15			35	<21>		Cavaglia
19	2			25	<28>		Fopel
20	5			40	<74>		Isolaccia *
21	110	S/A		200	<7+>		Corne del Palone *
22	3			25	<68>		Bagni Vecchi *
23	2			35	<70>		Migiondo
24	5			30	<40>		Vernuga
25	5			15	<11>		Val Belviso
26	5			20	<20>		Ponte Valtellina
27	18			20	<16>		Rifugio Zoia *
28	10			30	<35> <10>		Alpe Gera
29	?			90	<1>		Scerscen *
30	60			45	<70>		Rifugio Motta *
31	150			170	<2>		Val Giumellino
32	5			15	<9>		Spriana
33	2			20+	<63>		La Sasella
34	2			35	<21>		Fusine
35	15			80	<40>		Sirta *
36	90r			50+	<75+>		Val Gerola *
37	90	A/S		360	<3>		Averta *
38	10	S/A		30+	<350>		Remenno **
39	10	S/A		40	<30>		Val dei Bagni
40	15	A/S	747	450	<150>		Val di Mello ***

If you want a good outing into roofs, then visit Onore, plenty of pockets, but an awful angle.

 An area with more rolling hills than mountains, but it can be lovely and quiet during midweek

Topo: T63-1
Bergamo E Brescia
Eugenio Pesci; 1996 (reprint 2000)
369pp. 210mm x 150mm

T	I	?	5a-7a Info	🇬🇧	📷
🌲	★	★★★	★★		

⚠ 1 - 34 +++.
€ ???

SCHIAVI E CONTI 6a+, ??
Lantana Corna Rossa

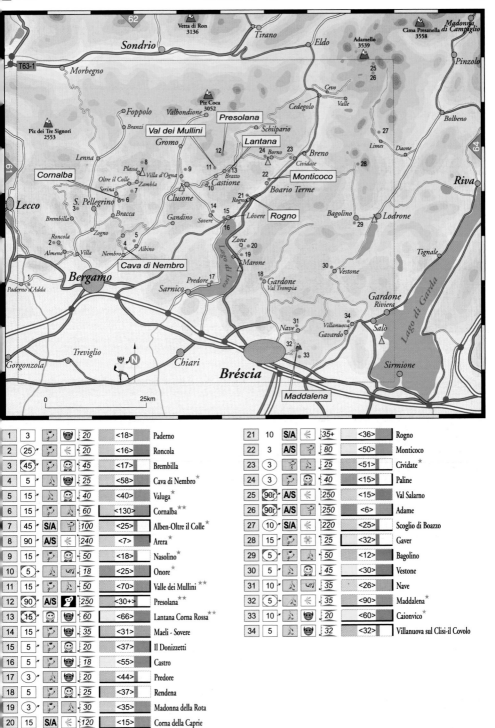

#					Name
1	3		20	<18>	Paderno
2	25		20	<16>	Roncola
3	45		45	<17>	Brembilla
4	5		25	<58>	Cava di Nembro*
5	15		40	<40>	Valuga*
6	15		60	<130>	Cornalba**
7	45	S/A	100	<25>	Alben-Oltre il Colle*
8	90	A/S	240	<7>	Arera*
9	15		50	<18>	Nasolino*
10	5		18	<25>	Onore*
11	15		50	<70>	Valle dei Mullini**
12	90	A/S	250	<30+>	Presolana**
13	15		60	<66>	Lantana Corna Rossa**
14	15		35	<31>	Maelì - Sovere
15	5		20	<37>	Il Donizzetti
16	5		18	<55>	Castro
17	3		20	<44>	Predore
18	5		25	<37>	Rendena
19	3		30	<35>	Madonna della Rota
20	15	S/A	120	<15>	Corna della Caprie
21	10	S/A	35+	<36>	Rogno
22	3	A/S	80	<50>	Monticoco
23	3		25	<51>	Cividate*
24	3		40	<15>	Paline
25	90	A/S	250	<15>	Val Salarno
26	90	A/S	250	<6>	Adame
27	10	S/A	220	<25>	Scoglio di Boazzo
28	15		25	<32>	Gaver
29	5		50	<12>	Bagolino
30	5		45	<30>	Vestone
31	10		35	<26>	Nave
32	5		35	<90>	Maddalena*
33	10		20	<60>	Caionvico*
34	5		32	<32>	Villanuova sul Clisi-il Covolo

ARTE SPAZIALE 8a, Onore;

BUFFALO BILL 6b+, Versasio (61); Wobbly

SCACCO AL RE 7c, Onore; ??

MONTE COLODRI

LAGO DI GARDA

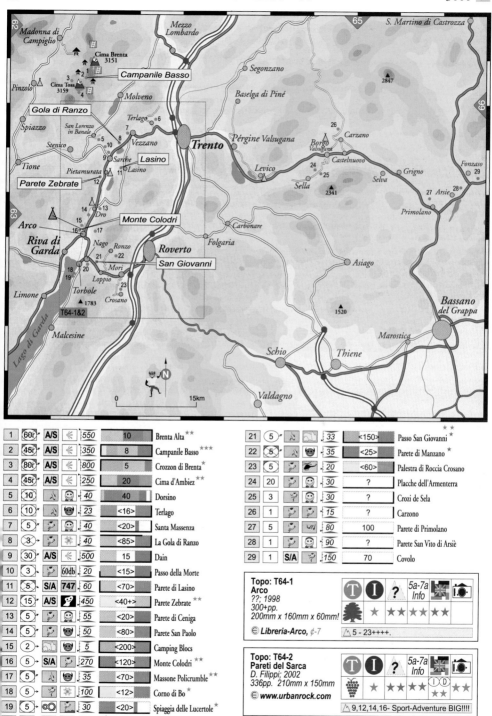

1	60r	A/S	←	550	10	Brenta Alta **
2	45r	A/S	←	350	8	Campanile Basso ***
3	80r	A/S	←	800	5	Crozzon di Brenta *
4	45r	A/S	←	250	20	Cima d'Ambiez **
5	10			40	40	Dorsino
6	10		23	<16>		Terlago
7	5		40	<20>		Santa Massenza
8	3		40	<85>		La Gola di Ranzo
9	30	A/S	←	500	15	Dain
10	3		60db	20	<15>	Passo della Morte
11	5	S/A	747	60	<70>	Parete di Lasino
12	15	A/S		450	<40+>	Parete Zebrate **
13	5		55	<20>		Parete di Ceniga
14	5		50	<80>		Parete San Paolo
15	2		5	<200>		Camping Blocs
16	5	S/A		270	<120>	Monte Colodri **
17	5		35	<70>		Massone Policrumble **
18	5		100	<12>		Corno di Bo *
19	5		30	<20>		Spiaggia delle Lucertole *
20	15		40	<200>		Nago ***

21	5		33	<150>		Passo San Giovanni **
22	5		35	<25>		Parete di Manzano *
23	5		20	<60>		Palestra di Roccia Crosano
24	20		30	?		Placche dell'Armenterra
25	3		30	?		Crozi di Sela
26	1		15	?		Carzono
27	5		80	100		Parete di Primolano
28	1		90	?		Parete San Vito di Arsiè
29	1	S/A	150	70		Covolo

Topo: T64-1
Arco
??; 1998
300+pp.
200mm x 160mm x 60mm!
€ **Libreria-Arco**, ¢-7

T I ? 5a-7a Info
★ ★★★★★★★
⚠ 5 - 23++++.

Topo: T64-2
Pareti del Sarca
D. Filippi; 2002
336pp. 210mm x 150mm
€ **www.urbanrock.com**

T I ? 5a-7a Info
★ ★★★★★ ★★
⚠ 9,12,14,16- Sport-Adventure BIG!!!!

CROZZON DI BRENTA

CASTELLETTO - Rifugio Tuckett, Brenta Dolomi.

ONTE COLODRI, & Camping Arco

SPIAGGIA DELLE LUCERTOLE

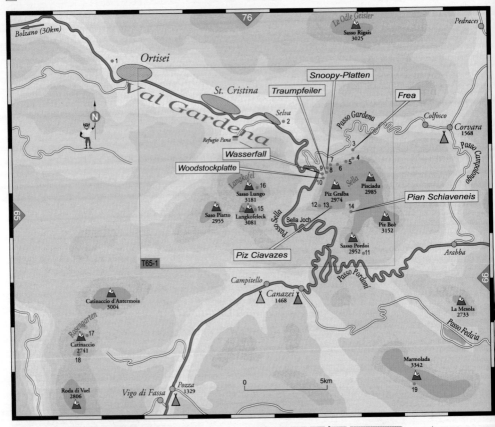

Map labels: Bolzano (30km), Ortisei, St. Cristina, Selva, Val Gardena, Refugio Pana, Passo Gardena, Colfosco, Corvara 1568, Passo Campolongo, Le Odle Geisler, Sasso Rigais 3025, Pedraces, Snoopy-Platten, Traumpfeiler, Frea, Wasserfall, Woodstockplatte, Langkofel, Sasso Lungo 3181, Sella, Piz Gralba 2974, Pisciadu 2985, Pian Schiaveneis, Saso Piatto 2955, Langkofeleck 3081, Sella Joch, Passo Sella, Piz Boe 3152, Piz Bob 3152, Sasso Pordoi 2952, Piz Ciavazes, Arabba, T65-1, Campitello, Canazei 1468, Passo Pordoi, Catinaccio d'Antermoia 3004, Rosengarten, Catinaccio 2741, La Mesola 2733, Passo Fedaia, Marmolada 3342, Roda di Vael 2806, Vigo di Fassa, Pozza 1329

#							Route
1	5			20	25		Cava
2	18			30	12		Palestra Bernardi
3	10			100	70		Frea **
4	15			250	5+		Frea Alpin *
5	15			200	11+		Meisulesturm *
6	20			250	18+		Meisules Biesces **
7	15			30	11		Snoopy-Placca *
8	15			150	23		Traumpfeiler *
9	Cal			35	8		Wasserfall *
10	10			40	17		Woodstock Placca **
11	45	A		300	10		Piz Maria *
12	20	A/S		250	17+		Sellaturm **
13	15	S/A		500	25		Piz Ciavazes **
14	15			30	27		Pian Schiaveneis *
15	80	A/S		350	15+		Cinque Dita *
16	30r	A/S		999	20+		Sasso Lungo - Langkofel *
17	40r	A/S		300	20+		Vajolet Towers
18	50r	A/S		350	10+		Catinaccio - Rosengarten
19	90r	A/S		850	100+		Marmolada ***

Topo: T65-1
Klettern rund ums Sellajoch
Stefan Stuflesser; 1997
174pp. 210mm x 150mm

T   I   ?   5a-7a Info

⚠ 1 - 14. + (Sport routen)

© Hobby Sport, S. Cristina, ¢-7

Topo: T65-2
Sella - Langkofel
R. Goedeke; 2001
416pp. 160mm x 120mm

Klassik routen

T   I   ?   5a-7a Info

⚠ 11 - 16.

© München, ¢-7

LANGKOFEL

How powerful are you? When it rains, go down to Erto, and you will be very impressed by the angle!

 If you enjoy a full alpine experience, then go to the Cinque Torri, good steep routes, big and small.

Topo: T66-1
Arramp.-sport a Cortina d'Ampezzo
Roberto Casanova; 1999
160pp. 210mm x 140mm

5a-7a Info

⚠ 1 - 10.

€ **Cooperativa di Cortina**, ¢-7

Topo: T66-2
Dolomiten
A. Köhler, N. Memmel; 1998
216pp. 230mm x 163mm

5a-7a Info

⚠ Klassik Dolomiten routen

€ **Cooperativa di Cortina**, ¢-7
München
GB version - www.urbanrock.com

⚠ Camping Olympia (1/1-31/12)
Fiames, 5km (N) Cortina.
Cortina d'Ampezzo

⚠ Camping Colfosco (1/1-31/12)
Covara, Trentino-Aldo Adige
39030 Italia

⚠ Camping Marmolada (1/1-31/12)
Via Pareda, Canazei

⚠ Camping Catinaccio
Rosengarten (1/6-?)
Avisio 15, Pozza di Fassa

WHITE LINE 6b, Crépe de Oucèra bassi; Jingo

TOFANA DI ROZES

TRE CIME DI LAVAREDO (Drei Zinnen)

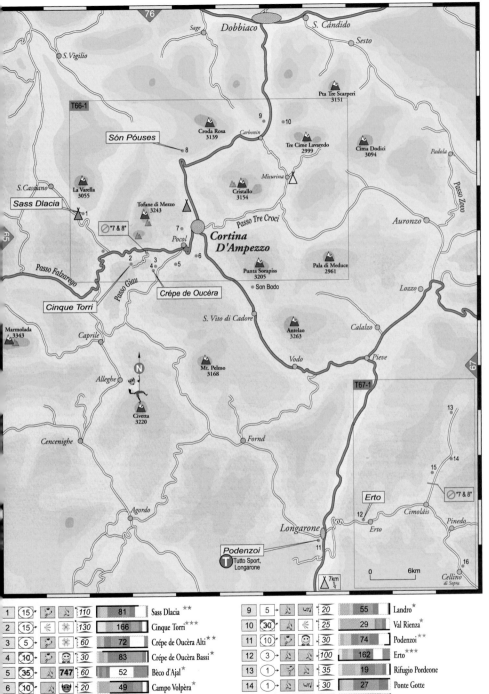

1	15			110	81	Sass Dlacia **	
2	15			130	166	Cinque Torri ***	
3	5			60	72	Crépe de Oucèra Alti **	
4	10			30	83	Crépe de Oucèra Bassi *	
5	35		747	60	52	Bèco d'Ajal *	
6	10			20	49	Campo Volpèra *	
7	5			12	12	Sasso di Colfiere *	
8	20			30	28	Són Póuses *	

9	5			20	55	Landro *	
10	30			25	29	Val Rienza *	
11	10			30	74	Podenzoi **	
12	3			100	162	Erto ***	
13	1			35	19	Rifugio Pordeone	
14	1			30	27	Ponte Gotte	
15	2			40	12	Parete dei Sediei	
16	15			60	23	Cellino	

SUDWAND III, Grosse Zinne-Grand Cime; Georg & Beate Schuster

ELEFONO AZZURRO 8a, Sasso Cubico, Cinque Torri; Marcella Santuz

Lots of good climbing in this sunny area.

 Why not try somewhere apart from Arco eh!

Topo: T67-1
Arrampicare in Friaul
Ingo Newmann; 1998
191pp. 210mm x 140mm

1 - 40.

€ **Österreich**
Tolmezzo ???, ¢-7

Camping Ai Poppi (15/4-31/10)
Via Bersaglio, Gemona. Friuli-Venezia Giulia
Tel: 0432 98038
Fax:
email:

ERTO, Longarone (66.1

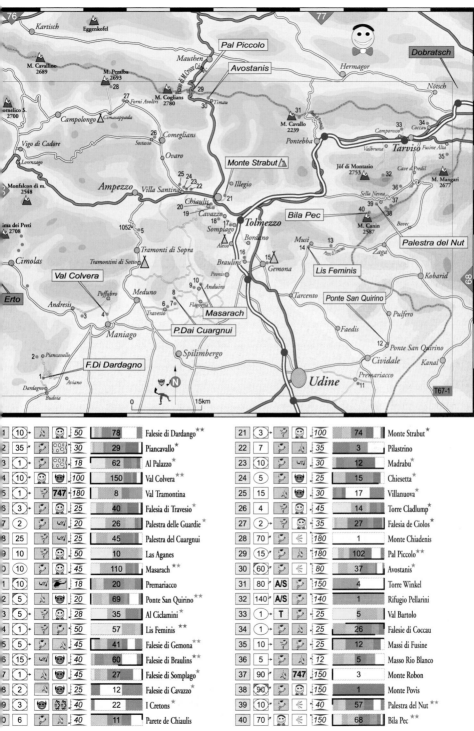

#							Name
1	(10)			50	78		Falesie di Dardagno**
2	35			30	29		Piancavallo*
3	(1)			18	62		Al Palazzo*
4	(10)			100	150		Val Colvera**
5	(1)		747	180	8		Val Tramontina
6	(3)			25	40		Falesia di Travesio*
7	(2)			20	26		Palestra delle Guardie*
8	25			25	45		Palestra del Cuargnui
9	10			50	10		Las Aganes
10	(10)			45	110		Masarach**
11	(10)			18	20		Premariacco
12	5			20	69		Ponte San Quirino**
13	(5)			28	35		Al Ciclamini*
14	(1)			50	57		Lis Feminis**
15	5			45	41		Falesie di Gemona**
16	(15)			40	60		Falesie di Braulins**
17	(1)			45	27		Falesie di Somplago*
18	2			25	12		Falesie di Cavazzo*
19	3			40	22		I Cretons*
20	6			40	11		Parete de Chiaulis
21	3			100	74		Monte Strabut*
22	7			35	3		Pilastrino
23	(10)			30	12		Madrabu*
24	(5)			25	15		Chiesetta*
25	15			30	17		Villanuova*
26	4			45	14		Torre Cladlump*
27	(2)			35	27		Falesia de Ciolos*
28	70			180	1		Monte Chiadenis
29	(15)			180	102		Pal Piccolo**
30	(60)			80	37		Avostanis*
31	80	A/S		150	4		Torre Winkel
32	140	A/S		140	1		Rifugio Pellarini
33	(1)	T		25	5		Val Bartolo
34	(1)			25	26		Falesie di Coccau
35	10			25	12		Massi di Fusine
36	5			12	5		Masso Rio Blanco
37	90		747	150	3		Monte Robon
38	(90)			150	1		Monte Povis
39	(10)			40	57		Palestra del Nut**
40	70			150	68		Bila Pec**

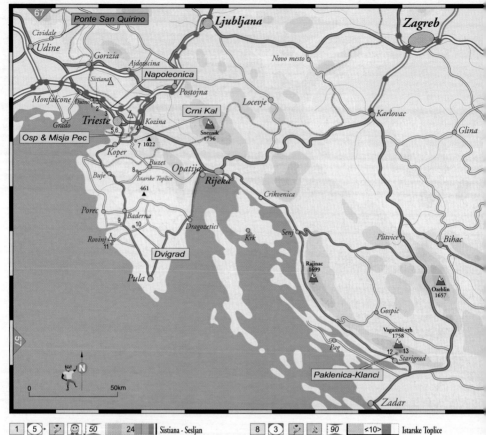

Map labels: 67, Ponte San Quirino, Ljubljana, Zagreb, Cividale, Udine, Gorizia, Ajdovscina, Novo mesto, Napoleonica, Sistiana, Monfalcone, Duino, Postojna, Locevje, Karlovac, Trieste, Kozina, Crni Kal, Snéznik 1796, Glina, Grado, Osp & Misja Pec, 7 1022, Koper, Buzet, Opatija, Karlovac, Buje, Istarske Toplice, Rijeka, Crikvenica, 461, Porec, Baderna, Dragozetici, Krk, Senj, Plitvice, Bihac, Rovinj, Dvigrad, Rajinac 1699, Pula, Ozeblin 1657, Gospic, Vaganski vrh 1758, 12 13 Starigrad, Pag, Paklenica-Klanci, Zadar

N 0 — 50km

1	5			50	24		Sistiana - Sesljan
2	2			40	40		Costiera[*]
3	1			30	<100>		Napoleonica[*]
4	10			20	80		Val Rosandra - Glinscia[*]
5	10			80	<110>		Osp[**]
6	5			40!	<90>		Misja Pec[**]
7	5			27	130		Crni Kal[**]

8	3			90	<10>		Istarske Toplice
9	3			25	<30>		Limski Kanal
10	10			23	<63>		Dvigrad[*]
11	10			16	<54>		Rovinj
12	10+			35	<50>		Vranjska Draga[*]
13	2+			35	<77>		Paklenica - Klanci[*]
14	30+		A/S	350	400		Paklenica National Park[**]

If you can float up vety steep and intimidating walls, then you must not miss out on a trip to Osp.

At the moment this is one of the quieter areas in Europe to climb, and plenty of new routes to find.

Topo: T68-1
Arrampicare senza frontiere
Sidarta; 2000
152pp. 210mm x 125mm

T I ? 5a-7a Info

★★★★ ★

△ 1-12.

€ **Technosport-Trieste**, ¢-7
www.urbanrock.com

(GB) Introductions   (D) Vorwort

Topo: T68-2
Paklenica
Boris Cujic, Sidarta; 1997
184pp. 210mm x 125mm

T I ? 5a-7a Info

★★★★★★ ★

△ 13,14

€ **Technosport-Trieste**, ¢-7
www.urbanrock.com

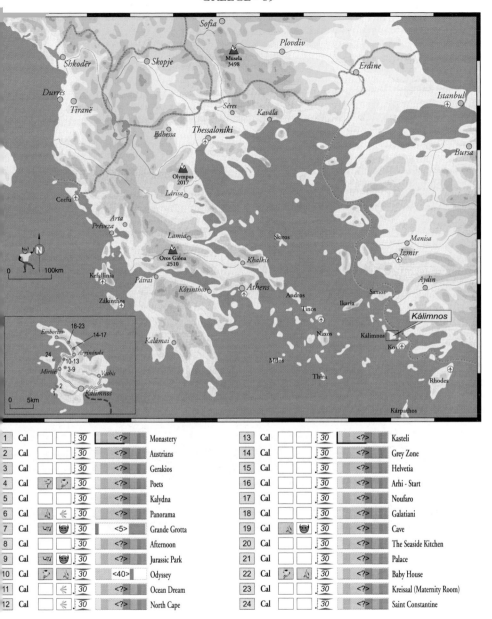

1	Cal		30	<?>	Monastery
2	Cal		30	<?>	Austrians
3	Cal		30	<?>	Gerakios
4	Cal		30	<?>	Poets
5	Cal		30	<?>	Kalydna
6	Cal		30	<?>	Panorama
7	Cal		30	<5>	Grande Grotta
8	Cal		30	<?>	Afternoon
9	Cal		30	<?>	Jurassic Park
10	Cal		30	<40>	Odyssey
11	Cal		30	<?>	Ocean Dream
12	Cal		30	<?>	North Cape
13	Cal		30	<?>	Kasteli
14	Cal		30	<?>	Grey Zone
15	Cal		30	<?>	Helvetia
16	Cal		30	<?>	Arhi - Start
17	Cal		30	<?>	Noufaro
18	Cal		30	<?>	Galatiani
19	Cal		30	<?>	Cave
20	Cal		30	<?>	The Seaside Kitchen
21	Cal		30	<?>	Palace
22	Cal		30	<?>	Baby House
23	Cal		30	<?>	Kreisaal (Maternity Room)
24	Cal		30	<?>	Saint Constantine

Andy Cave new routeing in the Bader valley, Patagonia. Photo: Simon Nadin

(**work hard, play hard**)

Work hard, play hard. That's our philosophy. Ever since we designed
our first gear in a Colorado work shed we've been driven to create
equipment that allows you to get out and focus on the experience.

lowealpine.com

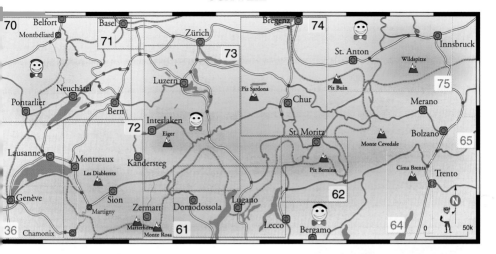

36: Cluses - Chamonix
61: Maggiore - Lecco
62: Chiavenna - Sondrio
64: Trento - Arco
65: Sella - Langkofel

70: Besançon - Neuchâtel
71: Basel
72: Martigny - Sion
73: Luzern
74: Chur
75: Tirol

LBATROS 6c, Ueschenen; Alois Aufschlager

The area of the Jura, is more of hills than mountains, and even though there is plenty of rainfall, it is a lot better than the Alps. Excellent & hard climbing on slightly steep rock, with good bolts almost everywhere.

 A very scenic area which is both in France and Suisse. Good for the wobbly, since there are many cliffs equipped for beginners. The valley of Ornans is not to be missed for some lovely lower grade, vertical -technical routes.

Topo: T70-1
Escalade en Haut Lieu
Philippe Gleizes; 1999
206pp. 210mm x 150mm

€ **Librairie-Presse,** ¢-7
Champagnole

5a-7a Info

⚠ 1,2,3,4. (+ 35.19,20,21)

Topo: T70-2
Escalades dans le Jura
Philippe Steulet; 1995
264pp. 210mm x 150mm

5a-7a Info

⚠ 11-37

€ **Librairie-Laufon,** ¢-7

Topo: T70-3
Jura Plaisir
Jürg von Känel; 1997
196pp. 185mm x 120mm

5a-7a Info

⚠ 2,3,4,25,30,31,36,37,40.

€ **Librairie-Bern,** ¢-7

La Barmaud
Xavier Petit; 1995
Mini Topo 24pp
⚠ 3,4.   🔨 **100**
€ **Ornans,** ¢-7

Pont de Roide
Grimpeur; 1997
Mini Topo 32pp
⚠ 10.   🔨 **144**
€ **O-De Tourisme-P de-Roi,** ¢-7

Montfaucon
P. Gleizes; 199?
Mini Topo 72pp
⚠ 5.   🔨 **200**
€ **?,** ¢-7

Rocher de Quint
?; 199?
Mini Topo 34pp
⚠ 6,7   🔨 **100**
€ **Tech- du Sport,** Baume I-D¢-7

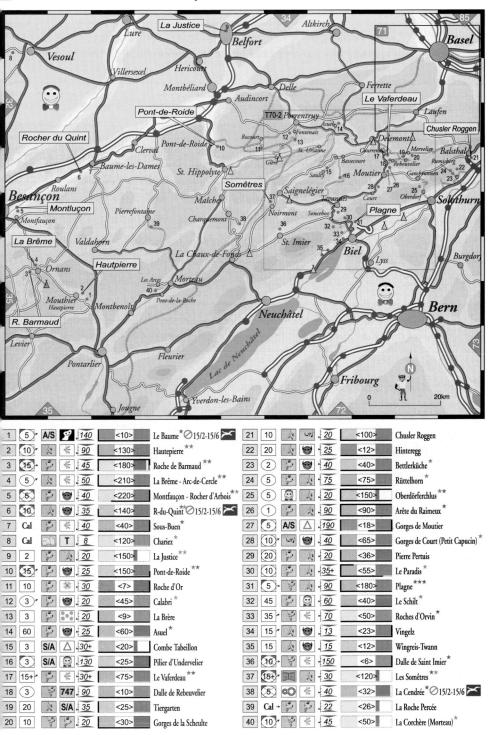

#						Name
1	(5)	A/S		140	<10>	Le Baume * ⊘15/2-15/6
2	(10)			90	<130>	Hautepierre **
3	(15)			45	<180>	Roche de Barmaud **
4	(5)			50	<210>	La Brême - Arc-de-Cercle **
5	(5)			40	<220>	Montfauçon - Rocher d'Arbois **
6	(10)			35	<140>	R-du-Quint ** ⊘15/2-15/6
7	Cal			40	<40>	Sous-Buen *
8	Cal	T		8	<120>	Chariez *
9	2			20	<150>	La Justice **
10	(15)			25	<150>	Pont-de-Roide **
11	10			30	<7>	Roche d'Or
12	3			20	<45>	Calabri *
13	3			20	<9>	La Brère
14	60			25	<60>	Asuel *
15	3	S/A	△	30+	<20>	Combe Tabeillon
16	(3)	S/A		130	<25>	Pilier d'Undervelier
17	15+			30+	<75>	Le Vaferdeau **
18	(3)	747		90	<10>	Dalle de Rebeuvelier
19	20		S/A	35	<25>	Tiergarten
20	10			20	<30>	Gorges de la Scheulte
21	10			20	<100>	Chusler Roggen
22	20			25	<12>	Hinteregg
23	2			40	<40>	Bettlerküche *
24	5			75	<75>	Rüttelhorn *
25	5			20	<150>	Oberdörferchlus **
26	1			90	<90>	Arête du Raimeux *
27	(5)	A/S	△	190	<18>	Gorges de Moutier
28	(10)			40	<65>	Gorges de Court (Petit Capucin) *
29	(20)			20	<36>	Pierre Pertuis
30	(10)			35+	<55>	Le Paradis *
31	(5)			90	<180>	Plagne ***
32	45			60	<40>	Le Schilt *
33	35			70	<50>	Roches d'Orvin *
34	15			13	<23>	Vingelz
35	15			15	<12>	Wingreis-Twann
36	(10)			150	<6>	Dalle de Saint Imier *
37	(15+)			30	<120>	Les Somêtres **
38	(5)			40	<32>	La Cendrée * ⊘15/2-15/6
39	Cal			22	<26>	La Roche Percée
40	(10)			45	<50>	La Corchère (Morteau) *

ROCHER DU QUINT

ORNANS (Rocher Barmaud)

ANDROGINE 6b+, pont de Roide; Jingo

The Calcaire of this area is very hard and compact, and it is very well suited, to very difficult bouldering; short, hard and steep routes. A lot of shade and cooler dark corners, but in summer, it can get too humid.

 Not the place for a soft holiday, a lot of the bolts are quite well spaced apart. The routes are very technical and require very good footwork indeed. Worth bringing a good crash pad for the bouldering grotto's. (Probably the best guidebook).

Topo: T71-1
Fluebible
P.Andrey, A. Luisier, M.Tscharner;
1997   348pp. 275mm x 140mm

"*WOW*"

5a-7a
Info

1-40.

© **Dynamo Sport,** ¢-?Kernmattstrasse 8,
Binningen, Basel: Lib-Laufen:
Adventure Sports, Freiburg, ¢-7

TOTALE ILLUSION 6c,
Dammenfelsen-Pelzmühletal;
Jingo

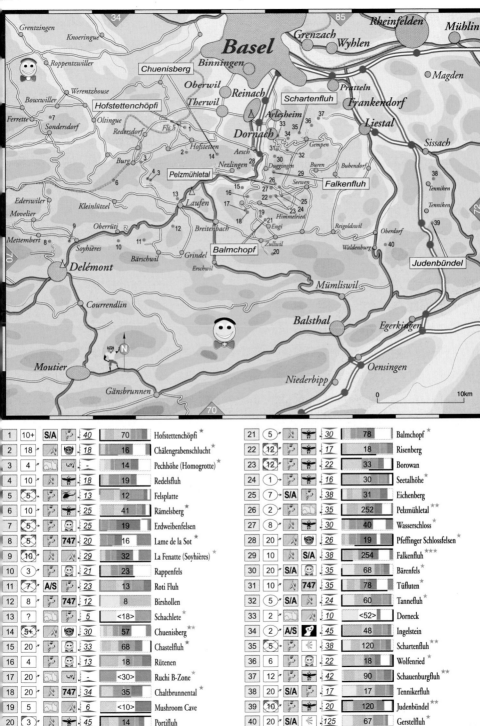

#							Name
1	10+	S/A		40	70		Hofstettenchöpfi *
2	18			18	16		Chälengrabenschlucht *
3	4			-	14		Pechhöhe (Homogrotte) *
4	10			18	19		Redelsfluh
5	8			13	12		Felsplatte
6	10			25	41		Rämelsberg *
7	8			25	19		Erdweibenfelsen
8	8		747	20	16		Lame de la Sot *
9	10			29	32		La Fenatte (Soyhières) *
10	3			21	23		Rappenfels
11	7	A/S		23	13		Roti Fluh *
12	8		747	12	8		Birshollen
13	?			5	<18>		Schachlete *
14	5+			30	57		Chuenisberg **
15	20			33	68		Chastelfluh *
16	4			13	18		Rütenen
17	20				<30>		Ruchi B-Zone *
18	20		747	34	35		Chaltbrunnental *
19	5			6	<10>		Mushroom Cave
20	3			45	14		Portifluh
21	5			30	78		Balmchopf *
22	12			17	18		Risenberg
23	12			22	33		Borowan
24	1			16	30		Seetalhöhe *
25	7	S/A		38	31		Eichenberg
26	2			35	252		Pelzmühletal **
27	8			30	40		Wasserschloss *
28	20			26	19		Pfeffinger Schlossfelsen *
29	10		S/A	38	254		Falkenfluh ***
30	20	S/A		35	68		Bärenfels *
31	10		747	35	78		Tüfluten *
32	5	S/A		24	60		Tannefluh *
33	2			10	<52>		Dorneck
34	2	A/S		45	48		Ingelstein
35	5			38	120		Schartenfluh **
36	6			22	18		Wolfenried *
37	12			42	90		Schauenburgfluh **
38	20	S/A		17	17		Tennikerfluh *
39	10			20	120		Judenbündel **
40	20	S/A		125	67		Gerstelfluh *

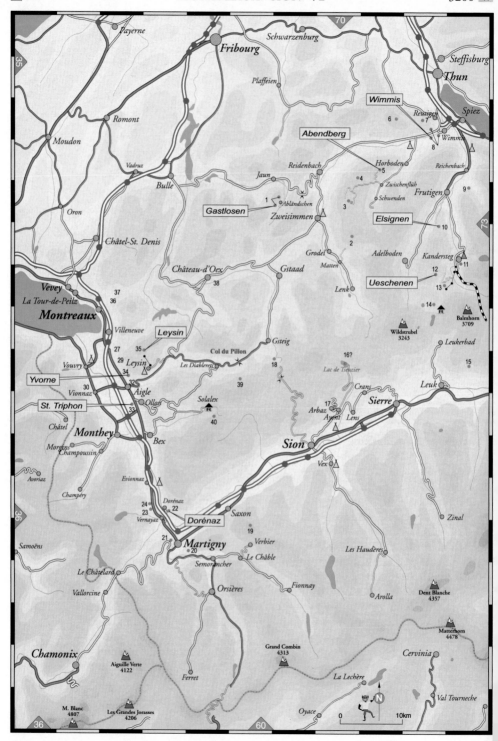

Lots of big powerful cliffs, but most are high up in the mountains, and need an expensive cable car ride! In the low valley of Monthey, there has been some good hard new bouldering areas worked out, most are brilliant.

 I love the view from Ueschenen, but remember in Schweiz, always have coins with you for the parking machines! Most of the cliffs have good climbing in the hard and easy grades; during midweek, the cliffs are really quiet and tranquil.

Topo: T72-1
Schweiz West *"Hard man"*
Timo Marschner; 1993
332pp. 200mm x 130mm

T | I | ? | 5a-7a Info
★ ★★★★★★ ★★ ★

△ 1, 5, 8,10-13, 21, 22, 33, 35.
€ ???

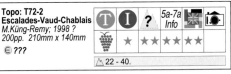

Topo: T72-2
Escalades-Vaud-Chablais
M.Küng-Remy; 1998 ?
200pp. 210mm x 140mm
€ ???

T | I | ? | 5a-7a Info
★ ★★★★★★

△ 22 - 40.

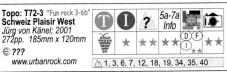

Topo: T72-3 "Fun rock 3-6b"
Schweiz Plaisir West
Jürg von Känel; 2001
272pp. 185mm x 120mm
€ ???
www.urbanrock.com

T | I | ? | 5a-7a Info
★ ★★★★★★ ★★

△ 1, 3, 6, 7, 12, 18, 19, 34, 35, 40

DORÉNAZ

UESCHENEN

#						Name	#						Name
1	60	S/A		35+	<100>	Gastlosen **	21	2			30	<40>	Ravoire
2	90	A/S		280	<6>	Rote Fluh *	22	1			35	<75>	Dorénaz *
3	40			25	<20>	Seebergsee - Diemtigtal	23	Gra			?	<43>	Miéville
4	20			35+	<50>	Buufal **	24	Gni			?	<33>	La Balmaz
5	30	cO		80	<80>	Abendberg **	25	Gni			?	<36>	Barme
6	10L			40	<30>	Stockhorn *	26	Cal			?	<8>	Vers-Court
7	15			80	<50>	Wissenfluh *	27				?	<22>	Roche
8	1			80	<120>	Wimmis **	28	Cal			?	<128>	Drapel
9	35			30	<60>	Gehrenen *	29				?	<15>	Corbeyrier
10	25			30+	<110>	Elsignen **	30				?	<20>	Vionnaz
11	10			25	<16>	Wildi *	31				?	<40>	Le Séchon
12	40			30+	<50>	Ueschenen **	32	Cal			?	<42>	Aigle
13	5			30	<50>	Winteregg *	33	2			25	<87>	St. Triphon *
14	20r			180	<21>	Schwarenbach *	34	30			30	<60>	Yvorne *
15	5			25	<30>	Brentschen *	35	20L	A/S		100	<252>	Leysin ***
16	?			40	<40>	Rawyl *	36	Cal			?	<21>	Les Avants
17	2			35	<40>	Arbaz	37	Cal			?	<7>	Dent de Jaman
18	25	S/A		250	<40>	Sanetsch **	38	Cal			?	<18>	Château d'Oex
19	30L			20	<30>	Pierre Avoi *	39	Cal	A/S		?	<147>	Les Diablerets
20	Gni			20	<35>	Chemin Dessus *	40	Cal	A/S		400	<20>	Miror de l'Argentine *

There has been a lot of development for hard climbing at the low cliffs of Interlaken, and more recently the area near Meiringen seems popular. Don't miss out on an excursion to the good climbing at Brig, or high up at Simplon.

 Many people will tell you of the easy slabs at Handegg and Eldorado. They are certainly good climbing, but if you have unsteady nerves, go with a very experienced and confident leader. The views are fantastic, but not in awful weather.

Topo: T73-1
Schweiz Plaisir West *"Hard man"*
Jürg von Känel; 2001
160+pp. 185mm x 120mm

🅣 🅘 ❓ 5a-7a Info 🏴󠁧󠁢󠁥󠁮󠁧󠁿 📷

🍇 ★ ★★ ★ ★★ ★★

⚠ 1-14, 36-40.

€ ???

Topo: T72-3
Schweiz Plaisir Ost *"Fun rock 3-6b"*
Jürg von Känel; 1997
260pp. 185mm x 120mm

🅣 🅘 ❓ 5a-7a Info 🏴󠁧󠁢󠁥󠁮󠁧󠁿 📷

🍇 ★ ★★ ★ ★★ ★★

⚠ 15,17,20,21.

€ ???

1	5			25	<42>		Beatenberg - Schmocken *
2	10			30	<124>		Lehn **
3	20			35+	<28>		Harder
4	10			25	<20>		Wilderswil
5	10			35	<8>		Lauterbrunnen
6	50L			25	<12>		Gimmenwald *
7	35	A/S		250	<30>		Hintisberg **
8	90	A/S		250	<30>		Engelhorn *
9	15			30	<31>		Lammi
10	40			45	<80>		Rosteini **
11	15			35	<42>		Schillingsflüe *
12	25			25	<32>		Cevi *
13	10			30	<32>		Bättlerbalm *
14	3			30	<13>		Lungern
15	60L			25+	<50>		Pilatus *
16	5		60db	20	<50>		Telli *
17	90L			30	<50>		Wissberg *
18	5			30	<7>		Chileflue Gersau
19	20			20	<14>		Sunneplättli
20	90	S/A		170	<10>		Rigi-Hochflue *

21	20			50	<20>		Gross Schijen *
22	2			40	<33>		Muotathal *
23	50L	A/S		90	<10>		Ganderfluh
24	Cal			60	<16>		Isleten
25	5			20	<50>		Erstfeld
26	2			45	<40>		Steingleschler
27	110	A/S		400	<10>		Wenden
28	20			?	<5>		Schöllenen
29	3	A/S		40	<20>		Göschereralp *
30	75	A/S		180	<10>		Graue Wand
31	90?	A/S		250	<10>		Bühlenhürner
32	15		747	250	<30>		Handegg
33	25			160	<10>		Gelmerfluh
34	90	A/S		600	<6>		Eldorado
35	60			200	<50>		Fieschertal *
36	15			40	<75>		Bitschji **
37	25			30	<50>		Naders *
38	15			30	<6>		Brigerbad
39	90			30	<20>		Wiwanni
40	10			35	<50>		Simplon Dorf *

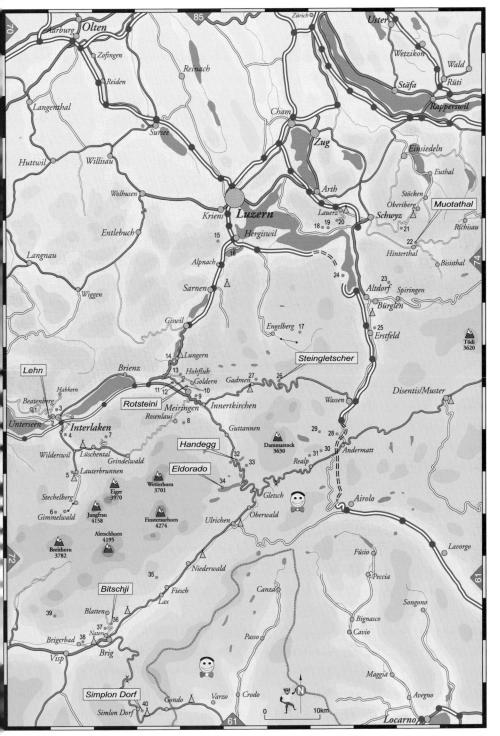

A good area for tough routes, mainly in the Vertical nature, but steep and sustained. Schafberg has plenty to entertain, and what a beautful setting. All out thugs, get a taste of Brüggler-Überhänge, very steep and powerful.

 If you want to find somewhere really special , try the Rätikon. The routes are difficult, but the position is superb, and good rock also. For the easier days out, don't miss a visit to Stoss, lots of big nice routes, and not very steep.

Topo: T74-1
Schweiz Ost
Timo Marschner; 1993
310pp. 200mm x 130mm

⚠ 1 - 3, 5 -13, 19 - 23.
€ ???

Topo: T74-2
Rätikon
Panico-Ravage; 1997?
60pp + topos. 180mm x 115mm

⚠ 15 - 18.
€ www.urbanrock.com

1	20L			25+	<30>	Schafberg*
2	60			45+	<25>	Stoss*
3	15L			100	<25>	Chäserrugg*
4	40L	S/A		150	<10>	Vord. Mattstock
5	2			25	<60>	Gallerie*
6	60			50	<20>	Wagenten
7	60			15	<15>	Brüggler-Überhänge
8	5			35	<12>	Ennenda
9	30L			18	<100>	Mettmen**
10	3			50	<40>	Obersiez-Weisstannen
11	5			15	<65>	Felsberger Blöcke*
12	5			100	<20>	Haldenstein
13	?			18	<20>	Tiefencastel
14	80	S/A		100	<25>	Seehorn*
15	120	A/S		250	<14>	Sulzfluh
16	90	A/S		380	<17>	Drusentürme
17	60			35	<10>	Schweizertor*
18	70			35+	<30>	Kirchlspitze*
19	2			12	<15>	Grüsch
20	15			20	<55>	Nussloch-Mastrisls
21	5			40	<20>	Fläsch*
22	?			20	<30>	Balzers
23	15			20	<70>	Brochne Burg*
24	40			35+	<130>	Löwenzähne**
25	?			80	<60>	Hängender Stein
26	5			40	<30>	Bürs*
27	15			30	<40>	Lorüns*

272

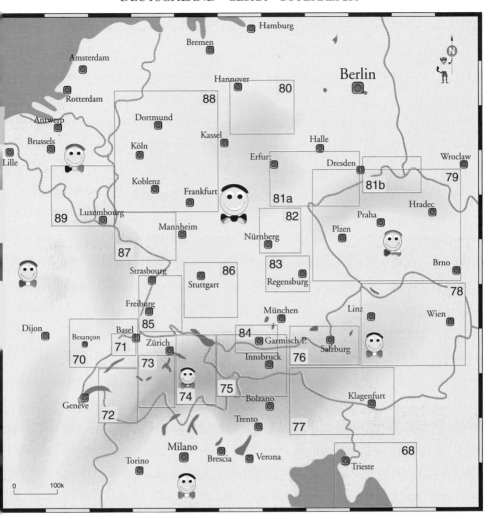

68: Trieste - Slovenia

70: Besançon-Neuchâtel

71: Basel

72: Montreaux - Sion

73: Luzern

74: Chur

75: Innsbruck

76: Salzburg

77: Klagenfurt - Villach

78: Wien

79: Ceska Republika

80: Hannover

81: Erfurt-Dresden

82: Nürnburg - Frankenjura

83: Regensburg

84: Garmisch Partenkirchen

85: Freiburg - Schwarzwald

86: Stuttgart

87: Annweiler - Pfalz

88: Bonn

89: Belgique

For those with oversize forearms, Dschungelbuch will offer plenty for a week or so!
Für alle mit starken Unterarmen bietet das Dschungelbuch genug Routen für eine Woche.

 If you climb and want a family picnic, go to Ewige Jagdgründe, a lovely place in good weather!
Ideal bei gutem Wetter: Klettern und ein Familien-Picknick in den Ewigen Jagdgründen.

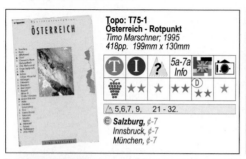

Topo: T75-1
Österreich - Rotpunkt
Timo Marschner; 1995
418pp. 199mm x 130mm

5a-7a Info

⚠ 5,6,7, 9,   21 - 32.

€ Salzburg, ¢-7
Innsbruck, ¢-7
München, ¢-7

Topo: T75-2
Alpine Sportkletterrouten
D. Elsner, Jochen Haase; 1996
168pp. 230mm x 162mm

5a-7a Info

⚠ 1, 2, 3, 8, 18, 23.

€ Salzburg, ¢-7
Innsbruck, ¢-7
München, ¢-7

Topo: T75-3
Karwendel
B. Eberle. A. Pasold; 1997
66pp. + 48 Topos 180mm x 115mm

5a-7a Info

⚠ 10 - 20

€ Innsbruck, ¢-7

Topo: T75-4
Klettersteige & Leichter Fels
Kurt Schall; 1996
240pp. 210mm x 150mm

5a-7a Info

⚠ 1, 2, 8, 10-20, ++++

€ Salzburg, ¢-7
Innsbruck, ¢-7

MARTINSWAND

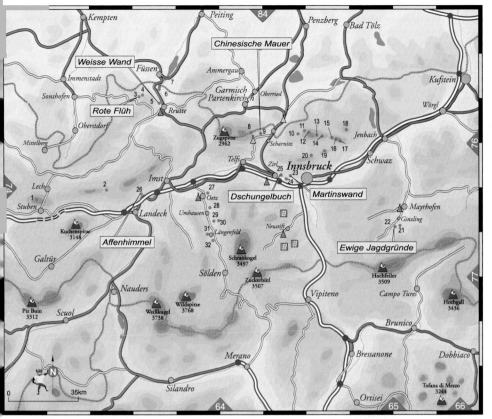

#						Route
1	90	A/S	⟵	170	5+	Rote Wand *
2	Cal	A/S	⟵	350	5+	Freispitze *
3	70	S/A	⟵	230	30+	Rote Flüh **
4	80	A	⟵	200	25	Gipfel *
5	5			60	40	Weisse Wand *
6	10			60	17	Pinswang
7	5			25	22	Kraftwerk *
8	20r	S/A	⟵	250	9+	Oberreintalturm *
9	25			35+	116	Chinesische Mauer **
10	60L	S/A		180	9	Gerberkreuz
11	30r	S/A		350	9	Kreuzwandspitze
12	25L		⟵	20	9	Damm-Rock
13	Cal →	A		850	9	Laliedererspitze
14	Cal →	A		750	8	Spritzkarspitze
15	Cal →	S/A		170	9	Mitterkarlspitze
16	Cal	A		250	11	Lamsenspitze
17	Cal	A/S		250	15	Rotwandlspitze
18	60	S/A		350	9	Sonnjoch
19	Cal	A/S		150	14	Speckarspitze
20	Cal	A		350	8	Kleiner Lafatscher

#						Route
21	20			25	26	Tulfer *
22	1			50	74	Ewige Jagdgründe *
23	25		⟵	220	21	Große Martinswand *
24	10		90db	35+	350	Martinswand-Felsen ***
25	5		90db	30+	173	Dschungelbuch ***
26	5			60	222	Affenhimmel **
27	Vol			30	14	Oetz
28	Vol			30	38	Tumpen
29	Vol			15	39	Au-Platte
30	Vol			25	20	Nösslach
31	Gra			25	?	Oberried
32	Gra			?	10	Astlehn

MOUNTAIN HARD WEAR

ROTE FLÜH

Afling, MARTINSWAND

KALKKÖGEL, Stubai, Neustift

Stubai, (Habicht)

)IREKTVAR.SW-WAND V-; Rote Flüh; Rainald Delille

There is no competition in this area for the hard climber, go directly to Schleier, and work out, hard.
Gehe direkt zum Schleier und gib Gas! Es gibt in der Gegend nichts vergleichbares für Spezialisten.

 There are many old beautiful climbing areas here, but the best newer routes are found at Torsäule.
In dieser Gegend gibt es viele alte gute Klettergebiete. Die besten neuen Routen findet man an der Torsäule.

Topo: T76-1
Kaisergebirge
Pit Schubert; 2000
399pp. 162mm x 113mm

⚠ 4.

€ **Kufstein**, ¢-7
Sport Eybl - Salzburg, ¢-7

Topo: T76-2
Dachsteingebirge
Kurt Schall, Thomas Jekel; 1996
368pp. 200mm x 137mm

⚠ 20,21,22,23. (+Dachstein)

€ **Schladming**, ¢-7
Sport Eybl - Salzburg, ¢-7

Topo: T75-1
Österreich - Rotpunkt
Timo Marschner; 1995
418pp. 199mm x 130mm

⚠ 1-3, 5-6, 8-9,16-19, 25

€ **Sport Eybl - Salzburg**, ¢-7
Innsbruck, ¢-7
München, ¢-7

Topo: T76-3
Out of Rosenheim
Markus Stadler; 2002
120pp. 185mm x 150mm

⚠ 1,2,3, ++ 17 cliffs near Rosenheim

€ **Montagne Sport, Rosenheim**, ¢-7
www.montagne.de

⛺ Egerbach (1/1-31/12) Camping Kufstein 2km SE - Kufstein (173 dir Going) Salurnerstr. 34

⛺ Michel'nhof (1/1-31/12) Weiberndorf, St. Johann

⛺ Camping Faninger, Harham 23, Saalfelden

⛺ Seeruhe im Talgrund (1/4-31/10) Hohenberg 2, Aigen i.Ennstal

1	5			30	23		Morsbacher*
2	10			50	44		Geisterschmiedwand**
3	5			35+	66		Sparchen**
4	120	A/S		250	600		Kaisergebirge*
5	80			40	50		Schleier Wasserfall-Links**
6	80			35	45		Schleier - White Winds**
7	35			150	23		Urlkopf*
8	5			50	16		Weissbach*
9	10			35	39		Seisenbergklamm*
10	120	A/S		250	27		Torsäule**
11	100	A		250	<30>		Watzmann
12	100	A		300	<40>		Reiteralpe
13	40	A/S		250	<60>		Göllmassiv

14	90	A/S		300	<30>		Untersberg/Hochthron**
15	10			30	60		Gitschenwand**
16	45			150	14		Falkenstein-St.Gilgen*
17	10			40	91		Rettenbachtal*
18	10			35	32		Ewige Wand*
19	20			60	19		Predigstuhl-Bad Goisern*
20	Cal	A		300	100		Gosaukamm**
21	20r			30	25		Hofpürgl Klettergarten
22	120	A		500	230		Dachstein**
23	20r	A		120	19		Krippenstein**
24	10		747	60	36		Burgstall-extrem*
25	3		90db	100	62		Burgstall**

Topo: T75-2
Alpine Sportkletterrouten
D. Elsner, Jochen Haase; 1996
168pp. 230mm x 162mm
△ 4,10,11,12,13.

Morsbacher Klettergarten

Cal: (E) (I) (O)

Morsbach
Zell Kufstein
Inn
P
◄— 1km —►

Geist-wand/Sparchen

Eichelmang
P
S
801
G
Kufstein
P
Cal: (F) (C)
◄— 150m —►

Schleier Wasserfall

Cal: (F) (M) (Z)

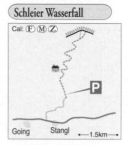

P
Going   Stangl
◄— 1.5km —►

Urlkopf

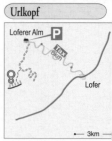

Loferer Alm   P
Tax
dagn
Lofer
◄— 3km —►

Torsäule

Cal: (I) (M)

Mitterfeldalm
Arthurhaus
P
Mülbach
◄— 2.5km —►

Gitschenwand

Hallein
Vigaun   Enzianhütte
St. Koloman   Trattberg
Tax
6km
P
Golling
◄— 150m —►

Ewige Wand

Cal: (T) (D)

Predigstuhl
P
Lasern
Bad Goisern
◄— 1.5km —►

Burgstall

Cal: (U) (T) (S)

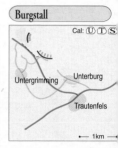

Untergrimming   Unterburg
Trautenfels
◄— 1km —►

TORSÄULE

8a+, SCHLEIER WASSERFAL

FLEISCHBANK, Kaisergebirge; Jingo

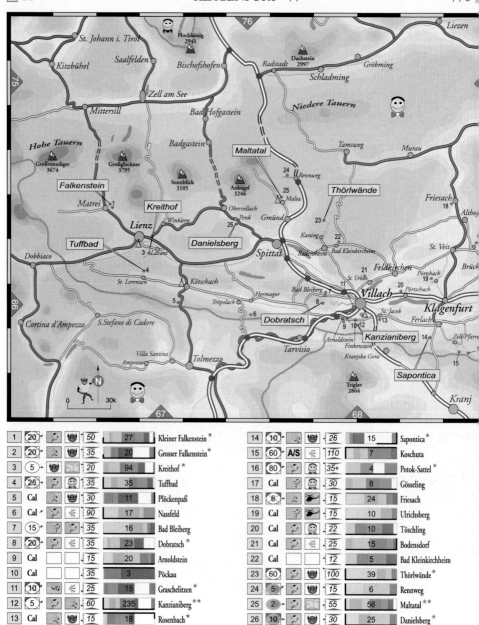

#					#				
1	20	50	27	Kleiner Falkenstein *	14	10	26	15	Sapontica *
2	20	35	20	Grosser Falkenstein *	15	60 A/S	110	7	Koschuta
3	5	20	94	Kreithof *	16	80	35+	4	Potok-Sattel *
4	25	35	35	Tuffbad	17	Cal	30	8	Gösseling
5	Cal	30	11	Plöckenpaß	18	6	15	24	Friesach
6	Cal	90	17	Nassfeld	19	Cal	15	10	Ulrichsberg
7	15	35	16	Bad Bleiberg	20	Cal	22	10	Töschling
8	20	35	23	Dobratsch *	21	Cal	25	15	Bodensdorf
9	Cal	15	20	Arnoldstein	22	Cal	12	5	Bad Kleinkirchheim
10	Cal	35	3	Pöckau	23	60	100	39	Thörlwände *
11	10	25	15	Graschelitzen *	24	5	15	6	Rennweg
12	5	60	235	Kanzianiberg **	25	2	55	56	Maltatal **
13	Cal	15	18	Rosenbach *	26	10	30	25	Danielsberg *

Some of the hard crags give 8c here, but the situation is not very good, stick to 7b's.
Es gibt hier einige 8c's, aber besser sind die 7b's.

 This whole area is generally very quiet, and offers some lovely climbing, take your pick.
Das ganze Gebiet ist sehr ruhig und bietet schöne Kletterei. Du hast die Qual der Wahl.

Topo: T71-1
Klettern in Kärnten
Ingo Neumann; 1995
176pp. 210mm x 150mm

5a-7a
Info

★ ★★★★★★★★

△ 3 - 11; 13 - 26.

€ *Buchhandlung-Heyn, Klagenfurt.* ¢-7
Hotel Zollner, Gödersdorf bei Villach

Kanzianiberg
Ingo Neuman; 1992
Mini Topo ? pp

△ 12.   🖉 **200**

€ *Hotel Zollner & Villach,* ¢-7

Österreich
T. Marschner; 1995
Topo 399 pp

△ 1,2,8,12,18,25   🖉 **200**

€ **Österreich**

△ Camping Gruber (1/5-30/9)
10km SE-Villach, (Faak am See)
Tel: 04254 2298
Fax: 04254 22987

△ Camping Maltatal (29/3-31/10)
Malta 6-7, Kärnten
Tel: 04733 234
E-mail pirker-toeristik@
lieser-maltatal.or.at

SAPONTICA

Dobratsch

Kanzianiberg

Sapontica

Maltatal

SCHUPPENRISS 5b, Friesach; Wobbly

GMÜND, Maltatal

WANDERSCHWEIN 6a+, Dobratsch; Jingo

There are lots of fantastic areas here to climb, with plenty for both the power climber and the vertical specialist. Don't miss out in the very good mountain rock to be found in the stunning Gesäuse range.

 The Sauzahn and Nixloch cliffs give some really good climbing in a lovely setting, great for the family. Sauzahn und Nixloch sind nette und familieu - freundliche felsen in schöner landschaft.

Topo: T78-1
Kletteratlas-Österreich Ost
Kurt Schall; 1996
256pp. 210mm x 150mm

? | 5a-7a Info

8,9,10,11; 13-17; 18, 25, 31, 32-35.

€ **Wien**, ¢-7
Salzburg, ¢-7

Topo: T75-1
Österreich - Rotpunkt
Timo Marschner; 1995
418pp. 199mm x 130mm

? | 5a-7a Info

1-7, 12-17, 19-29, 36-40

€ **Wien**, ¢-7
Innsbruck, ¢-7
Salzburg, ¢-7

HAINDLKARHÜTTE, GESÄUSE

Kletterfelsen von Wien bis Semmering
Chrisian Hacker

Topo | 25-32 | € ??? | 900

LAUSA

6b, Nixloch; Andreas Essl

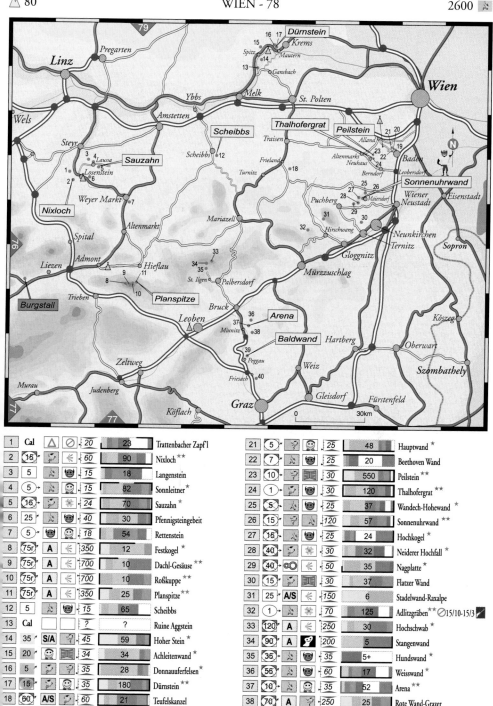

#				value	Name
1	Cal	△ ⊘	20	23	Trattenbacher Zapf'l
2	15		60	90	Nixloch **
3	5		15	18	Langenstein
4	5		15	82	Sonnleitner *
5	15		24	70	Sauzahn *
6	25		40	30	Pfennigsteingebiet
7	5		18	54	Rettenstein
8	75r	A	350	12	Festkogel *
9	75r	A	700	10	Dachl-Gesäuse **
10	75r	A	700	10	Roßkuppe **
11	75r	A	350	25	Planspitze **
12	5		15	65	Scheibbs
13	Cal		?	?	Ruine Aggstein
14	35	S/A	45	59	Hoher Stein *
15	20		34	34	Achleitenwand *
16	5		35	28	Donnauuferfelsen *
17	15		35	180	Dürnstein **
18	60	A/S	60	21	Teufelskanzel *
19	5		25	29	Jannerwandl-Helenental *
20	2		20	11	Engelsfels *
21	5		25	48	Hauptwand *
22	7		25	20	Beethoven Wand
23	10		30	550	Peilstein **
24	1		30	120	Thalhofergrat **
25	5		25	37	Wandech-Hohewand *
26	15		120	57	Sonnenuhrwand **
27	15		25	24	Hochkogel *
28	40		30	32	Neiderer Hochfall *
29	40		50	35	Nagplatte *
30	15		30	37	Flatzer Wand
31	25	A/S	150	6	Stadelwand-Raxalpe
32	1		70	125	Adlitzgräben ** ⊘15/10-15/3
33	120	A	250	30	Hochschwab *
34	90	A	200	5	Stangenwand
35	35		35	5+	Hundswand *
36	55		60	17	Weisswand *
37	10		35	52	Arena **
38	70	A	250	25	Rote Wand-Grazer
39	3		90db 35	34	Baldwand *
40	35		35	26	Hasenstein *

GENUSS 5a, Sauzahn; Andrea Kinau

The size of the sandstone towers are incredible, they are completely overpowering. The routes are all on a theme of, climb the crack to the first bolt at 15 metres! For added enjoyment, the rock is soft and wears, so grades change!

 Oh, what beautiful scenery. Perfect for walking, and true botanical involvement. I tried to climb, but was so scared, that all I wanted to do was to go home! I did see a lot of other wobblies top roping though.

Topo: T79-1
Horolezecky Pruvodce (2483 routes)
Pavel Cerny
232pp. 205mm x 145mm

⚠ Elbetal (4), Labské, Udoli a Bela

€ **Hudy Sport @ Hrensko,**
Hudy Sport @ Teplice
www.hudy.cz

Topo: T79-2 & 3 Weird Grades!!!!
Adrspach-1 & 2
Stanislav Lukavsky; 2001
288pp. 205mm x 145mm

⚠ 19

€ **Redpoint @ Teplicke,**
Camping Stransky @ Ardspach,

Topo: T79-4
Böhmischer Sandstein
Pádlo Werdermann; 1994
263pp. 185mm x 145mm

⚠ 1 - 19

€ **Palm & Enke @ Erlangen (D),**

⚠ Camping Stransky (15/4-30/9)
Dolní Ardspach, Pod Skalama 99, Teplicke.
Tel: 0441 48 32 67

⚠ Camping Malá Scála (1/5-30/9)
Malá Scála, c.p. 509.
Tel: 0428 39 21 57

⚠ Intercamp (1/4-30/10)
Jetrovice,.
Tel:

⚠ Camping Tisá (15/4-15/10)
Tisá
Tel: 047 512 02 54

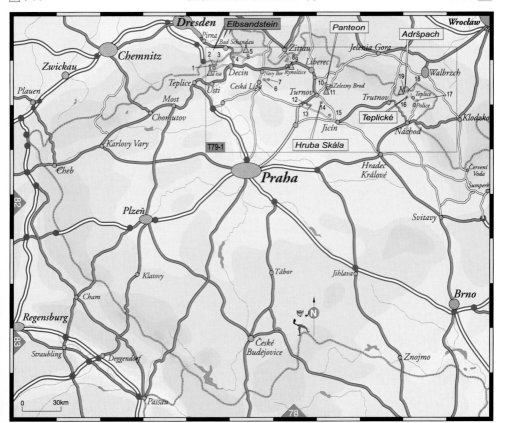

1	10 →	C	🧗	60	<60(C)>	Rájec
2	5 →	C	🧗	50	<200(C)>	Tisá
3	5 →	C	🧗	90	<70(C)>	Ostrov
4	5 →	C	747	60	<2483(C)>	Labské Udoli, Bela
5	15 →	C	🧗	50	<60(C)>	Jetrichovice
6	San	C	🧗	40	<20(C)>	Sloup
7	San	C	🧗	?	<30(C)>	Svojkov
8	San	C	🧗	?	<30(C)>	Horni Skály
9	San	C	🧗	?	<30(C)>	Krkavci Skály
10	10 →	⇐	🧗	35	<90(C)>	Panteon**
11	San	C	🧗	55	<130(C)>	Suche Skály
12	San	C	🧗	?	<40(C)>	Drabske Svetnicky
13	San	C	🧗	55	<120(C)>	Prihrazy
14	1 →	C	🧗	70	<400(C)>	Hruba Skála *
15	San	C	🧗	70	<80(C)>	Prachov
16	15 →	Zzz	🧗	40	<200(C)>	Horni Laybrint *
17	30 →	⇐	🧗	150	<400(C)>	Teplické Skály *
18	15 →	Zzz	🧗	30	<90(C)>	Krížový Vrch *
19	5 →	☀	🧗	70	<2500(C)>	Adršpach *

ARDSPASSKE SKALY

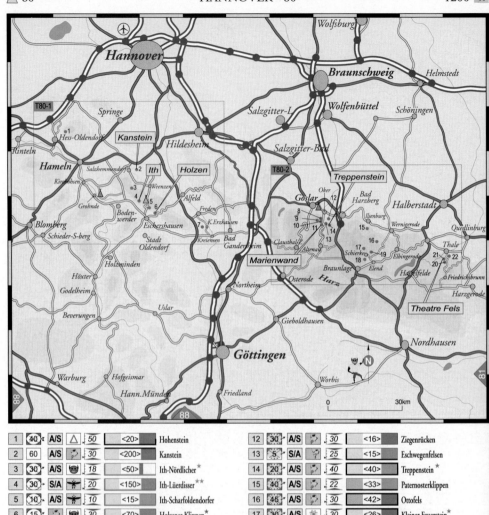

1	40	A/S	△	50	<20>	Hohenstein
2	60	A/S		30	<200>	Kanstein
3	30	A/S		18	<50>	Ith-Nördlicher *
4	30	S/A		20	<150>	Ith-Lüerdisser **
5	10	A/S		10	<15>	Ith-Scharfoldendorfer *
6	15			30	<70>	Holzener Klippen *
7	30	S/A		20	<30>	Selter *
8	10	A/S		30	<48>	Alderklippe
9	20	A/S		40	<18>	Uhuklippe
10	5	A/S		30	<27>	Schlafender Löwe
11	5	S/A		50	<44>	Marienwand - Okertal *
12	30	A/S		30	<16>	Ziegenrücken
13	5	S/A		25	<15>	Eschwegenfelsen
14	20	A/S		40	<40>	Treppenstein *
15	40	A/S		22	<33>	Paternosterklippen
16	45	A/S		30	<42>	Ottofels
17	30	A/S	❄	30	<26>	Kleiner Feuerstein *
18	20	A/S		20	<35>	Schnarcherklippe *
19	30	A/S		15	<25>	Vogelherdklippe
20	10	A/S		15	<24>	Hintere Wand
21	15	A/S		30	<45>	Theatre Fels *
22	10	A/S		14	<13>	Feuerschiff - Steinbachtak

The area of the Ith is good, powerful Calcaire. A lot of the cliffs are in the trees and can stay damp in winter. A lot of the routes have bolts, but a full rack of gear is very usefull. Can get very popular at weekends, but still great fun.

 The Harz mountains are really oversize hills, with very thick and dense forests. You need a map to find the cliffs. A lot of the cliffs are very quiet and even though they are small, they offer good small routes; the mosquitos can be very annoying.

Topo: T80-1
Deutschland Vertical
H-D Brunner, M. Lochner; 1987
320pp. 210mm x 150mm

Ⓣ Ⓘ ? | 5a-7a
Info | 🏴 | 📷

⊙⊙ ★ ★★★ ★ Ⓓ★★ ★

△ 1, 2, 4, 6, 7, +++Deutschland

€ ???

Topo: T80-2
Wo die Felsennasen schnarchen
W. Brandt, G. Wiechmann; 1998
216pp. 200mm x 140mm

Ⓣ Ⓘ ? | 5a-7a
Info | 🏴 | 📷

🌳 ★★★★★★ Ⓓ★★ ★★

△ 8 - 22 ++

€ **Brumby Buchhandlung**
Breite Str. 7, 38640 Goslar, ¢-7
info@brumby.de

△ Camping Grohnder Fährhaus (1/1-31/12)
An der Fähre 1, 31860 Emmerthal, Grohnde.
East (Ost) - Wesser river.

△ Camping Ith (1/1-31/12)
4km N, Eschershausen.

△ Camping Harz (1/1-31/12)
Göttingerode, 38667 Bad Harzburg.
4km E, Goslar.

KAMEL, Ith

DRACHENTÖTER 7, Holzen; Holger Koch

GROHNDE

GOSLAR

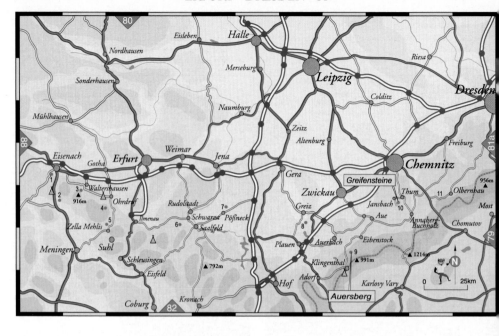

FALKENSTEIN   *SCHRAMMSTEIN*

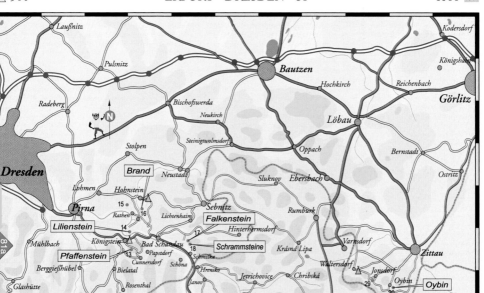

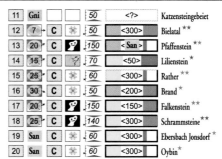

1	?	A		50	<16>	Eisnach
2	?			20	<?>	Bad Liebenstein
3	Vol			60	<100>	Taberz
4	Vol	A/S		100	<50> ?	Tambach-Dietharz
5	Vol			?	<?>	Zella Mehlis
6				?	<?>	Schwarzatal
7	Cal			10	<?>	Döbritzer Kalkfels
8	Sch	△		40	<?>	Steincht
9	10	A/S		30	<60>	Auersberg
10	10	A/S		45	<100>	Greifensteine *

11	Gni			50	<?>	Katzensteingebeiet
12	7	C		50	<300>	Bielatal **
13	20	C		150	< San >	Pfaffenstein **
14	15	C		70	<50>	Lilienstein *
15	25	C		60	<300>	Rather **
16	30	C		50	<200>	Brand *
17	20	C		150	<150>	Falkenstein **
18	25	C		140	<300>	Schrammsteine **
19	San	C		60	<300>	Ebersbach Jonsdorf *
20	San	C		60	<300>	Oybin *

There is no shortage of good routes and good cliffs here. There are very few bolts! and the first one, is usually very high up indeed! A tremendous place, with a fantastic feeling and atmosphere. Very worrying for leading though!!!

The Sandstein of the Elbe valley is quite soft, and there is hardly any good bouldering. Most protection is from knotted slings, and this is essential. Fall factor 1 and upwards is possible around hanging belays, use an 11mm rope at least!

Topo: T81: 1-10
Elbsandsteingebirge
Various; 1995-2000
200pp. 162mm x 120mm
ⓔ **Bergsport Arnold**
  Hohnstein, ¢-7

5a-7a
Info

△ 12 - 20 +++.

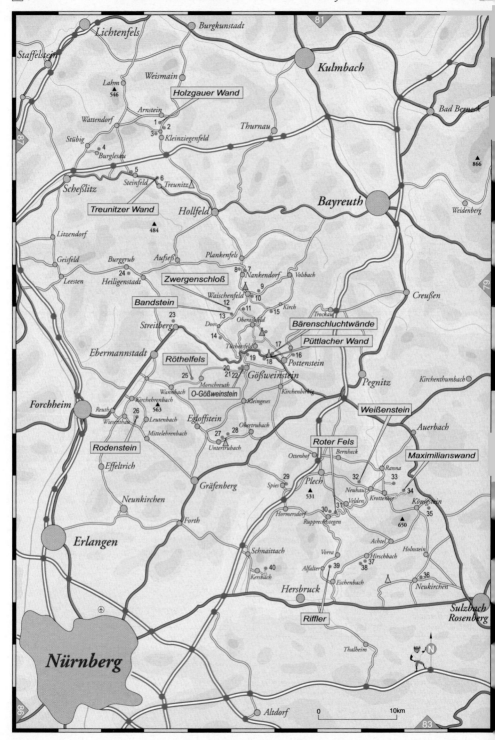

The most important power area in Germany, but the handholds get increasingly painful after each day.
Das wichtigste Kraft-Klettergebiet Deutschlands, aber die Griffe werden mit jedem Klettertag schmerzhafter.

 You need technique here as well as strength. A lot of the quieter cliffs are lovely, so stay a while to discover more.
Du brauchst hier sowohl Technik als auch Kraft. Viele der ruhiger gelegenen Gebiete sind sehr schön, also lass dir Zeit zum Entdecken.

Topo: T82-1
Nördlicher Frankenjura
Bernhard Thum; 2003
700pp. 210mm x 150mm

5a-7a
Info

△ 1-40 ++++++

© *Camping Eichler @ U/trubach,*
Sports @ Pottenstein, ¢-7
Palm & Enke @ Erlangen, ¢-7
www.frankenjura.de
info@frankenjura.de

Topo: T82-2
Frankenjura Band 2 - South
Sebastien Schwertner; 2002
344pp. 185mm x 150mm

5a-7a
Info

△ 25-40 ++++

© *Camping Eichler @ U/trubach,*
Sports @ Pottenstein, ¢-7
Palm & Enke @ Erlangen, ¢-7

Nord-Band 1
S.Schwertner; 2003
376

Topo

△ 1-24   600

© *Camping Eichler*

Camping Bärenschlucht (01/1-31/12)
91278 Pottenstein.
Tel: +49 (0) 9243 206
Fax: +49 (0) 9243 880

△ *Camping Eichler (01/4-01/10)*
Wolfsberg 43, Obertrubach.
Tel: +49 (0) 9245 1383
Fax: +49 (0) 9245 19116

⊘ *Dogs, Chien, Hund, Cane, Perro.*

△ *Camping Jurahöe (01/1-31/12)*
Kleinlesau 9, 91278 Pottenstein.
Tel: +49 (0) 9243 9173
Fax: +49 (0) 9243 9174

HELDBRÄU 'DUNKEN PARADISE'

#	Grade					Name
1	(10)		31	31		Holtzgauer Wand **
2	(5)		28	28		Rote Wand
3	(5)		23	15		Ziegenfelder Wand *
4	(5)		18	43		Burglesaur Wand *
5	(1)		20	24		Steinfelder Turm *
6	(2)		16	39		Treunitzer Wand *
7	Cal		25	8		Mader Ged.-Wand *
8	Cal		18	17		Freunenhaus-Aalkorber Wände *
9	(2)		15	8+(9 F7c)		Waischenfelder Turm *
10	(1)		20	4		Freistein *
11	(5)		30	9		Dooser Wand *
12	(15)		20	17		Zwergenschloß *
13	(5)		35	13		Bandstein *
14	Cal	747	45	16		Wolkensteiner Wand *
15	(2)		25	12		Heldwand *
16	Cal		15	34		Marientaler Wand *
17	(2)		22	36		Bärenschluchtwände **
18	(2)	90db	28	29		Püttlacher Wand **
19	Cal		30	15		Dornröschwand *
20	(5)		22	65		Eibenwände *
21	(5)		30	21		Napoleon *
22	(4)	747	20	32		Obere Goßweinsteiner Wände *
23	(5)		30	22		Streitberger Schild *
24	Cal		30	29		Rotenstein *
25	(15)	A	32	110		Röthenfels *
26	(10)	A	23	44		Rodenstein *
27	(2)		22	20		Richard Wagner Fels *
28	(5)		30	27		Zehnerstein *
29	Cal		15	24		Hohe Reute *
30	Cal		25	25		Ankatalwand *
31	(5)		40	43		Roter Fels *
32	(1)		15	31		Weißenstein *
33	Cal		28	12		Rabenfels *
34	(5)	747	20	73		Maximillian's/Krottensee Turm **
35	Cal		16	40		Kühlochfels *
36	Cal		16	36		Hartenfels *
37	Cal		24	61		Schlaraffenland *
38	Cal	747	27	27		Mittelbergwand *
39	( )		30	27		Riffler *
40	Cal		28	24		Glatzenstein *

Holzgauer Wand

Wallersberg
Arnstein
Gr-
Ziegenfeld
Kl-

Cal: **Z F T** ◄—800m—►

Bandstein

Zwergenschloß
Bandstein
Doos

Cal: **Z H** ◄—150m—►

Obere Gößweinsteiner Wände

Gößweinstein

Cal: **F R** ◄—150m—►

Maximillianswand

Krottensee
Maximilliansgrotte

Cal: **F Z H** ◄—500m—►

STREITBERGER SCHILD

SEKUNDANT 7-, Rodenstein; Johannes Ottl

FÜR CONNY 7, Roter Fels; Carmen Barske

KRAMPFHAMMER 9, Weißenstein; Christian Schart

ZWERGENSCHLOSS

GUNTHER PRIEM U 42, 9, Heldwand; Michaela Karrasch

SUDWESTKANTE 6-, Steinfelder Turm; Detlef Fuchs

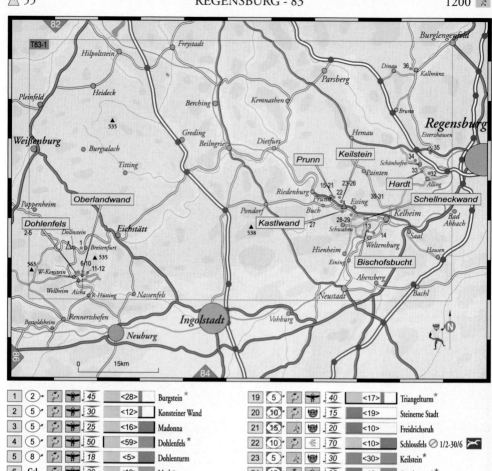

1	②		☀	45	<28>		Burgstein*
2	⑤		☀	30	<12>		Konsteiner Wand
3	⑤		☀	25	<16>		Madonna
4	⑤		☀	50	<59>		Dohlenfels*
5	⑧		☀	18	<5>		Dohlenturm
6	Cal		☀	30	<19>		Merltürme
7	Cal		☀	30	<21>		Weiße Wand
8	Cal		☀	30	<18>		Fensterlwand
9	Cal	S/A		20	<36>		Oberlandwand
10	Cal	S/A		17	<17>		Zahn
11	Cal	S/A		18	<21>		Lochwand
12	Cal	S/A		17	<33>		Oberländer Wandl
13	⑮		🐟	70	<34>		Bischofsbucht*
14	⑳	⑤	←	80	<16>		Römerwand*
15	⑤	✗	S/A	45	<24>		Prunner Turm
16	⑤	✗	S/A	40	<28>		Prunner Wand
17	⑤		😊	30	<31>		Mühltor*
18	⑤		747	26	<25>		Felskirchl
19	⑤		☀	40	<17>		Triangelturm*
20	⑩		😊	15	<19>		Steinerne Stadt
21	⑮	✗	😊	20	<10>		Freidrichsruh
22	⑩		←	70	<10>		Schlossfels ⊘ 1/2-30/6 🐟
23	⑤		😊	30	<30>		Keilstein*
24	⑩		☀	35	<16>		Quaderwand*
25	⑩	✗		20	<9>		Waldkopf
26	⑩		😊	40	<26>		Bärenkopf*
27	⑩		747	60	<65>		Kastlwand**
28	⑩		😊	35	<10>		Mayfels*
29	⑩		😊	30	<10>		Klausfels
30	①	✗	😊	25	<6>		Schellneckkopf* ⊘1/2-30/6 🐟
31	④		☀	50	<40>		Schellneckwand* ⊘1/2-30/6 🐟
32	Cal		😊	17	<31>		Allinger Wände
33	Cal	✗		20	<50>		Hardt
34	Cal	S/A	😊	35	<51>		Labertal
35	Cal		😊	15	<17>		Etterzhausener Wände
36	Cal		😊	15	<25>		Vilstal

A lot of the rock at Prunn is polished, and you need a lot more strenght than normal. The harder routes are mostly very technical on small pockets and are very sustained.

 Lots of technical desperate classics (S-neck). Also, there are many esoteric spots by the Danube, if you can find them!

Topo: T83-1
Südlicher Frankenjura
Hans-Dieter Brunner; 1999
272pp. 210mm x 150mm

| T | I | ? | 5a-7a Info | | |

△ 1 - 36.

€ **Gasthaus Zur Krone-Prunn,**
Buchhandling Bauer - Kelheim, ¢-7

Landgasthof Kastlhof (1/1-31/12)
Pillhausen (3km-Essing dir Riedenburg)
Tel: 094 47 698

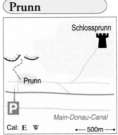

Prunn

Schlossprunn

Prunn

P

Main-Donau-Canal

Cal: E W ←500m→

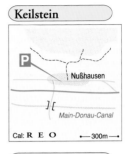

Keilstein

P

Nußhausen

] [

Main-Donau-Canal

Cal: R E O ←300m→

Kastlwand

Nußhausen

Pillhausen
△

] [
Main-Donau-Canal

P

Cal: F O ←1.5km→

Schellneckwand

Essing
1/2-30/6

] [

Main-Donau-Canal

P

Cal: F O ←800m→

SCHELLNECKWAND >

KASTLWAND

DEUTSCHLAND - 84

6+, FRAUENWASSERL

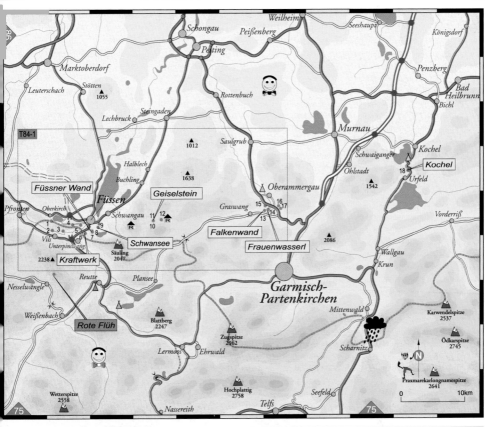

1	20			30?	<15>	Neufundland
2	25	S/A		100	<4>	Bui Wand
3	15	S/A		30?	<15>	Müllplatzplatten
4	20			35	<20>	Schwärzer Wand *
5	15			?	<20>	Bad Faulenbach
6	10			40	<50>	Kraftwerk *
7	15			35+	<50>	Füssner Wand *
8	15			35	<50>	Schwanseeplatten *
9	20			?	<10>	Schatzkiste
10	90r	A/S		250	<20>	Geiselstein-Südwand **
11	90r	A/S		250	<20>	Geiselstein-Nordwand **
12	40r	A/S		175	<10>	Kenzenkopf *
13	15			35+	<50>	Falkenwand **
14	2			80	<25>	Frauenwasserl *
15	20			35+	<36>	Kofel *
16	2			35	<10>	Bärenhöhle
17	10			35	<30>	Kraxentrager *
18	5			35	<60>	Kochel *

Topo: T84-2:   Kochel - 2003
Mini Topo   120pp   www.panico.de

Topo: T84-1
Ammergau
M. Lutz, R. Heiland; 1999
68pp + 40 topo. 180mm x 115mm

5a-7a
Info

⌂ 1 - 17.

Ⓔ *Füssen*, ¢-7
www.panico.de
www.urbanrock.com

FALKENWAND

Not a very good area for the full-on power monkey. There are a few spots to get pumped, but nothing to rival the bouldering and ferocity of Basel Jura cliffs. Battert still gives some quite hard routes though.

 The Black forest (Schwarzwald) are big, high rolling hills. A lot of the cliffs are in the trees, and just the top of the rock sticks out. A lovely quiet area with a lot of the routes in the easier grades being well equipped.

Topo: T85-1
Klettern im Dreiländereck
Christian Frick; 1998
288pp. 150mm x 210mm

€ **Freiburg:**
Adventure Company
₵-7

5a-7a
Info

⚠ 6,7,8,9,10,11,12,13,14.

KNAUTSCHZONE 6-, Scheibenfelsen; Tobias Hauser

FREIBURG

#							Name
1	Vol			65	<200>		Battert**
2	Gra	A/S		50	<20>		KGB Türme-Falkenwand*
3	Gra	A/S		50	<20>		Wiedenfelsen*
4	Gra	A/S		40	<25>		Ruine Berneck
5	Gra	A/S		40	<40>		Schloßfelsen
6	Gni			30	<35>		Kostgefäll
7	Gni			25	<32>		Kandelfels
8	10			35	<32>		Scheibenfelsen*
9	25			30	<90>		Gefällfelsen*
10	3			18	<40>		Harzlochfelsen
11	2			25	<20>		Altvogelbach
12	10			30	<85>		Schwimmbad**
13	3			35	<45>		Windbergfels*
14	5			25	<50>		Albbruck*
15	Vol			20	<30>		Falkenstein
16	Gra			100	<20>		Tannholzfluh

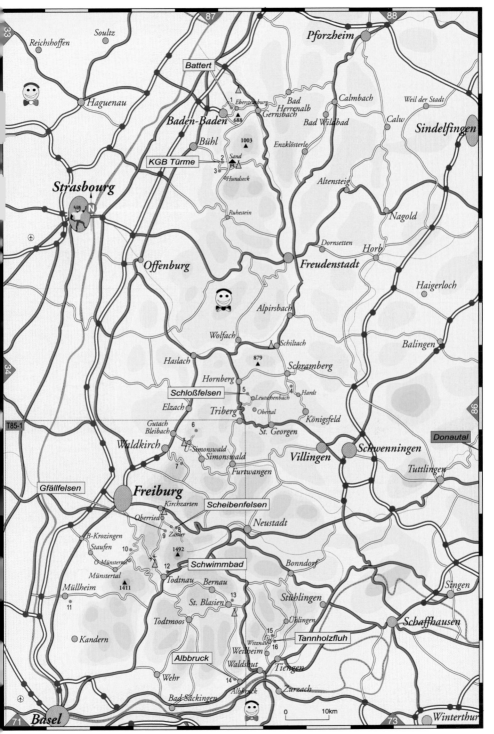

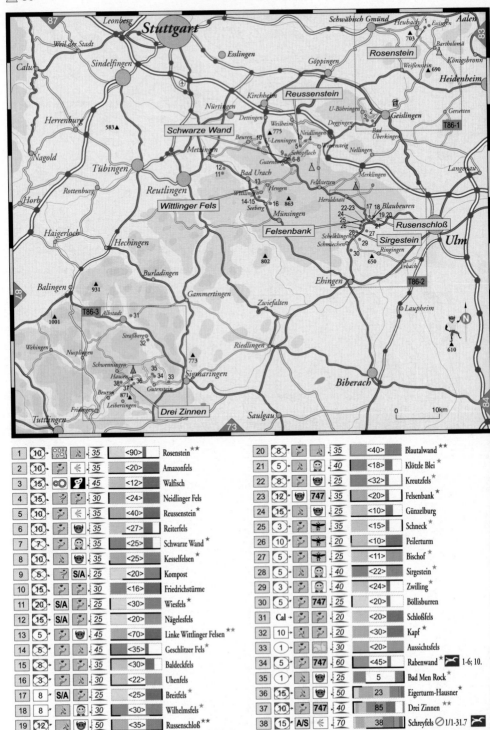

1	(10)			35	<90>	Rosenstein **
2	(10)			35	<20>	Amazonfels
3	(15)			45	<12>	Walfisch
4	(15)			30	<24>	Neidlinger Fels
5	(10)			35	<40>	Reussenstein *
6	(10)			35	<27>	Reiterfels
7	(7)			35	<25>	Schwarze Wand *
8	(10)			35	<25>	Kesselfelsen *
9	(5)		S/A	25	<20>	Kompost
10	(15)			30	<16>	Friedrichstürme
11	(20)	S/A		25	<30>	Wiesfels *
12	(15)	S/A		25	<20>	Nägelesfels
13	(5)			45	<70>	Linke Wittlinger Felsen **
14	(5)			45	<35>	Geschlitzer Fels *
15	(8)			35	<30>	Baldeckfels
16	(3)			30	<22>	Uhenfels
17	8	S/A		25	<25>	Breitfels *
18	8			30	<30>	Wilhelmsfels *
19	(12)			50	<35>	Russenschloß **

20	(8)			35	<40>	Blautalwand **
21	(5)			40	<18>	Klötzle Blei *
22	(8)			25	<32>	Kreutzfels *
23	(12)		747	35	<20>	Felsenbank *
24	(15)			25	<10>	Günzelburg
25	(3)			35	<15>	Schneck *
26	(10)			20	<10>	Peilerturm *
27	(5)			25	<11>	Bischof *
28	(5)			40	<22>	Sirgestein *
29	(3)			40	<24>	Zwilling *
30	(5)		747	25	<20>	Böllisburren *
31	Cal			20	<20>	Schloßfels
32	10			20	<30>	Kapf *
33	1			30	<20>	Aussichtsfels
34	5		747	60	<45>	Rabenwand * 1-6; 10.
35	1			25	5	Bad Men Rock *
36	(15)			50	23	Eigerturm-Hausner *
37	(10)		747	40	85	Drei Zinnen **
38	(15)	A/S		70	38	Schreyfels ⊘ 1/1-31.7

Lots of superb climbing here. If you are on the strong side, it is best to go to Blautal, lots of very good hard climbing, and some very steep, daunting moves above bolts! Some very good hidden gems, so spend time discovering this area.

 Some lovely exposed climbing above the Donau, and with a great rural aspect. Some of the cliffs have total bird restrictions, but the best rock is virtually unaffected. Very quiet and peaceful in the summer, and usually - not too hot either.

Topo: T86-1 *Updated 2002*
Ostalb
A. Eller, A. Pasold, L. Weber; 1997
152pp. 185mm x 150mm

5a-7a Info

⚠ 1 - 3, + 🏠

€ Stuttgart, ¢-7
www.panico.com

Topo: T86-2 *Updated 2002*
Blautal
A. Buck, A. Lonhard, B. Richter; 1997
128pp. 185mm x 150mm

5a-7a Info

⚠ 17 - 30 +++

€ Stuttgart, ¢-7
www.panico.com

Topo: T86-3 *Updated 2003*
Donautal
M. Pegler, R. Stöhr; 1998
168pp. 185mm x 150mm

5a-7a Info

⚠ 31 - 38.

€ Stuttgart, ¢-7
www.panico.com

Lenninger
Panico; 2003
144pp

Mini Topo

⚠ 4 - 10   250

€ ??

Uracher
Panico; 2000
168pp

Mini Topo

⚠ 11-16   250

€ ??

BOULDER, SCHNURRPULUS 7-, Aussichtsfels;

SÜDRIß 8+, Felsenbank;

RENAISSANCE 6+, Zweite Zinne, Drei Zinnen; Sue Füellemann

REUSSENSTEIN

ALTE BLAUTALWAND 8, Blautalwand; Sybille Bessor

EIGERTURM SUPERDIREKT 6+, Drei Zinnen; Jürgen Füellemann

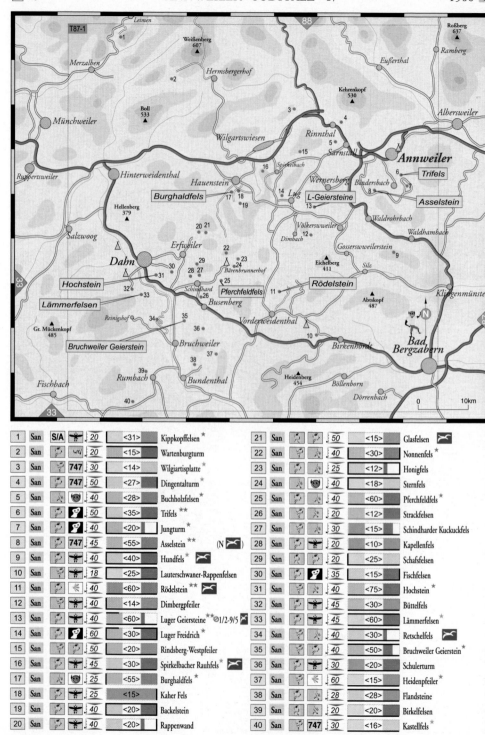

1	San	S/A	20	<31>	Kippkopffelsen *		21	San	50	<15>	Glasfelsen
2	San		20	<15>	Wartenburgturm		22	San	40	<30>	Nonnenfels *
3	San	747	30	<14>	Wilgiartisplatte *		23	San	25	<12>	Honigfels
4	San	747	50	<27>	Dingentalturm *		24	San	40	<18>	Sternfels *
5	San		40	<28>	Buchholzfelsen *		25	San	60	<60>	Pferchfeldfels *
6	San		50	<35>	Trifels **		26	San	20	<12>	Strackfelsen
7	San		40	<20>	Jungturm *		27	San	30	<15>	Schindharder Kuckuckfels *
8	San	747	45	<55>	Asselstein ** (N)		28	San	20	<10>	Kapellenfels
9	San		40	<40>	Hundfels		29	San	20	<25>	Schafsfelsen
10	San		18	<25>	Lauterschwaner-Rappenfelsen		30	San	35	<15>	Fischfelsen
11	San		40	<60>	Rödelstein **		31	San	40	<75>	Hochstein *
12	San		40	<14>	Dimbergpfeiler		32	San	45	<30>	Büttelfels
13	San		40	<60>	Luger Geiersteine ** ⌀1/2-9/5		33	San	45	<60>	Lämmerfelsen *
14	San		60	<30>	Luger Freidrich *		34	San	40	<30>	Retschelfels
15	San		50	<20>	Rindsberg-Westpfeiler		35	San	40	<50>	Bruchweiler Geierstein *
16	San		45	<30>	Spirkelbacher Rauhfels *		36	San	30	<20>	Schulerturm
17	San		25	<55>	Burghaldfels *		37	San	60	<15>	Heidenpfeiler *
18	San		25	<15>	Kaher Fels		38	San	28	<28>	Flandsteine
19	San		40	<20>	Backelstein		39	San	20	<20>	Birkelfelsen *
20	San		40	<20>	Rappenwand		40	San	747	30	<16>	Kastellfels *

This is an area with some of the best Sandstein climbing on the whole planet! Some of the bolts are quite far apart, but there is usually one just beneath the real hard and powerful moves. A lot of climbing in the shade of the trees also.

 Sandstein is always technical, and here you have an excellent combination of longer hard routes, and individual hard boulder moves. Sometimes you just pull on a tiny pebble embedded in the Sandstein - if you can. Humid in summer.

Topo: T87-1
Südpfalz
Jürgen Wesley; 1996
276pp. 210mm x 150mm

5a-7a
Info

🔺 1 - 40

€ **Bärenbrunnerhof (24)**

Pfalz-Boulder
Panico; 2003
116pp 148x185mm
Mini Topo

🔺?.

€ ? NEW

PERESTROIKA 6+, Luger Friedrich; Jingo

Not much climbing, but at least there is some. At Nideggen, you can have a frightening time on Burgfelsen, very airy; or you can go to the much steeper Effels, but as with all conglomerate, very tiring to on-sight.

 Morgenbachtal is a very popular crag with the weekend, lower grade climbers, and is in a nice setting too. A few restricitons so watch out for any notices, if in doubt; go for a beer instead.

EIFELWEG 7-, Burgwand, Burgfelsen; Wobbly

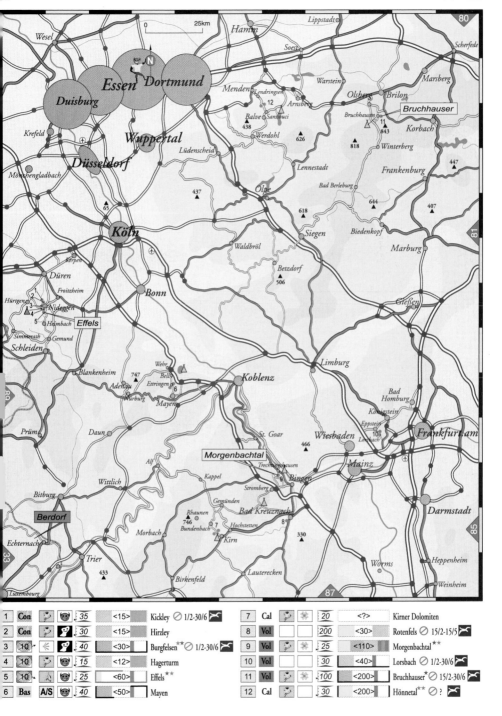

1	Con			35	<15>		Kickley ⊘ 1/2-30/6
2	Con			30	<15>		Hirzley
3	10			40	<30>		Burgfelsen** ⊘ 1/2-30/6
4	10			15	<12>		Hagerturm
5	10			25	<60>		Effels**
6	Bas	A/S		40	<50>		Mayen
7	Cal			20	<?>		Kirner Dolomiten
8	Vol			200	<30>		Rotenfels ⊘ 15/2-15/5
9	Vol			25	<110>		Morgenbachtal**
10	Vol			30	<40>		Lorsbach ⊘ 1/2-30/6
11	Vol			100	<200>		Bruchhauser* ⊘ 15/2-30/6
12	Cal			30	<200>		Hönnetal** ⊘ ?

NINA HAGEN 7a, Freyr; Barry Knight (Photo Brian Par

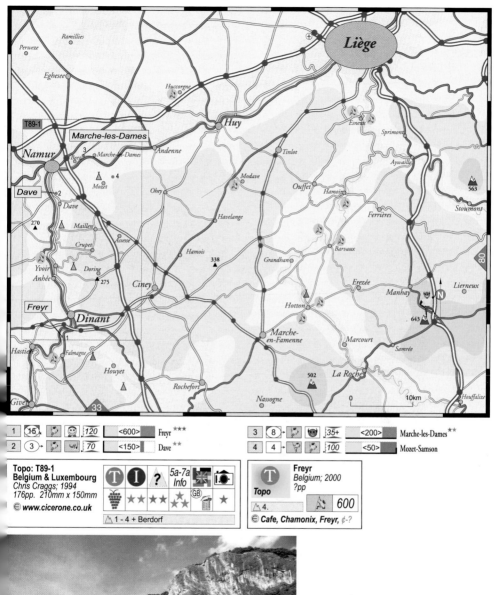

| 1 | (15) | | | 120 | <600> | Freyr ★★★ |
| 2 | (3) | | | 70 | <150> | Dave ★★ |

| 3 | 8 | | | 35+ | <200> | Marche-les-Dames ★★ |
| 4 | 4 | | | 100 | <50> | Mozet-Samson |

Topo: T89-1
Belgium & Luxembourg
Chris Craggs; 1994
176pp. 210mm x 150mm
Ⓒ **www.cicerone.co.uk**

T | I | ? | 5a-7a Info | |
★★★★ | | | GB | | ★
⛰ 1 - 4 + Berdorf

Freyr
Belgium; 2000
?pp
Topo
⛰ 4.   600
Ⓒ **Cafe, Chamonix, Freyr, ¢-?**

FREYR

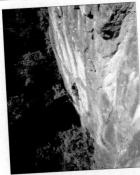

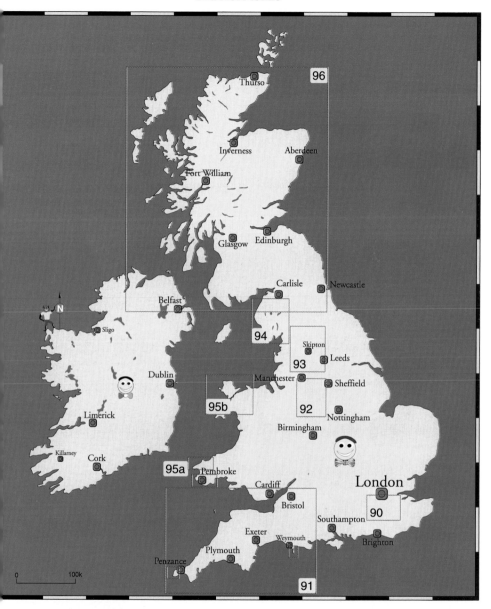

90: Tunbridge Wells
91: Plymouth (Cornwall-Devon)
92: Sheffield - Peak District
93: Leeds - Skipton
94: Keswick - Lake District
95a: Pembroke -Wales
95b: Bangor - Wales
96: Scotland

Urban Rock Shop
The Westway Climbing Centre
1 Crowthorne Road, London W10 6RP.
Tel: 020 8964 0185

Urban Rock Shop
The Castle Climbing Centre
Green Lanes, Stoke Newington,
London N4 2HA Tel: 020 8211 0475

Winter is not a good time at the rocks, but from March until the end of October, the tempertature is perfect. Nothing really hard, but beware of the locals who know all the tricks to the hard crux's.

 This Sandstone can be quite a handfull to the beginner. It does offer quite brilliant technical climbing, but you must always keep your feet clean friction is vital, so bring a mat to stand on. It's fun top roping also; and the pubs are great.

Topo: T90-1
Sandstone - South East England
David Atchison-Jones; 2000
336pp. 210mm x 150mm

T I ? | 5a-7a Info | 🏴󠁧󠁢󠁥󠁮󠁧󠁿 📷

🌳 ★ ★★★ ★★★ ★★★ ★★

⚠ 1-11.

£ Junction Inn @ Groombridge,
Huntsman Pub @ Eridge,
Village Shop @ Groombridge ¢-pm7
www.urbanrock.com

🔺 Camping Julie Tullis (1/1-31/12)
Car Park , Harrison's Rocks
🔺 Crowborough C&C Site (2/2-21/12)
Goldsmith Recreation Club,
Crowborough, East Sussex
Tel: 01892 664 827

HENRY the NINTH, 5c, High Rocks; Kim Tulli

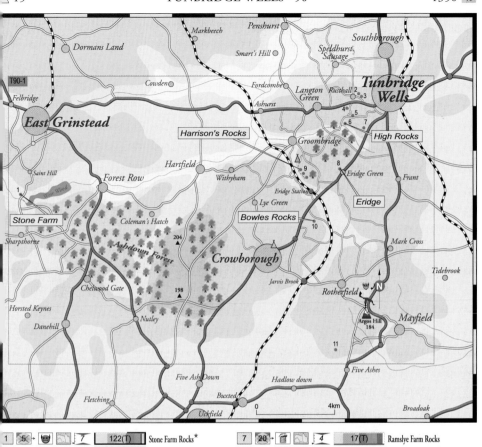

1	5	7	122(T)	Stone Farm Rocks*
2	1	3	32(B)	Toad Rock - Denny Bottom
3	4	8	58(T)	Bulls Hollow
4	5	9	42(T)	Happy Valley Rocks
5	4	6	58(T)	High Rocks Annexe *
6	1	11	296(T)	High Rocks **

7	20	4	17(T)	Ramslye Farm Rocks
8	2	8	170(T)	Eridge Green Rocks *
9	17	8	353(T)	Harrison's Rocks ***
10	1	9	160(T)	Bowles Rocks **
11	15	8	38(T)	Under Rocks *

Harrisons Rocks

San: |—1.5km—|
G P N-51,06,392~E-000,11,342
G N-51,05,846~E-000,11,195

Bowles Rocks
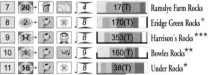
San: |—750m—|
G P N-51,04,564~E-000,12,110
G N-51,04,524~E-000,11,938

High Rocks
San: |—600m—|
G P N-51,07,306~E-000,13,502
G N-51,07,371~E-000,13,593

SILVA *Multinavigator*

HENNESEY HEIGHTS 5b, Bowles Rocks; Jo da Silva

TOUCH TOO MUCH 6b, High Rocks; Dave Pot

SHATTERED 6b, High Rocks; Barry Knight

REPUBLIC 6b, Guy McLelland

BIRCHDEN WALL 5b, Malcolm McPherson

LEFT CIRCLE 5c, Gerry Gilmartin

SMOOTH AND SLIPPERY CHIMNEY 3b, Remus Gerrar

GENESIS 5c+, Eridge Green Rocks, Virginie Percival

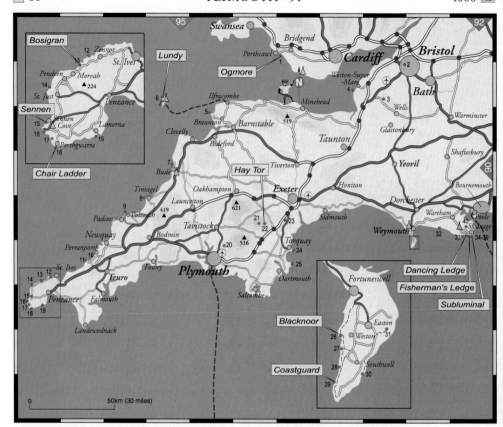

No.					Grade	Name
1	15			45	<200(N)>	Ogmore*
2	5	90db		80	<100(N)>	Avon Gorge
3	2+			100	<300(N)>	Cheddar Gorge ⊘ 1/3 - 31/10
4	45			30	<60(N)>	Brean Down*
5	15			80	<50(N)>	Baggy Point*
6	45			100	<400(N)>	Lundy*** ⊘ 1/4-31/6
7	15			45	<40(N)>	Lower Sharpnose Point*
8	15			80	<15(N)>	Tintagel*
9	20			65	<7(N)>	Pentire Head*
10	15			40	<?(N)>	Cligga Head
11	15			100	<6(N)>	Carn Gowla
12	10			100	<20(N)>	Gurnard's Head*
13	10			60	<100(N)>	Bosigran**
14	10			50	<12(N)>	Kenidjack Castle Cliffs*
15	10			10	<150(N)>	Sennen Cove**
16	10			40	<130(N)>	Land's End**
17	10			30	<150(N)>	Carn Barra-Pordenack*
18	15			60	<110(N)>	Chair Ladder**
19	30		Zzz	35	<40(N)>	Tater Dû
20	20			40	<50(N)>	Dewerstone
21	15+			4	<200>	Dartmoor Boulders**
22	20	747		24	<50(N)>	Hay Tor*
23	45			30	<40(N)>	Chudleigh
24	15			35	<40>	Anstey's Cove*
25	15			70	<20(N)>	Berry Head
26	15			30	<180>	Blacknoor**
27	10			30	<90>	Battleship Edge*
28	20			30	<80>	Wallsend*
29	20			30	<140>	Coastguard Cliffs*
30	10			30	<120>	Cheyne Cliffs
31	20			25	<25>	The Cuttings
32	20			35	<52>	Lulworth Cove* ?? ⊘
33	18			25	<37>	Winspit Quarry
34	18			35	<80>	Dancing Ledge*
35	45			50	<41(SA)>	Blackers Hole*
36	40			35	<90(N)>	Fisherman's Ledge*
37	25			35	<25(N)>	Cattle Troughs
38	20			50	<110(N)>	Boulder Ruckle
39	10			25	<60(N)>	Subluminal Cliff
40	20			8	<15>	The Agglestone

No shortage of terror here; Ogmore will scare you silly, if the tide and the rocks don't get you; Tintagel takes no prisoners; Carn "Growler" can also be particularly mean; and Bosigran 'Great Zawn' is just, swell in a storm!

 Just the place for excellent August and September holidays. Cornish granite is fantastic for all levels of climbing, Devon granite is great for bouldering, and Portland as a sports climbing oasis in England. Don't for get the sun tan cream.

Topo: T91-1
Cornish Rock
R. Edwards, T. Denell; 1997
266pp. 210mm x 150mm

△ 12 - 19
£ www.cicerone.co.uk
www.urbanrock.com

Topo: T91-2
West Cornwall (2 volumes)
John Hooper & Chums; 2000
338+328pp. 165mm x 105mm

△ 26 - 39.
£ www.urbanrock.com
❶ www.climbers-club.co.uk
❶ www.cordee.co.uk

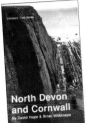

Topo: T91-3
North Devonn & Cornwall
David Hope, Brian Wilkinson; 2000
368pp. 165mm x 105mm

△ 26 - 39.
£ www.urbanrock.com
❶ www.climbers-club.co.uk
❶ www.cordee.co.uk

Topo: T91-4
Dorset
Pete Oxley; 2000
272pp. 210mm x 150mm

△ 26 - 39.
£ www.rockfax.com

THE DEVIL'S SLIDE, Lundy

SHIT ACTUALLY HAPPENS IF YOU GO OFF ROUTE 6a+++, Blacknoor: Sandy Ogilvie

Blacknoor Edge, Portland

REPTILE SMILE 6a+, Blacknoor; Guy Townsend

HELIX 3a, Fisherman's Ledge; Steve Williams

329

The bouldering is very good here, but you need to be very powerful - and have a good steady head to get the best from the larger boulders. Most of the limestone suffers from water seepage - until late June, only sport-routes above 7a!!

 Jamming of Gritstone cracks is unique to this area, using the fingers, hands, and body - very physical. There is also some friction routes, the best of these must be the gritstone arete's. Most people top rope their hard problems first, it's safer!!!!

Topo: T92-1
Peak Bouldering
Allen Williams, Alan James; 1998
224pp. 210mm x 150mm

5a-7a Info

★★ ★★ ★☆ ★★★★

△ 6, 8 - 13, 15, 18, 23-25, 31,33,36

£ **Outside Shop, Hathersage,**
Joe Royle Shop, Buxton, 7: 10-4pm
The Edge Wall, Sheffield
www.rockfax.com

Topo: T92-2
Peak Limestone   New: 2003
Alan James; 1992
224pp. 210mm x 150mm

5a-7a Info

★ ★ ★★★ ★★

△ 16, 20, 21, 26 - 36 ++++.

£ **Outside Shop, Hathersage,**
Joe Royle Shop, Buxton, 7: 10-4pm
The Edge Wall, Sheffield
www.rockfax.com

Topo: T92-3   BMC Series
Stanage
David Simmonite; 2002
376pp. 170mm x 105mm

5a-7a Info

★ ★★★★ GB ★

△ 6

£ **Outside Shop, Hathersage,**
Joe Royle Shop, Buxton, 7: 10-4pm
The Edge Wall, Sheffield

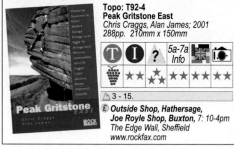

Topo: T92-4
Peak Gritstone East
Chris Craggs, Alan James; 2001
288pp. 210mm x 150mm

5a-7a Info

★★★ ★☆ ★★★★★★

△ 3 - 15.

£ **Outside Shop, Hathersage,**
Joe Royle Shop, Buxton, 7: 10-4pm
The Edge Wall, Sheffield
www.rockfax.com

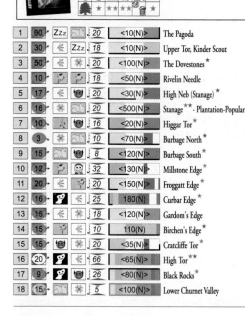

BMC Series
Stanage-Millstone; Derwent Gritstone,
Peak Limestone - 2 Vols;
Chew Valley; Staffordshire Gritstone.

5a-7a Info

★ ★★★★ GB ★

#						Name
1	60	Zzz		20	<10(N)>	The Pagoda
2	30		Zzz	18	<10(N)>	Upper Tor, Kinder Scout
3	50			20	<100(N)>	The Dovestones *
4	10			18	<50(N)>	Rivelin Needle
5	17			20	<30(N)>	High Neb (Stanage) *
6	16			20	<500(N)>	Stanage ** - Plantation-Popular
7	10			16	<20(N)>	Higgar Tor *
8	3			10	<70(N)>	Burbage North *
9	15			8	<120(N)>	Burbage South *
10	12			32	<130(N)>	Millstone Edge *
11	20			20	<150(N)>	Froggatt Edge *
12	16			25	180(N)	Curbar Edge *
13	15			18	<120(N)>	Gardom's Edge *
14	15			10	110(N)	Birchen's Edge *
15	15			20	<35(N)>	Cratcliffe Tor *
16	20			66	<65(N)>	High Tor **
17	9			26	<80(N)>	Black Rocks *
18	15			5	<100(N)>	Lower Churnet Valley
19	15		Zzz	18	<20(N)>	Harston Rock
20	20	Zzz		30	<60(N)>	Dovedale Valley
21	10			40	<40(N)>	Beeston Tor *
22	15			35	<110(N)>	Hen Cloud
23	16			40	<120(N)>	The Roaches **
24	5			10	<150(N)>	Ramshaw Rocks *
25	10			8	<60(N)>	Newstones-Baldstones
26	20			40	<20(N)>	Plum Buttress *
27	25			15	<25(S)>	Embankment
28	35			30+	<70(SN)>	Two Tier Buttress *
29	45			40	<80(N)>	Chee Tor *
30	45			30	<80(S)>	Cornice-Cheedale *
31	1			35+	<50(S)>	Raven Tor *
32	20			25	<30(S)>	Water-cum-Jolly (Cornice)
33	7			18	<45(S)>	Rubicon Wall *
34	18			50	30(N)	Ravensdale
35	15			35	<50(S)>	Horseshoe Quarry
36	10			60	<150(N)>	Stoney Middleton **

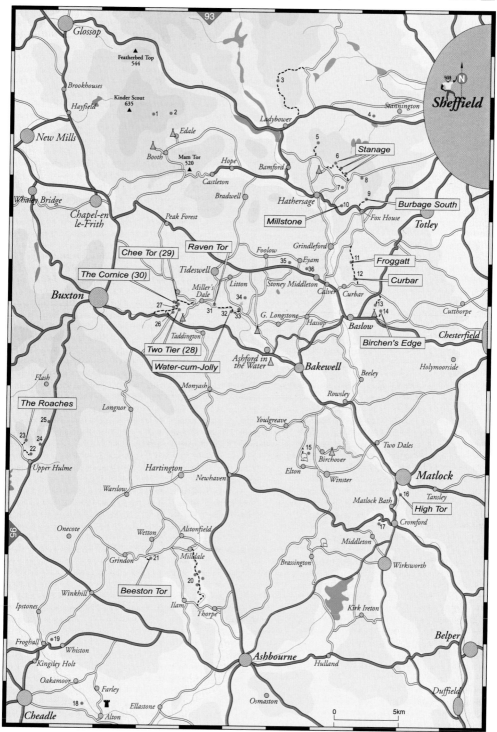

TOPAZ E4 6a, Stanage Edge; Ed Cox

MECCA 8b+, Raven's Tor; Mark Leach

HUBBLE 8c+, Raven's Tor; Ben Moon

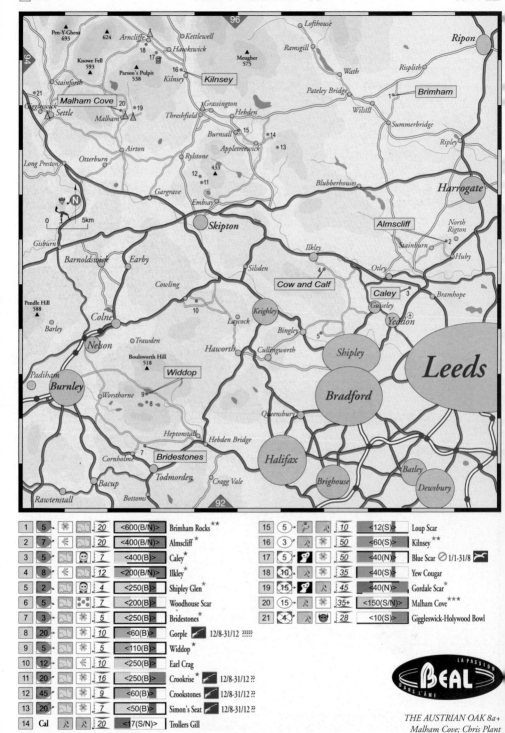

1	5	❄		20	<600(B/N)>	Brimham Rocks ★★
2	7			20	<400(B/N)>	Almscliff ★
3	5		😀	7	<400(B)>	Caley ★
4	8			12	<200(B/N)>	Ilkley ★
5	2		😀	4	<250(B)>	Shipley Glen ★
6	5		⠿	7	<200(B)>	Woodhouse Scar
7	3		❄	5	<250(B)>	Bridestones ★
8	20		❄	10	<60(B)>	Gorple 12/8-31/12 ?????
9	5		❄	5	<110(B)>	Widdop ★
10	12			10	<250(B)>	Earl Crag
11	20		❄	16	<250(B)>	Crookrise ★ 12/8-31/12 ??
12	45		❄	9	<60(B)>	Crookstones 12/8-31/12 ??
13	20		❄	7	<50(B)>	Simon's Seat 12/8-31/12 ??
14	Cal			20	<17(S/N)>	Trollers Gill
15	5			10	<12(S)>	Loup Scar
16	3			50	<60(S)>	Kilnsey ★★
17	5			50	<40(N)>	Blue Scar ⊘ 1/1-31/8
18	10		❄	35	<40(S)>	Yew Cougar
19	15			45	<40(N)>	Gordale Scar ★
20	15		❄	35+	<150(S/N)>	Malham Cove ★★★
21	4		😀	28	<10(S)>	Giggleswick-Holywood Bowl

THE AUSTRIAN OAK 8a+
Malham Cove; Chris Plant

There are plenty of Gritstone-urban dead quarries, but the small outcrops on the top of the moors, offer wonderful bouldering, and in lovely remote settings. Some are a bit on the high side, so a rope and gear can be useful.

 You need to be strong to get the best out of the limestone in Yorkshire, Malham for sun and Kilnsey for shade- both are very impressive. There are many other crags in the area, but the rock tends to be shattered and loose, nice and quiet.

Topo: T93-1
Yorkshire Gritstone Bouldering
Alan Cameron-Duff; 2000
320pp. 210mm x 150mm

1 - 13. (+)

£ **The Leeds Wall, (Armley) W-Leeds.**
True North, 26 Otley Road, Leeds.
www.rockfax.com

Topo: T93-2 New edition 8'2002
Yorkshire Limestone
Mick Ryan; 1989
94pp. 210mm x 150mm

14 - 21.

£ **The Leeds Wall, (Armley) W-Leeds.**
True North, 26 Otley Road, Leeds.
www.rockfax.com

FREE AND EVEN EASIER 7a+, Malham Cove; Simon Nadin

GREAT WESTERN VS, Almscliff; Nigel Birtwell

There is some tough bouldering in the lakes, but not much in the way of steep routes. The main difficulty remains in the mental attitude of using natural protection, and keeping your legs from shaking! Route finding is also very tricky.

 The Lake District is pictorially gentle, and the best climbing is to be ,found on tricky, technical walls or slabs. The views are mostly stunning, and the approach walks - usually quiet! Climbing in the low grades, is some of the best in Britain.

Topo: T94-1
The Lakes
A. Hyslop, P. Cornforth; 1994
192pp. 210mm x 150mm

| T | I | ? | 5a-7a Info | | |

| ★ | ★★ | ★★★ | ★★ |

⚠ 1, 7, 8, 9, 39, 40.

💷 *Rock & Run, Ambleside, ¢-7*
Needle Sports, Keswick, ¢-7
www.rockfax.com

T94-2 Buttermere & Eastern Crags
T94-3 Borrowdale
T94-4 Langdale
T94-5 Scafell, Wasdale & Eskdale
T95-6 Gable and Pillar
T95-7 Dow, Duddon, Slate
Fell and Rock Club. 1994-2000
364pp. 165mm x 102mm

| T | I | ? | 5a-7a Info | | |

| ★ | ★ | ★★ GB | ★★ |

⚠ T94-2 [2-5,14-18]; T94-3 [6, 9-13]
T94-4 [19-24]; T94-5 [25,26,31-33]
T94-6 [27-30]; T94-7 [35-38]

💷 *Rock & Run, Ambleside, ¢-7*
Needle Sports, Keswick, ¢-7
www.frcc.co.uk

THE DANGLER, E2 5c,
Lower Falcon Crag, Borrowdale;
Rob Knight

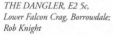

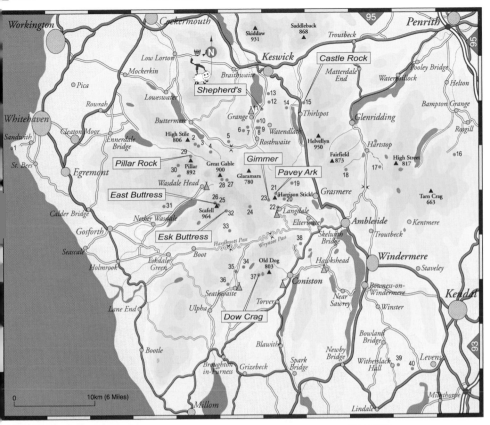

1	10	60	<50>	St. Bees Head
2	80	Zzz 55	<22(N)>	Eagle Crag*
3	80	Zzz 60	<30(N)>	High Crag*
4	50	80	<12(N)>	Green Crag
5	14	80	<17(N)>	Buckstone How
6	15	90	<40(N)>	Goat Crag*
7	45	20	<20>	Dalt Quarry
8	45	6	<50>	Bowderstone*
9	15	50	<8(N)>	Hell's Wall
10	20	Zzz 100	<45(N)>	Black Crag*
11	5	60	<100(N)>	Shepherd's Crag**
12	15	70	<25(N)>	Lower Falcon Crag*
13	10	40	<30(N)>	Recastle Crag*
14	18	70	<20(N)>	Raven Crag
15	10	90	<51(N)>	Castle Rock*
16	15	Zzz 40	<50(N)>	Gouther Crag*
17	40	40	<16(N)>	Raven Crag - Threshwaite Cove*
18	80	60	<30(N)>	Dove Crag*
19	80	60	<18(N)>	Deer Bield Crag
20	40	60	<46(N)>	White Ghyll*

21	60	100	<75(N)>	Pavey Ark**
22	15	90	<50(N)>	Raven Crag*
23	50	100	<73(N)>	Gimmer Crag**
24	110	100	<17(N)>	Bowfell Buttress*
25	110	Zzz 70	<67(N)>	East Buttress**
26	100	120	<40(N)>	Scafell Crag*
27	70	60	<30(N)>	Kern Knotts*
28	90	Zzz 100	<70(N)>	Napes - Gable Crag*
29	120	150	<100(N)>	Pillar Rock*
30	120	Zzz 80	<10(N)>	Haskett Buttress
31	40	60	<50(N)>	Buckbarrow Crags*
32	110	130	<40(N)>	Esk Buttress*
33	35	60	<20(N)>	Heron Crag
34	20	30	<14(N)>	Burnt Crag*
35	5	Zzz 20	<20(N)>	Troutal Gorge
36	15	Zzz 60	<28(N)>	Wallowbarrow Crag
37	90	120	<120(N)>	Dow Crag**
38	10	50	<60(N/S)>	Hodge Close*
39	45	S/A 35	<60(S)>	Chapel Scar*
40	45	35	<12>	White Scare

LIFE IN THE FAST LANE, E5 6b, Hodge Close Quarry; Ed Cleasby

INCANTATIONS E6 6b, Gable Crag, Napes-Great Gable; Pete Whillance

This area offers sea cliff climbing at its best. All the walk in's are nice and flat, and most of the cliffs are easy to walk down to. Very sharp rock, West facing, and incredibly quiet during midweek. Plenty of steep, routes too.

 The South Coast is quite popular because of the huge concentration of good cliffs. But don't forget the North coast for those esoteric quiet spots. Not a lot of technical routes, mainly long, steep, on huge holds.

Topo: T95a-1
Pembroke
Alan James; 1995
112pp. 210mm x 150mm

T	I	?	5a-7a Info		
🍇	★	★★★★★	★★★	🗑	★

⚠ 1, 3-14.
£ **www.rockfax.com**

Topo: T95a-2
Pembroke - 2 Vols.
J Harwood, D. Viggars; 1996
414pp + 414pp. 165mm x 105mm

T	I	?	5a-7a Info		
🌲	★	★★★	★★	🗑	★

⚠ 1 - 20, +++++
£ **Mrs. Westons Teashop,Bosherston**
www.urbanrock.com

THE GREAT WHITE, E7 6c, White Tower, Mother Carey's Kitchen; Mick Lovatt

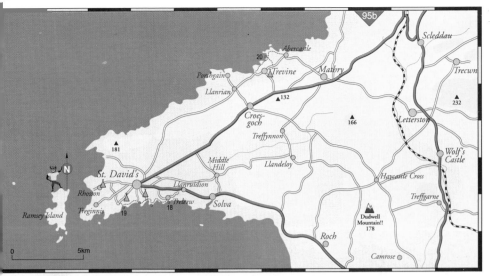

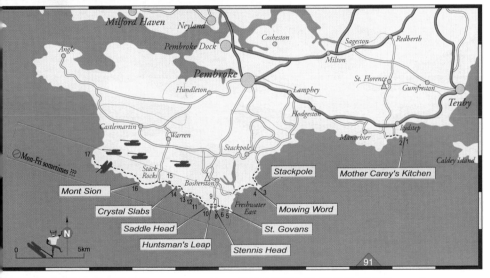

1	10	∞		60	<50(N)>	Mother Carey's Kitchen **	
2	5	∞		50	<100(N)>	Lydstep West *	
3	30	∞		50	<60(N)>	Stackpole Head ** ⊘1/2-31/6	
4	30	∞		50	<50(N)>	Mowing Word ** ⊘1/2-31/6	
5	15		*	50	<150(N)>	Saint Govan's Head **	
6	10			45	<100(N)>	Trevallen Cliff **	
7	10	∞		50	<20(N)>	Stennis Ford *	
8	15		*	50	<35(N)>	Stennis Head *	
9	15	∞		45	<70(N)>	Huntsman's Leap **	
10	20		*	60	<40(N)>	Saddle Head *	
11	30		*	40	<75(N)>	The Castle *	
12	25	∞		35	<60(N)>	Crickmail Point *	
13	24	∞		60	<50(N)>	Mewsford * ⊘1/3-31/6 (50%)	
14	12			50	<50(N)>	Flimston & Crystal Slabs **	
15	10	∞		50	<25(N)>	The Cauldron *	
16	18		*	50	<100(N)>	Mont Sion ** ⊘ 1/2-15/8	
17	15			32	<120(N)>	Western Walls ** ⊘1/2-15/8	
18	5			60	<120(N)>	Carreg-y-Barcud *	
19	10			25	<40(N)>	Porthclais - Ffynnon *	
20	45			50	<10(N)>	Craig Llong	

Feeling powerful? Go to the limestone on the coast, very hard sport routes and lots to do, but generally cold and dismal. The best hardish routes are big walls on Gogarth, Llanberis, and on the slate. Good climbing for natural gear.

 The Slate is certainly demanding, and on some of the routes you get a long way above the gear, on very creaky holds. For normal people, there is a wealth of middle grade climbing all over North Wales. Watching rain, is popular too here!

Topo: T95b-1
Tremadog
D.Ferguson,I Jones, P.Littlejohn; 2000
285pp. 165mm x 105mm

⚠ 21, 22, 23. ++

£ **Cotswold, Ultimate; Betws-y-Coed**
Joe Brown Capel Curig,
Joe Brown & Outside, Llanberis

Topo: T95b-2
Llanberis
Paul Williams; 1987
305pp. 165mm x 105mm

⚠ 26 - 30.

€ **Cotswold, Ultimate; Betws-y-Coed**
Joe Brown Capel Curig,
Joe Brown & Outside, Llanberis

Topo: T95b-3
Gogarth
Andy Newton & Pals; 1990
302pp. 165mm x 105mm

⚠ 37 - 40 +++

€ **Joe Brown Shop, Capel Curig**
Joe Brown Shop & Outside, Llanberis,
www.climbers-club.co.uk

Topo: T95b-4
North Wales Limestone & Bouldering
A. James, P. Evans, J. Barton; 1997
224pp. 210mm x 150mm

⚠ 34 - 36; +++++ Bloc

€ **Joe Brown Shop, Capel Curig**
Joe Brown Shop & Outside, Llanberis,
www.rockfax.com

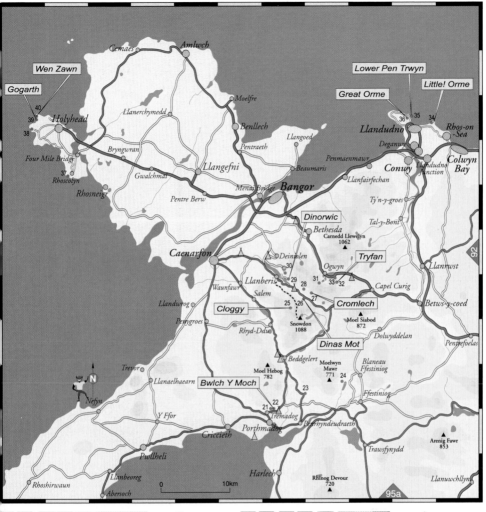

21	10			70	<80(N)>	Pant Ifan **
22	5			70	<100(N)>	Bwlch Y Moch **
23	1			60	<30(N)>	Carreg Hyll Drem *
24	15			80	<30(N)>	Clogwyn Yr Oen *
25	90		Zzz	80	<115(N)>	Cloggy **
26	15			80	<70(N)>	The Mot & The Wings *
27	35			75	<60(N)>	The Cromlech **
28	15			60	<40(N)>	The Grochan *
29	5+			35+	<100(SA)>	Llanberis Slate Quarries
30	15+			35+	<200(SA)>	Dinorwic Slate Quarries ***

31	25			120	<60(N)>	Idwal Slabs *
32	70			130	<30(N)>	Tryfan East Face *
33	8			70	<40(N)>	Milestone Buttress
34	45			60+	<130(SA)>	Little Orme *
35	10			45	<50(S)>	Lower Pen Trwyn *
36	5			30+	<200>	Pen Trwyn - Upper Tier *
37	10		Zzz	35	<60>	Rhoscolyn *
38	5			60	<20>	Castell Helen *
39	20			100	<140>	Gogarth Main Cliff ***
40	25			120	<20>	Wen Zawn *

COMES THE DERVISH, E3 6a
Vivien Slate Quarries, Llanberis.
Kev Howett

CITADEL, E5 6b, Gogarth Main Cliff; Joe Healey

OCTO, HVS 5a, Cloggy 6 am! Dave Lawson

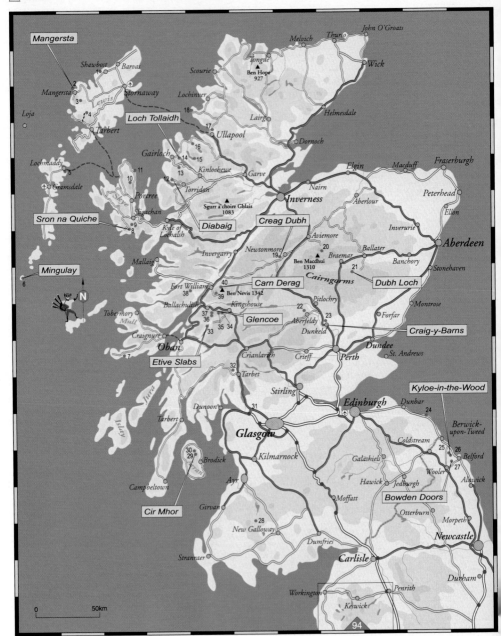

Mangersta

Shawbost   Barvas

Melvich   Thurso   John O'Groats

Tongue   Wick

Scourie   Ben Hope 927

Mangersta   Lewis   Stornaway

Lochinver

Loja   Lairg   Helmesdale

Loch Tollaidh   Ullapool

Lochmaddy   Dornoch

Gairloch   Kinlochewe   Garve

Gramsdale   Skye   Torridon   Elgin   Macduff   Fraserburgh

Portree   Sligachan   Nairn   Inverness   Aberlour   Peterhead   Ellon

Sgurr a'choire Ghlais 1083   Aviemore   Inverurie   Aberdeen

Sron na Quiche   Kyle of Lochalsh   Diabaig   Creag Dubh   Ben Macdhui 1310   Braemar   Ballater   Banchory   Stonehaven

Mingulay   Invergarry   Newtonmore   Dubh Loch

Mallaig   Carn Derag   Cairngorms

Fort William   Ben Nevis 1342   Pitlochry

Tobermory   Mull   Ballachulish   Kingshouse   Aberfeldy   Forfar   Montrose

Craignure   Glencoe   Dunkeld   Craig-y-Barns

Oban   Dundee   St. Andrews

Etive Slabs   Crianlarich   Crieff   Perth

Jura   Tarbet   Stirling   Kyloe-in-the-Wood

Dunoon   Dunbar   Berwick-upon-Tweed

Tarbert   Glasgow   Edinburgh   Coldstream   Belford   Wooler   Alnwick

Islay   Kilmarnock   Galashiels   Bowden Doors

Brodick   Ayr   Hawick   Jedburgh

Cir Mhor   Campbeltown   Girvan   Moffatt   Otterburn   Morpeth

New Galloway   Newcastle

Dumfries   Carlisle

Stranraer   Durham

Workington   Penrith

Keswick

94

0   50km

A great area for climbing, with some savage sea cliffs on the Isles. The traditional hard climbs need more of a strong head and good route finding. Glencoe and Ben Nevis are superb, but don't miss out on the rest, it's unique.

 A lot of beautiful spots to climb, away fom the crowds. Has been known to rain on occasions! A lot of surprisingly demanding slabs. Good boots needed for walk to cliffs, camping with midges, is not my idea of fun.

Topo: T96-1 etc,,,,
SMC Series
McClimbers;
1995-2002
350pp.
162mm x 103mm
New series
195mm x 103mm

£ **Nevisport,**
Fort William, ¢??-7
www.smc.org.uk

△ Skye & Hebrides: 1-11, ++++.
Highland Outcrops: 19,22,23 ++39.
Lowland Outcrops: 24,28,31, ++++.
Glencoe & Ben Nevis (New series)
North East Outcrops
www.smc.org.uk

Topo: T91-2 etc,,,,
Wester Ross, (Laminated)
J.Buchanan, P.Tattersall; 2002
2-8pp. 294mm x 210mm

WildWest TOPOS

£ **The Coffee shop,**
Poolewe;
The Old Inn, Gairloch;
Rubha Reidh lighthouse,
Melvaig;
www.wildwesttopos.com

△ 12, 13, 14, 16, ++++

Topo: T91-4
Northumberland
J. Earl + chums; 1989
337pp. 160mm x 105mm

△ 25, 26, 27, +++++++++

€ **Newcastle Upon Tyne, ???**

Topo: T96-3
Rock Climbing in Scotland
Kevin Howett; 2001
504pp. 170mm x 110mm

△ 1 - 15, 19 - 21, 29, 30, 32 - 40.

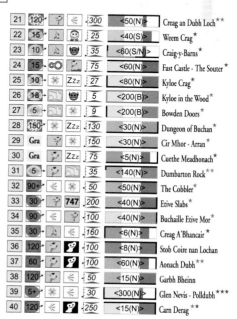

#						Name
1	10			50	<60(N)>	Dalbeg Bay*
2	5+			50	<150(N)>	Mangersta**
3	150		747	180	<15+(N)>	Creag Dubh Dabadale*
4	180			200	<30(SA)>	Sron Ulladale*
5	Bas			35	<50(N)>	Madah Mor Island*
6	Gni			100	<50+(N)>	Mingulay**
7	15			25	<70(N)>	Scoor (Mull)*
8	120			200	<70(N)>	Sron na Ciche**
9	180			35	<5(N)>	Bhastier Tooth*
10	40			6	<99+(N)>	Carn Liath*
11	10			50	<40(N)>	Kilt Rock*
12	15			70	<50(N)>	Diabaig - Torridon*
13	Vol	Zzz		?	<70(N)>	Stone Valley Crags*
14	10+	Zzz		35	<150(N)>	Loch Tollaidh**
15	150			100	<30(N)>	Carnmore*
16	30			50	<12(N)>	Gruinard - Lochan Dubh*
17	Vol	Zzz		?	<?(N)>	Ardmair Crags
18	Gra			30	<400(N)>	Reiff **
19	10			60	<100(N)>	Creag dubh - Newtonmore**
20	60L			140	<30(N)>	Shelter Stone*
21	120			300	<50(N)>	Creag an Dubh Loch**
22	15			25	<40(S)>	Weem Crag*
23	10			35	<60(S/N)>	Craig-y-Barns*
24	15			75	<60(N)>	Fast Castle - The Souter*
25	10	Zzz		27	<80(N)>	Kyloe Crag*
26	18			5	<200(B)>	Kyloe in the Wood*
27	5			9	<200(B)>	Bowden Doors*
28	150	Zzz		130	<30(N)>	Dungeon of Buchan*
29	Gra			150	<30(N)>	Cir Mhor - Arran*
30	Gra	Zzz		75	<5(N)>	Cuethe Meadhonach*
31	5			35	<140(N)>	Dumbarton Rock**
32	90+			50	<50(N)>	The Cobbler*
33	30		747	200	<40(N)>	Etive Slabs*
34	90			100	<40(N)>	Buchaille Etive Mor*
35	30			160	<6(N)>	Creag A'Bhancair*
36	120			100	<8(N)>	Stob Coire nan Lochan*
37	60			100	<60(N)>	Aonach Dubh**
38	120			50	<15(N)>	Garbh Bheinn
39	5+			30	<300(N)>	Glen Nevis - Polldubh***
40	120			250	<15(N)>	Carn Derag**

THE OVERHANGING CRACK, 5c (F6b), Bowden Doors; Bob Smith

REQUIEM, E7 6c, Dumbarton Rock; Dave Cuthebertson

Hoz de Jucar, Montanejos, Patones, Riglos, Chaos de Targasonne, Vingrau, Seynes, Chambotte, Ablon, Céüse. Presles, Gorges du Verdon, Gogarth.

Desplomlandia, Ayna, El Yelmo, Pelúgano, Ramales, Zerkuppe, Troubat, Céou, Guignoterie, Ailefroide, Groti, Andonno, Schleier Wasserfall, Planspitze, Bosigran, Gimmer Crag, Dow Crag, Mother Carey's Kitchen, Bwlch Y Moch, The Cromlech, Mangersta, Mingulay, Creag an Dubh Loch.

Socueva, Torralba de los Frailes, Foz de Escalete, Mondarrain, Camps, Franchard-Crête Sud, Rocher des Molliats, Super Vanoise, Barrachin, Dobratsch, Ogmore, Froggatt Edge, Raven Tor, Black Rocks, Bridestones, Dove Crag, Kern Knotts, Stennis Head, Bowden Doors. The Cobbler, Etive Slabs.

Sella, Leiva, Chuilla, Horata de Saint Joan, Arguibelle, Pic du Jer, Russan, Gorges d'Apremont, Saint Pancrasse, Orpierre, Cimai, Châteauvert, Ferentillo, Harrison's Rocks, Glen Nevis-Polldubh.

Sa Gubia, Los Cahorros, Jerica, Pedrosa, Rochers du Parc, La Justice, Séloge, Saint Crépin, Crépe de Oucèra, Blautalwand, Blacknor, Scafell East Buttress, Pavey Ark, Sron na Ciche, Loch Tollaidh.

Priañes, Liendo, Arboli, Alquezar, Rouziet, Vergisson, Lignerolles, Clécy, Bois Rond, Tamié, Gravaille, Reussenstein, Hay Tor, Black Crag-Lakes, Esk Buttress, Idwal Slabs, The Grochan.

Saffres, Saint Egrève, Les Vouillants, Volx, Dshungelbuch, Martinswand, Dinorwic Slate Quarries.

Los Cotos, Les Gaillands, St. Martin la Porte, Comboire, Sisteron, Tetto di Sarre, Ith, Püttlacher Wand, Stoney Middleton, Cloggy, Dumbarton Rock.

Mijas, La Riba, Ravin d'Urrio, Sarazine, Brison-St. Innocent, Virieu-le-Grand, Saint Marcel, Espace Comboire, Le Claps, Roche de Rame, Norma, Sasso del Drago, Onore, Dorénaz, Kraftwerk, Selter, Cornice Cheedale, Ilkley Quarry, White Ghyll, The Cauldron, Lower Pen Trwyn.

GUIDEBOOK STARS

One of the best aspects to the climbing guidebooks of Europe, is the sheer range and diversity of publications on offer; dog eared notebooks in bars, club journals, prose accounts, laminated topos, artistic impressions! photographic gargantunums etc. They all attempt to offer the 'Climbing Guidebook experience.' So, whilst the guidebooks are all good fun to local climbers who know their 'patch,' we try to give a fair and unbiased opinion, for those climbers visiting an unknown area for the first time. By giving 5 different categories, we show what is great - and what is awful; and hopefully encourage the right people to buy the guides. We try to include any guidebooks sent to us, and ask people to let us know of new editions; and also good places where you can locally buy the topos.

ⓘ Information

★ Basic climbing information, rock types, style of bolts and protection required, notes of access problems; if the cliffs are affected by tides; any loose rock; local climbing walls.

★★ General overall information, local shops, car repairs, petrol stations. Where to stay; campsites, caravans to rent, apartments, hotels; best drinking taverns, nightclubs!

★★★ Extra information; such as geology cross sections, wild flowers and plants in the area; details on birds and their habitat. A history of the local area, and recommended tours.

? Crag location

★ Information in the guidebook to actually find the crag!!! A one star is not a good rating, and you almost definitely will need to buy a map, and maybe have some luck too!

★★ There should be enough information to actually find the crag, but don't leave your map at home, since the maps in the guide rely on a few vague details.

★★★ This is not easy to award - we think that you do not need to buy a map, since the directions are very good, and the maps work for people of all languages.

5a-7a Info Route information

★ The guide must have routes in it! Names of climbs are given, or are marked on the topo, and the grades for each route are given. (We have no opinion on the grades given.)

★★ Good specific information; length of route, length of rope needed, type of bolts and number of quick draws per route; style of climbing on each route.

★★★ Very detailed info; where the crux of the route is, the hard sections, any long run outs, difficulty for short people, best time of year for condition of route (it's almost cheating).

Interlinguality perception

★ Very basic! You will not be able to understand very much in this guide, but you should be able to work out where the routes go, the grades that they are, and have a 'OK' day out.

★★ An effort has really been made by the writer to enable all languages to use the guide, so all the format is easy to understand, and as a pure 'climbing guide' it really works.

★★★ This guide is actually designed for multi language use, with good introductions in different languages (sometimes specified). A proper topo layout, with climbing icons.

📷 Photography, design and feel good factor

★ Generally Black and white photography, just to get an idea of the crag and the routes; A good small selection of colour photos, generally gets 1 red star.

★★ A nice and whizzy guide; lots of photos and nice layout; Crag shots as well as climbing action shots, gives you a very good impression of the climbing on offer.

★★★ Wow factor - you are now looking at almost a collectors book, great graphic design, hundreds of colour photos, proper sewn binding; a dream come true!

🗑 The Dustbin

This is our comedy award, nobody is usually good at everything, and most guidebooks have a real Achilles heel, so we award **THE DUSTBIN**, to a really dodgy aspect of any guide. (To delete a dustbin, please send large quantities of free beer to us.)

We had a lot of people telling us about different types of calcaire, such as, urgonien, jurassic, cretaceous, etc. The fact is, that generally only geologists know anything about rock, and their descriptions have simply nothing to do with climbing. We instead looked at the general different effect of CALCAIRE, with climbing interest: Such as:- slipperyness - which we all hate; rounded texture - good for worn skin; sharp 'cimai' teeth - bad for worn skin, etc. We then distilled all the different types to a reasonable quantity - 25, and gave them a letter each. Nobody, except 'those typical retentives,' were going to remember the letters. So we decided to use the first letter from the name of a cliff, where that type of rock is present. It's never going to be perfect, since many cliffs have quite a few different types of calcaire, and some are not precise examples. However, we feel it is a lot more useful than just saying 'calcaire.' We hope it works as a quick to use reference system. The graphic icons on the cover will help, but the photos on these 4 pages, should help even more.

A - Alaro

B- Buoux

C - Cimai

D - Dolomiti

E - Erto

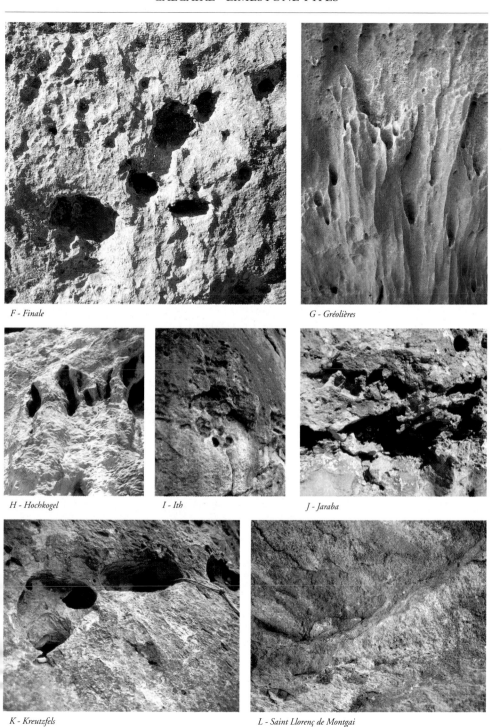

F - Finale

G - Gréolières

H - Hochkogel

I - Ith

J - Jaraba

K - Kreutzfels

L - Saint Llorenç de Montgai

M - Malham Cove

N - Gorges du Nesque

O - Oillaskoa

P - Pouponne

Q - Quié

R - Rosenstein

S - Stoney Middleton

V - Vignettes

T - Troubat

U - Ubrieux

W - Water-Cum-Jolly

X ?

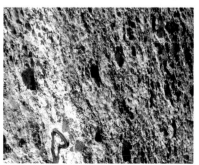

Y - Yenne

Z - Zwergenschloß

INDEX

JINGO WOBBLY tours started back in the early 1960's, in the golden days of travel. There was no need for a tunnel to the continent, or grubbly little hire cars in those days. We took the grandest style of fly drive. You simply booked in at the check-in desk, where they informed you that today's luggage allowance - was around 1500 kilos, per family. The front of the plane opened up, and it could take around 4 cars! It was all very English, "We will be boarding in a few minuites so hurry along, if you please; the plane takes off at five and twenty to three, and the hostess will have a thermosflask of hot tea for you."

JINGO WOBBLY tours 2001, on the way over the Col d'Iseran 2764m, with the 'Escargot of Love'. After many years of suffering in tents and massive alpine storms, we took a leap into social insanity in the 1990's, and became dreaded cara-vanners! Fortunately for us, we claw back some self esteem, by towing it with our racy little sports car. This way we can leave the giant 'Romford Palace' in the valley, and tear up and down the sun filled mountains in the open air.

There has been no shortage of hard work and dedication to the collection of material for this book, David here doing some particularly fine research at Vers, France - tough life somedays.

Carrie in the Pays Basque. We both seem to be non-stop photgraphers, here sending a kiss to those back home.

Outward travel-ticket/flight number, date, time:

Return travel-ticket/flight number, date, time:

Car Hire company & telephone no:

1) Credit card emergency no:

1) Credit card emergency no:

Climbing insurance telephone:

Policy number:

Tickets · Money · Travellers Cq · Credit Card 1 · Credit Card 2 · Passport · E111 · Alpine hut card · Camera · Film · Rope 1 · Rope 2 · Harness · Quickdraws · Descender · Gri Gri · Maillons & · Wrench · Rock shoes · Chalk Bag · Crash matt · Guidebooks · Rucksac · Tent · Sleeping bag · Sleeping mat · Cooker · Pots · Plates · Cutlery · Clothes · Wash bag · Warm jacket · Sun tan lotion · Shades · Mosquito rep · Compass (GPS)

□□□□□□□□□□□□□□□□□□□□□□□□□□□□□□□□□□□□□□□

Outward travel-ticket/flight number, date, time:

Return travel-ticket/flight number, date, time:

Car Hire company & telephone no:

1) Credit card emergency no:

1) Credit card emergency no:

Climbing insurance telephone:

Policy number:

Tickets · Money · Travellers Cq · Credit Card 1 · Credit Card 2 · Passport · E111 · Alpine hut card · Camera · Film · Rope 1 · Rope 2 · Harness · Quickdraws · Descender · Gri Gri · Maillons & · Wrench · Rock shoes · Chalk Bag · Crash matt · Guidebooks · Rucksac · Tent · Sleeping bag · Sleeping mat · Cooker · Pots · Plates · Cutlery · Clothes · Wash bag · Warm jacket · Sun tan lotion · Shades · Mosquito rep · Compass (GPS)

□□□□□□□□□□□□□□□□□□□□□□□□□□□□□□□□□□□□□□□

Outward travel-ticket/flight number, date, time:

Return travel-ticket/flight number, date, time:

Car Hire company & telephone no:

1) Credit card emergency no:

1) Credit card emergency no:

Climbing insurance telephone:

Policy number:

Tickets · Money · Travellers Cq · Credit Card 1 · Credit Card 2 · Passport · E111 · Alpine hut card · Camera · Film · Rope 1 · Rope 2 · Harness · Quickdraws · Descender · Gri Gri · Maillons & · Wrench · Rock shoes · Chalk Bag · Crash matt · Guidebooks · Rucksac · Tent · Sleeping bag · Sleeping mat · Cooker · Pots · Plates · Cutlery · Clothes · Wash bag · Warm jacket · Sun tan lotion · Shades · Mosquito rep · Compass (GPS)

□□□□□□□□□□□□□□□□□□□□□□□□□□□□□□□□□□□□□□□

	ENGLISH	FRANÇAIS	ESPAÑA	ITALIA	
	Powerful climbing-Big holds, steep rock	Puissant - Bonnes prises, dévers	Escalada atlética - cazos, roca vertical	Arrampicata fisica	
	Technique, balance and experience required	Technique, équilibre et expérience nécessaires	Técnica, requiere equilibrio y experiencia	Tecnica	
★	An exceptional location with memorable routes	Endroit exceptionnel avec des voies inoubliables	Excepcional localización con escaladas memorables	Incredibile	★
★	A good location, and good climbing moves	Bien situé et de bons mouvements	Buena localización, y buenos movimientos de escalada	Molto bello	★
★	Good routes, but a bad area, a quarry, etc.	Bonnes voies mais mal situé (carrière, etc)	Buenas vías, pero un mal sitio, una cantera, etc	Bello	★
3★	3 Stars - Lots to climb worth a special holiday	Beaucoup de voies très bien pour des vacances	3 estrellas - muchas escaladas para unas buenas vacaciones	-	3★
2★	2 Stars - A lot of climbs, all of high quality	beacoup de voies de très bonne qualité	2 estrellas - muchas escaladas, todas de buena calidad	-	2★
1★	1 Star - Good routes, worth a special detour	1 étoile - bonnes voies qui valent un détour	1 estrella - buenas escaladas como alternativa	-	1★
	Complete choss, not worth a visit	Ne vaut pas la peine de visiter	Fracaso, no merece la pena	Non bello	
	A wonderful view, often in the mountains	Vue magnifique, souvent en montagne	Maravillosas vistas, a menudo entre montañas	ottimo panorama	
	A beautiful natural setting, countryside	Joli site naturel, campagne	Marco natural, campo	Bel posto	
S/A	Mostly sport routes, but nuts should be carried	Terrain sportif, plus coinceurs.	Mayoritariamente deportiva, pero es conveniente llevar empotradores	SPORT & adv	S/A
A/S	Natural protection mainly, with some bolts	Protection naturelle, quelques broches	Seguros naturales, con algunos parabolts	AVENT & sport	A/S
A	Terrain adventure - roofs are done with aid	Terrain adventure !!!!!!!	Terreno de aventura - techos con ayuda	-	A
N	Natural protection only, no pegs or bolts	Protection naturelle, aucune broche	Sólo con autoprotección, sin spits ni parabolts	-	N
C	Czech style - only knots on slings, insitu bolts	Czech style	Estilo checo - sólo nudos en anillas, en lugar de parabolts	-	C
T	Top roping, and you may need slings	Corde a la tête	Top-rope, pudiendo necesitar anillas	-	T
	Via ferrata in the nearby area, good fun	Via ferrata à proximité, divertissant	Vía ferrata en la zona, muy divertido	Via Ferrata	
	Very well protected crux, bolt above move	Mouvement clé très bien protégé	Muy bien protegido el paso clave, parabolt por encima del paso	volo piccolo	
	A good 2 metre fall from crux will be expected	Du mouvement clé chute de 2 mètres possible	Puedes caer dos metros desde el paso clave	volo corto	
747	A whopper fall 5-10 metres - wheeeee	Longue chute de 5-10 mètres	Sartenazo de 5 a 10 metros	volo lungo	747
	If you fall !! you will go a very long way, 30 metres	Si vous tombez, énorme chute de 30 mètres	Si caes, tendrás un gran vuelo, 30 metros	volo gigantesco	
	A very scary cliff, will completely terrify you	Falaise qui vous donnera la chair de poule	Pared escalofriante, te aterrorizará...	Pericoloso	
△	General warning, loose rock, wear helmets etc.	Roche instable, portez un casque	Precauciones generales, roca suelta, llevar casco, etc.	-	△
⊘	No climbing during the restriction please	Pas d'escalade pendant la période de restriction	No escalar durante las restricciones	-	⊘
	Climbing restrictions for bird nesting season	Restrifications pour nidification	Restricciones de escalada por nidificación	limitazione per i volatili	
	Shooting season - you may get shot!	Période de chasse - attention aux balles perdues	Temporada de caza - te pueden disparar	-	
90db	A rating for car traffic noise 30-99 db	Côte pour les bruits de circulation 30-99 db	Intervalo de ruido de coches, entre 30 y 99 db	rumori di automobili	90db
90db	Really loud river noise	Rivière très bruyante	Ruido de río realmente fuerte	-	90db
Zzz	A very quiet crag	Une falaise très calme	Zona muy tranquila	Silenzioso	Zzz
	Humidity warning, often on overcast days	Attention à l'humidité surtout les jours couverts	Cuidado humedad, a menudo nublado	Rocca unida	
	Nuclear reactor closeby watch out!	Réacteur nucléaire proche - Attention!	Reactor nuclear en las cercanías. ¡Cuidado!	-	
△	Open field - camping, no facilities at all	Camping dans un champ, aucun équipement	Campo abierto - escasez de servicios	Camping	△
△	Very basic camping, with toilets and water	Camping de base avec toilettes et eau	Camping básico, con baños y agua	Camping	△
△	Normal campsite, hot showers, basic	Camping avec eau chaude, douches	Camping normal, agua caliente, básico	Camping	△
△	Excellent campsite with shop, bike hire, etc.	Excellent camping avec magasins, location vélos	Camping excelente, con tienda, alquiler de bicis, etc.	Camping	△
△	Amazing, top facilities, swimming pool, dancing	Camping de luxe avec piscine, discothèque	Impresionante, todo tipo de servicios, piscina, baile	Camping	△
F	Languages used in a guidebook	Langues utilisées dans le guide	Idiomas utilizados en la guía	-	F

ENGLISH	FRANÇAIS	ESPAÑA	ITALIA	
Boulders for good bouldering	Bons blocs	Buenos boulders	Bloc	
Slab climbing	Dalle	Escala en placa	-	
Vertical, climbing - bad for resting	Vertical - pas de repos	Escalada vertical, sin reposos	-	
Leaning rock, the wrong side of vertical	Le - Ooohmph	Roca desplomada, el lado malo de la vertical	-	
Really leaning and steep rock, grottos	grottos	Muy vertical, incluso desplomada, cuevas	Grotto	
Roof climbs, or sections with roofs	Toit ou sections avec toit	Techos, o secciones con techos	Strapiombante	
Sea cliff climbing above the water	Falaises, escalade au-dessus de la mer	Acantilado en el que se escala sobre el agua	-	
You must swim to the route, or take a boat	Rejoindre la voie à la nage ou par bateau	Hay que nadar hasta pie de vía o coger un bote	-	
Approach by abseil	Approche en rappel	Aproximación rapelando	cordia doppia	
A chimney	Cheminée	Chimenea clásica	Camino	
Very pocketed rock	Roche avec beaucoup de trous - gruyère	Roca muy agujereada - como un queso	Arrampicare su buchi	
An arête, here shown climbed on the right	Une arête, montrée ici à droite	Arista, aquí se muestra escalada por la derecha	Dulfer a dx	
A mantleshelf, no holds to pull over on	Un rétablissement aucune prise pour la sortie	Paso de mostrador, sin agujeros para traccionar	Ristabilimento	
Foot lock, hooking a heel to do a problem	Le technique - pour le pied	Talonaje para resolver el paso	Tallonagio	
A real friction problem, no good holds	Beaucoup d'adhérence, aucune bonne prise	Paso de adherencia sin buenos agarres	Rocca Unta	
Dynamic lunge, leaping for holds	Mouvement dynamique Sauter pour les prises	Lanzamiento dinámico para encontrar los agarres	Dinamica	
A climb with corners and grooves	Une voie avec dièdres et cannelures	Escalada con aristas y fisuras	Diedro	
A route which wakes up to morning sunshine	Une voie avec le soleil le matin	Una vía para madrugar	Al Mattino	
A route in the sun all day	Une voie avec le soleil toute la journée	Vía al sol durante todo el día	Tutto il giorno	
A route that gets afternoon, evening sun	Une voie avec le soleil l'après-midi et soir	Vía para no madrugar, sol hasta tarde	Al pomeriggio	
A route that keeps out of the sun	Une voie non exposée au soleil	Vía en sombra	All'ombra	
Trees in the area to give shade in summer	Arbres qui donnent de l'ombre en été	Arbolado que da sombra en verano	A'll ombra estivo	
Cal	Limestone; All seabed sedimentary fossils	Calcaire sédimentaire, fossiles	Caliza, toda llena de fósiles sedimentarios	Calcare	Cal
Gra	Granite; all quality from white hard - brown poor	Granit	Granito; de todas las calidades, desde el blanco duro al marrón más pobre	Granito	Gra
Gni	Green hard gneiss, often in natural folds	Gneis	Gneis verde duro, a menudo en fallas	Gneiss	Gni
Sch	Schist; low quality gneiss, flakey and poor	Schist, rocher mauvais	Esquisto, gneis roto, de baja calidad	-	Sch
Vol	General volcanic rocks; rhyolite, dolerite, tuff	Volcanique - trés adherence	Rocas volcánicas; riolita, diolita, lava	Roccia vulcanica	Vol
Qua	Quartzite; hard and very slippery, soapy rock	Quartz, dur et glissant comme du savon	Cuarcita; dura y resbaladiza, lavada	Quarzite	Qua
Con	Conglomerate; like stones in concrete	Congloméré comme des pierres dans du béton	Conglomerado;	Conglomerato	Con
Gri	Very hard and gritty sandstone, abrasive	Grès - unique	Arenisca dura y rugosa, abrasiva	Arenaria calcarea	Gri
San	Sandstone, soft grainy rock, takes deep bolts	Grès, granuleux doux	Arenisca, roca blanda, necesita parabolts largos	Arenaria	San
Bas	Bassalt; similar feel to sandstone, ex-volcanic	Basalte, même sensation que le grès	Basalto; tacto similar a la arenisca, origen volcánico	-	Bas
Sla	Slate, smooth and dark slippery rock, tiny edges	Ardoise, lisse et sombre roche glissante	Pizarra, roca oscura y pulida con los cantos finos	-	Sla
P	Free parking normally	Parking gratuit normalement	Parking gratuito habitualmente	Parch. gratuito	P
P	Pay parking, have coins for slot machines	Parking payant avec horodateurs	Parking de pago, ten monedas para las máquinas	Parch. apagamento	P
▲ 222	General spot height for a high point	Point de altitude	Visión general de la zona desde un punto alto	-	▲ 222
SF £	Currency accepted	Devises acceptées	Se acepta efectivo	-	SF £
CC	Credit cards	Cartes de crédit	Tarjetas de crédito	-	CC

	DEUTSCHLAND	ČESKÁ	JAPAN	
	Athletische Kletterei - große Griffe, steiler Fels	silové lezení - velké chyty, strmé lezení	パワークライミング　ガバ　前傾壁	
	Klettertechnik und Gleichgewichtsgefühl nötig	technika, rovnováha a zkušenosti jsou nutné	テクニカルクライミング、バランス系、垂壁、スラブ	
★	Außergewöhnliches Gebiet mit unvergesslichen Routen	výjimečná oblast s nezapomenutelnými cestami	最高の環境、記憶に残るエリア	★
★	Schönes Gebiet mit guten Routen	pěkná oblast a dobré lezení	非常に良い環境、面白いエリア	★
★	Gute Routen, aber unschöne Lage	dobré cesty, ale špatná oblast, lom, atp.	ルートは面白いが エリアとしてはいまいち	★
3★	3 Sterne - sehr viele Routen, gutes Urlaubsziel	3 hvězdičky - dostatek lezeckých cest na celou dovolenou	3ツ星ー特別なルート	3★
2★	2 Sterne - viele schöne Routen	2 hvězdičky - mnoho cest vysoké kvality	2ツ星ーほとんどのルートが ハイクオリティ	2★
1★	1 Stern - gute Routen, sind einen Abstecher wert	1 hvězdička - cesty stojí za výjezd	1ツ星ー良いルート	1★
	Totaler Müll, kann man vergessen	špatné lezení, nestojí za návštěvu	良くない　行く価値無し	
	Schöne Aussicht, oft in den Bergen	nádherný výhled, často v horách	眺めが非常に良い	
	Landschaftlich reizvolles Gebiet	nádherná příroda, prostředí, krajina	自然が豊富	
S/A	V.a. Sportkletterrouten, aber Klemmkeile nötig	převážně sportovní cesty, ale nutno dojistit	ほとんどがボルトルート、ただしナチプロ類も必要	S/A
A/S	V.a. selbst abzusichern, mit ein paar Bohrhaken	převážně ne přírodní jištění, občas nýty	ほとんどがナチプロ、部分的にボルト	A/S
A	Abenteuergelände - in Dächern Technorouten	dobrodružnéž cesty, stropy se lezou s umělými pomuckami	冒険的、エイドも混ざる	A
N	Komplett selbst abzusichern	pouze přírodní jištění, bez nýtu a skob	ナチプロのみ、ボルト類は一切無い	N
C	Tschechischer Stil - nur Ringe und Knotenschlingen	český styl - pouze smyčky a kruhy	旧東ドイツスタイル、プロテクションはスリングのみ	C
T	Toprope, eventuell Schlingen nötig	top rope, možná budete potřebovat smyčky	トップロープ、スリングは持参	T
	Spaßiger Klettersteig in der Nähe	nedaleko via ferrata (klettersteig), dobrá zábava	岩場にハシゴや橋が かかって遊べるエリアあり	
	Sehr gut abgesicherte Schlüsselstelle	velmi dobře zajištěná oblast, nýty na každém kroku	プロテクション非常に良し、核心部はボルト下	
	An der Schlüsselstelle ist ein Sturz von 2 Metern drin	bezpečné pády kolem 2 metru	プロテクション良し、核心部は2m以内の墜落	
747	Große Sturzweite: 5-10 Meter	pády 5-10 metru	5-10mの墜落の可能性あり	747
	Megasturz möglich: bis 30 Meter	pokud spadnete, tak se docela proletnete, pády až 30 metru	30m程度の大墜落の 可能性あり	
	Moralisch sehr anspruchsvolles Gebiet	hruzostrašná skála, určite vás vyděsí	恐怖感満点のエリア	
△	Vorsicht! Brüchiger Fels, Helm nötig.	všeobecné varování, zvětralá skála, volné bloky, helma nutná, atp.	要注意、脆い岩 ヘルメット必携など	△
⊘	Bitte während Vogelschutzzeiten nicht klettern	zákaz lezení v době omezení	クライミング禁止 期間あり	⊘
	Kletterverbot während der Vogelbrutzeit	omezení lezení v období hnízdění ptáku	鳥の巣がある期間は クライミング禁止	
	Jagdsaison - Vorsicht Lebensgefahr!	střelecká sezóna - můžete být zastřeleni!	狩のシーズンあり 撃たれるかも！	
90db	Starker Verkehrslärm	hluk aut kolem 30-99 db	車の騒音あり 30-99db	90db
90db	Sehr lauter Fluss	velmi hlučná řeka	川の音が大きい	90db
Zzz	Sehr ruhiges Gebiet	velmi klidá oblast	とても静かな岩場	Zzz
	Fels bei bedecktem Himmel oft feucht	varování ohledně vlhkosti, často během zamračených dnu	湿気高し、特に海風の日	
	Atomkraftwerk in der Nähe	nedaleko atomový reaktor - pozor!	近くに核施設あり	
△	Campingplatz ohne sanitäre Einrichtungen	otevřená plocha pro táboření, žádné sociální zařízení	ただの原っぱのキャンプ場、施設は何も無い	△
△	Einfacher Campingplatz mit Toiletten und Wasser	táboriště se základním vybavením - toalety a voda	シンプルなキャンプ場 トイレと水はある	△
△	Normaler Campingplatz mit heißen Duschen	kemp se základním vybavením - teplá voda, sprchy	普通のキャンプ場 お湯の出るシャワーあり	△
△	Guter Campingplatz mit Einkaufsmöglichkeit etc.	vynikající kemp s obchodem, půjčovnou kol atd.	とても良いキャンプ場 売店などもある	△
△	Luxus-Campingplatz mit Swimming pool etc.	nadstandardní vybavení - bazén, diskotéka	豪華なキャンプ場 プールなど何でもある	△
(F)	Im Kletterführer verwendete Sprachen	jazyky použité v pruvodci	ガイドブックで記載されている 言語	(F)

Deutschland	Česká	Japan
Gute Boulderfelsen	dobré bouldrování	ボルダリングエリアあり
Plattenkletterei	plotnové lezení	スラブ
Klettern in senkrechtem Fels, kaum Ruhepunkte	kolmé lezení - špatné pro odpočívání	垂壁
Überhängender Fels	ukloněná skála do převisu	薄被りの傾斜
Stark überhängender und steiler Fels, Höhlendächer	velmi ukloněná skála, strmé lezení, jeskyně	前傾壁、ケイブ
Dachkletterei, oder Teilbereiche mit Dächern	lezení ve stropech nebo části cest vedou stropem	ルーフ、もしくはルーフ部分あり
Routen direkt über dem Meer	lezení na mořských útesech nad vodou	シークリフ
Schwimmend oder per Boot zum Einstieg	k cestě je nutné doplavat nebo si vzít lodičku	ルートまで泳ぐかボートが必要
Per Abseilen zum Einstieg	přístup ke slanění	取りつくのに懸垂下降が必要
Klassischer Kamin	klasický komín	チムニー
Sehr löchriger Fels - wie Schweizerkäse	skála s kapsami - jako ementál	ポケットホールドがたくさん
Grat, hier auf der rechten Seite beklettert	hrana, zde lezena zprava	カンテ
Mantlemove, keine Griffe zum Hochziehen	římsa bez chytu	マントル
Foothook	stup pro zahákování paty	ヒール、トゥフック
Reibungsproblem, gute Griffe sind Mangelware	kroky na tření, žádné dobré chyty	フリクションクライム、ホールドなし
Dynamischer Zug, Griff anspringen	dynamické kroky k chytum	ランジ
Verschneidungskletterei	lezení v koutě, žlebem	コーナー
Route mit Morgensonne	na cestu svítí slunce pouze ráno	朝から日が当る
Route ganztags sonnig	na cestu svítí slunce celý den	1日中、日当たり良し
Route mit Nachmittags- oder Abendsonne	na cestu svítí slunce pouze odpoledne a večer	午後から日向
Route liegt immer im Schatten	na cestu nikdy nesvítí slunce	1日中日陰
Im Sommer Schatten durch Bäume	v létě je cesta ve stínu stromu	夏は日陰のアリア
Marine Kalke	vápenec; všechny usazené fosílie z mořského dna	石灰岩　二子山、備中と同じ
Granit; von weiß und hart bis braun und brüchig	žula; všech kvalit od bílé tvrdé po hnědou měkkou	花崗岩　小川山と同じ
Grüner harter Gneis, oft gefaltet	zelená tvrdá rula	チャート系
Kristalliner Schiefer; »schlechter« Gneis, abblätternd	rula špatné kvality, měkká, odlupuje se	かなり脆い火山岩
Vulkanisches Gestein; Rhyolith, Dolerit, Tuff	vulkanická vyvřelina; ryolit, dolerit, tuf	火山岩　場ヶ崎と同じ
Quarzit; harter, sehr rutschiger, seifiger Fels	křemenec; tvrdý a velmi kluzký	スムーズな砂岩　フォンテーヌブロなど
Konglomerat; wie in Beton gebettete Steine	slepenec; jako kameny v betonu	レキ岩　メイプルキャニオン(ユタ)など
Sehr harter, grobkörniger Sandstein, hautfeindlich	velmi tvrdý a hrubý pískovec, drsný	非常に堅い砂岩
Weicher, körniger Sandstein; lange Bohrhaken nötig	pískovec, měkká zrnitá skála, hluboko zapuštěné kruhy	柔らかい砂岩　鷹取山など
Basalt; fühlt sich an wie Sandstein	bazalt; podobný pískovci, vulkanického puvodu	安山岩　湯河原幕岩
Schiefer, dunkles, rutschiges Gestein, winzige Kanten	břidlice, hladká a tmavá, kluzká skála, malé lišty	不明
Parken normalerweise gebührenfrei	obvykle park. zdarma	通常は駐車無料
Parken gegen Gebühr, Münzen nötig	placené parkování, připravte si minci do park. hodin	有料駐車場　小銭が必要な場合もある
Höhe über dem Meeresspiegel	nadmořská výška nejvyššího místa	標高
Fremdwährungen werden akzeptiert	hotovost akceptována	使用可能通貨
Kreditkarten	kreditní karty	クレジットカードOK

Name:

House:

Street:

Town:

City & Code:

Country:

Home telephone:

Work telephone:

Mobile telephone:

Medical conditions:

Birthdate:

Age:

Regular doctor:

Allergy's:

Passport Number:

Issue place:

Expiry date:

Driving licence:

Issue place:

Expiry date:

Emergency contact:

Next of kin:

Relationship:

Address:

Address:

Telephone:

Work Telephone: